VOLUME 534

JULY 1994

THE ANNALS

of The American Academy *of* Political
and Social Science

RICHARD D. LAMBERT, *Editor*
ALAN W. HESTON, *Associate Editor*

STRATEGIES FOR IMMIGRATION CONTROL: AN INTERNATIONAL COMPARISON

Special Editor of this Volume

MARK J. MILLER

University of Delaware
Newark

 SAGE Periodicals Press *THOUSAND OAKS   LONDON   NEW DELHI*

THE ANNALS

© 1994 *by* The American Academy *of* Political *and* Social Science

Editorial Office: 3937 Chestnut Street, Philadelphia, PA 19104.

For information about membership* (individuals only) and subscriptions (institutions), address:

SAGE PUBLICATIONS, INC.
2455 Teller Road
Thousand Oaks, CA 91320

From India and South Asia,		*From the UK, Europe, the Middle*
write to:		*East and Africa, write to:*
SAGE PUBLICATIONS INDIA Pvt. Ltd.		SAGE PUBLICATIONS LTD
P.O. Box 4215		6 Bonhill Street
New Delhi 110 048		London EC2A 4PU
INDIA		UNITED KINGDOM

SAGE Production Staff: ERIC L. LAW, LIANN LECH, DORIS HUS, and JANELLE LeMASTER
*Please note that members of The Academy receive THE ANNALS with their membership.
Library of Congress Catalog Card Number 93-85877
International Standard Serial Number ISSN 0002-7162
International Standard Book Number ISBN 0-8039-5591-X (Vol. 534, 1994 paper)
International Standard Book Number ISBN 0-8039-5590-1 (Vol. 534, 1994 cloth)
Manufactured in the United States of America. First printing, July 1994.

The articles appearing in THE ANNALS are indexed in *Academic Index, Book Review Index, Combined Retrospective Index Sets, Current Contents, General Periodicals Index, Public Affairs Information Service Bulletin, Pro-Views,* and *Social Sciences Index.* They are also abstracted and indexed in *ABC Pol Sci, America: History and Life, Automatic Subject Citation Alert, Book Review Digest, Family Resources Database, Higher Education Abstracts, Historical Abstracts, Human Resources Abstracts, International Political Science Abstracts, Managing Abstracts, Periodica Islamica, Sage Urban Studies Abstracts, Social Planning/Policy & Development Abstracts, Social Sciences Citation Index, Social Work Research & Abstracts, Sociological Abstracts, United States Political Science Documents,* and/or *Work Related Abstracts,* and are available on microfilm from University Microfilms, Ann Arbor, Michigan.

Information about membership rates, institutional subscriptions, and back issue prices may be found on the facing page.

Advertising. Current rates and specifications may be obtained by writing to THE ANNALS Advertising and Promotion Manager at the Thousand Oaks office (address above).

Claims. Claims for undelivered copies must be made no later than three months following month of publication. The publisher will supply missing copies when losses have been sustained in transit and when the reserve stock will permit.

Change of Address. Six weeks' advance notice must be given when notifying of change of address to ensure proper identification. Please specify name of journal. Send address changes to: THE ANNALS, c/o Sage Publications, Inc., 2455 Teller Road, Thousand Oaks, CA 91320.

The American Academy of Political and Social Science

3937 Chestnut Street   Philadelphia, Pennsylvania 19104

Board of Directors

ELMER B. STAATS   ANTHONY J. SCIRICA
MARVIN E. WOLFGANG   FREDERICK HELDRING
RICHARD D. LAMBERT   LYNN CURTIS
LLOYD N. CUTLER   MARY ANN MEYERS
HENRY W. SAWYER, III   SARA MILLER McCUNE

Officers

President
MARVIN E. WOLFGANG

Vice Presidents
RICHARD D. LAMBERT, *First Vice President*
STEPHEN B. SWEENEY, *First Vice President Emeritus*

Secretary   **Treasurer**   **Counsel**
ANTHONY J. SCIRICA   ELMER B. STAATS   HENRY W. SAWYER, III

Assistant to the President
MARY E. HARRIS

Editors, THE ANNALS

RICHARD D. LAMBERT, *Editor*   ALAN W. HESTON, *Associate Editor*
THORSTEN SELLIN, *Editor Emeritus*   ERICA GINSBURG, *Assistant Editor*

Origin and Purpose. The Academy was organized December 14, 1889, to promote the progress of political and social science, especially through publications and meetings. The Academy does not take sides in controverted questions, but seeks to gather and present reliable information to assist the public in forming an intelligent and accurate judgment.

Meetings. The Academy occasionally holds a meeting in the spring extending over two days.

Publications. THE ANNALS is the bimonthly publication of The Academy. Each issue contains articles on some prominent social or political problem, written at the invitation of the editors. Also, monographs are published from time to time, numbers of which are distributed to pertinent professional organizations. These volumes constitute important reference works on the topics with which they deal, and they are extensively cited by authorities throughout the United States and abroad. The papers presented at the meetings of The Academy are included in THE ANNALS.

Membership. Each member of The Academy receives THE ANNALS and may attend the meetings of The Academy. Membership is open only to individuals. Annual dues: $42.00 for the regular paperbound edition (clothbound, $60.00). Add $9.00 per year for membership outside the U.S.A. Members may also purchase single issues of THE ANNALS for $13.00 each (clothbound, $18.00). Add $2.00 for shipping and handling on all prepaid orders.

Subscriptions. THE ANNALS (ISSN 0002-7162) is published six times annually—in January, March, May, July, September, and November. Institutions may subscribe to THE ANNALS at the annual rate: $145.00 (clothbound, $172.00). Add $9.00 per year for subscriptions outside the U.S.A. Institutional rates for single issues: $25.00 each (clothbound, $30.00).

Second class postage paid at Thousand Oaks, California, and additional offices.

Single issues of THE ANNALS may be obtained by individuals who are not members of The Academy for $14.00 each (clothbound, $19.00). Add $2.00 for shipping and handling on all prepaid orders. Single issues of THE ANNALS have proven to be excellent supplementary texts for classroom use. Direct inquiries regarding adoptions to THE ANNALS c/o Sage Publications (address below).

All correspondence concerning membership in The Academy, dues renewals, inquiries about membership status, and/or purchase of single issues of THE ANNALS should be sent to THE ANNALS c/o Sage Publications, Inc., 2455 Teller Road, Thousand Oaks, CA 91320. Telephone: (805) 499-0721; FAX/Order line: (805) 499-0871. *Please note that orders under $30 must be prepaid.* Sage affiliates in London and India will assist institutional subscribers abroad with regard to orders, claims, and inquiries for both subscriptions and single issues.

Printed on recycled, acid-free paper

THE ANNALS

of The American Academy *of* Political
and Social Science

RICHARD D. LAMBERT, *Editor*
ALAN W. HESTON, *Associate Editor*

--------- **FORTHCOMING** ---------

THE ARMS TRADE: PROBLEMS AND
PROSPECTS IN THE POST-COLD WAR WORLD
Special Editors: Robert E. Harkavy and Stephanie G. Neuman
Volume 535   September 1994

EMPLOYEE DISMISSAL: JUSTICE AT WORK
Special Editor: Stuart Henry
Volume 536   November 1994

ETHICS IN AMERICAN PUBLIC SERVICE
Special Editor: Harry W. Reynolds, Jr.
Volume 537   January 1995

See page 3 for information on Academy membership and
purchase of single volumes of **The Annals.**

CONTENTS

BOOK DEPARTMENT CONTENTS

SOCIOLOGY

ECONOMICS

PREFACE

International migration, the movement of people across borders, has affected states and societies since time immemorial. It is one of history's great constants. Yet its role in forging states and societies not infrequently is neglected or forgotten. The oft repeated slogan that Germany is not an immigration land perhaps best testifies to the commonplace disregard of migration history. As late as the early 1970s, study of international migration appeared an esoteric pursuit, save perhaps for historians of countries like the United States, Canada, Argentina, or Australia. Major subdisciplines of the social and political sciences, like international relations, despite the richness of their theory, had little to say about international migration and scarcely took note of it. Now, as more and more states are wont to declare that the boat is full, it finally is becoming clear that, with respect to one of the principal determinants of global order and disorder in the late twentieth century, international relations theory missed the boat. Fortunately, more generous assessments can be made: anthropology and demography fared better.

The contemporary migratory epoch dates from the late nineteenth century, when industrial states of the North Atlantic began to regulate international migration. The predominance of migration for employment defines the current period. Mass international migration linked to industrialization, changing labor markets, and transnational employment networks, however, has taken place along with concomitant flows of refugees, family reunification, and settler migration. One of the hallmarks of late-twentieth-century migration is the blurring of various, formerly more distinctive, types of migrants. Western democracies in particular face increasingly difficult tasks, for instance, in distinguishing refugees from economically motivated migrants.

No one is certain how many international migrants there are; 100 million recent international migrants is a figure commonly heard. If this is anywhere near the mark, migrants would represent only about 2 percent of the world's population. Clearly, the vast majority of the world's population resides at home. But virtually all available information suggests that a major quantitative upsurge in international migration has occurred over the past several decades. In addition, more so than in the past, international migration is a global phenomenon, affecting all areas of the world. As late as 1988, international migration specialists could joke that, if the world consisted of states like Japan and Albania, the former understood to be a land without immigrants and the latter a state from which it was virtually impossible to leave, there would not be a need for students of international migration. Only several years later, Japan finds itself grappling with difficult issues related to preventing a rising tide of illegal immigrants, and a substantial fraction of the Albanian population has gone abroad, mainly to nearby Greece and

8

Italy. One indication of the global migration upsurge can be found in the doubling of the estimated global refugee population from roughly 8 to 17 million over the decade of the 1980s. Moreover, international population movements play a growing role in the international political economy. The estimated $67 billion in migrant wage remittances ranks labor migration only behind oil in terms of its significance to world trade.

Increasingly, major events in domestic and international politics directly or indirectly involve migration. The Gulf War and its sequels, for instance, displaced an estimated 5-6 million persons, with sometimes catastrophic effects on the most fragile of the world's economies. The transformation of the Warsaw bloc area was precipitated in part by the movement of ethnic Hungarian refugees from Romania through Hungary to Austria. When Austria moved to stem the inflow of these and other refugees and asylum seekers, Hungary, confronted by a growing alien and refugee population in its territory, moved to eradicate the barriers separating Hungary and Austria. This, in turn, created opportunities for exit by citizens of the German Democratic Republic and set into motion a chain of events that led to the fateful East German decision to dismantle the Berlin Wall in order to permit "temporary" exit of its citizens to the Federal Republic of Germany.

Events like these have thrust international migration issues to the top of governmental agendas in the post-Cold War period. There is every reason to expect the number of international migrants to increase in coming years if global disparities in wealth, life chances, political order, and demography continue to sharpen rather than attenuate. Globalization of the economy and continued advances in transportation and communication make more rather than less international migration in future decades a safe bet. However daunting this prospect may be from the perspective of governmental regulation, it is a far cry from overly alarmist scenarios of uncontrollable mass migration. Even in plausible situations like the collapse in great disorder of the military-backed secular government in Algeria, it is difficult to see how events there would result in uncontrollable mass migration to a country like France. There has been a steady inflow of the Algerian middle class into France since the rise of the fundamentalist Islamic Salvation Front in the late 1980s and many more Algerians would like to emigrate if they could. But the hard reality is that most cannot get out now and will not be able to do so in the future. Events since 1989 suggest that only a fraction of the vast pool of aspiring migrants worldwide succeed in making it to a country like France. Others succeed in making it to less desirable places abroad. But most simply do not. If the mass migrations were to materialize, they would have done so already.

Still, what might be termed the new high politics of migration appears warranted. One of the reasons why governments are belatedly paying more attention to international migration arises from the uneven effects of international migration on societies. Migration affects major cities and certain areas, usually those that are most economically dynamic, much more than other areas. Various industries and socioeconomic milieus also tend to be quite unevenly affected. The concentration of migrants in particular areas and industries has contributed to sociopolitical tensions that in some societies have exploded into violence and in others have fed anti-immigrant political movements. International migration possesses both negative and positive potential for societies. Political and socioeconomic circumstances and the policies of governments determine how international migration will affect societies. Perceptions of those effects can change rapidly and, over the long run, dramatically.

The immediate post-Cold War period witnessed a commingling of, on the one hand, celebration of international migration and its putative beneficial economic effects, most clearly seen in the adoption of the Immigration Act of 1990 in the United States, with, on the other hand, a deepening gloom over prospects for successful governmental regulation of international migration. The 1990 law increased legal immigration to the United States by 35 percent and allotted additional visas on employment grounds in particular. For some, the celebration of international migration as a positive economic factor and skepticism as to the capacity of democratic states to prevent unwanted international migration went hand in hand. They were two faces of a triumphant affirmation of liberal ideology and the corollary vision of post-Cold War world order. In this vision, the new realities and imperatives created by the globalization of the economy necessitated liberalization of trade and the creation of regional trading blocs. The sovereign state seemed anachronistic and its inability to regulate international migration provided further evidence of its obsolescence.

Thus serious doubts have arisen as to the ability of governments, particularly Western democratic ones, to regulate international migration at a time when global migratory propensities are on the rise. The articles in this volume address various facets of what looms as a principal foreign and domestic policy issue worldwide in the foreseeable future. With the exception of the overview by Gary Freeman, each article endeavors to address a specific empirical dimension of the global question. Units of analysis vary, as do the presuppositions and policy orientations of the contributors. What emerges is a mixed record. Some states have quite successfully regulated international migration while others have not. Certain types of migration seem more amenable to control than others. All the cases studied suggest a growing governmental response to what W. R. Böhning has termed unwanted migration.

Gary P. Freeman breaks down the broad question of state or governmental capacity to regulate international migration into four policy areas: legal immigration, illegal migration, asylum seekers, and temporary foreign workers. While he finds an uneven record of evidence in the four areas, his major thrust is to warn against facile notions of governmental inability to affect international migration flows. The range of his comparisons mirrors those of the ensuing articles and attests to the convergence of international migration policy concerns among Western democracies. While the problems and issues faced are analogous, various governments operate in distinctive institutional, geographical, and historical contexts that affect how effectively they deal with migration control challenges.

The next three articles examine the effects of the Immigration Reform and Control Act (IRCA) of 1986 in the United States. Rosanna Perotti reviews evidence concerning implementation of three major provisions of the act, which are employer sanctions, measures to ensure nondiscrimination in the wake of penalization of unauthorized employment of aliens, and the legalization of alien farm workers. She finds that implementation faltered badly in all three areas but that the law was but a first step toward curbing illegal migration.

In broad comparative terms, adoption of the 1986 immigration law brought the United States closer to Western Europe, where similar measures typically were enacted in the mid-1970s. This has prompted some to regard the adoption of sanctions in the United States as a European import and a misguided one at that. In fact, however, adoption of employer sanctions by the U.S. government was advocated during the Bracero period, in the 1940s and early 1950s, by Mexico, which saw in sanctions a way to ensure U.S. employer compliance with the terms of the bilateral labor program. Under the so-called Texas Proviso of the 1952 legislation, which, as amended, still serves as the basis of U.S. immigration law, employers were specifically exempted from punishment for hiring aliens entitled to work in the country. Whatever the shortcomings in the implementation of the 1986 law, it overcame an enormous hurdle to a credible governmental response to growing concern over illegal migration by doing away with the Texas Proviso. While her assessment of the implementation of the three provisions provides little comfort to the vast majority of Americans who want to see illegal migration curbed, Professor Perotti clearly seems to feel that the future will witness more serious efforts to control illegal migration.

Philip L. Martin focuses on the effects of the 1986 law on one industry, agriculture. His analysis deepens that of Perotti and likewise provides little comfort to those who hoped that IRCA would significantly reduce illegal migration. He makes a damning analysis of the Special Agricultural Worker legalization program, which must rank among the most fraud-ridden and counterproductive policies ever adopted by the U.S. government. This particular legalization opportunity, however, was the sine qua non for passage of IRCA. It was a bitter pill to swallow for proponents of immigration reform as it was not debated and was crafted to assuage powerful agricultural interests. Martin, who served as a member of the Commission on Agricultural Workers authorized by IRCA, bemoans the growing incidence of poverty among farm workers and increasing employer reliance on farm labor contractors who engage illegal aliens. Essentially, IRCA did little to change the underlying system in which certain growers receive a labor subsidy in the form of poorly remunerated, frequently illegal alien labor. Indeed, this sector is expanding, with untoward socioeconomic and moral effects for American society.

David S. North expands upon and deepens Perotti's analysis in another way. While Martin examined a particular industry heavily affected by migration, North makes Los Angeles County his unit of analysis. He reasoned that, if IRCA were to have measurable effects, they assuredly would manifest themselves in the area of the United States that is perhaps the most affected by international migration. North studied enforcement of the minimum wage and employer sanctions by investigating four agencies. His conclusions are grim, a proponent of immigration reform's equivalent of Zola's *J'accuse*. North's inclusion of minimum wage enforcement is particularly significant because increased enforcement of such laws is frequently advocated as an alternative to employer sanctions. North found little interagency cooperation, hence next to none of the complementary enforcement imperative to effective deterrence of illegal alien employment and other violations of labor law. The legislative and administrative reforms proposed by North on the basis of his research merit the careful scrutiny of all concerned Americans. They could well serve as the basis for an effort to strengthen employer sanctions enforcement by the Clinton administration.

The second group of articles has a focus on asylum seekers and refugees. Christopher Mitchell's analysis of U.S. policy toward Haitian entrants serves as a bridge between the U.S. case studies and the international comparisons that constitute the rest of the volume. Mitchell tackles one of the most controversial and sensitive issues in U.S. foreign and domestic politics in the 1980s and 1990s. He finds that the U.S. government does possess a capacity to prevent what is viewed as economically motivated migration, but that the deterrence comes at a considerable moral and ethical price in terms of U.S. commitments to refugees and asylees.

The fine line walked by the United States, of course, closely resembles the situation in Europe, which is the topic of Catherine Wihtol de Wenden's study of French responses to the asylum seeker influx in recent years. Her conclusions dovetail with those of Mitchell. French reforms of asylum policy have resulted in a drop in asylum applications, despite France's having a rate of asylum applicant recognition much higher than those of many of its neighbors. De Wenden's article also mentions the most recent of a long succession of French legalization programs, this last one for asylum applicants who were denied refugee status but who stayed on long enough to be considered integrated into French society. Since circa 1968, French legalization programs have been viewed as exceptional. Yet they recur. As was the case in the early 1990s with asylum seekers who were denied refugee status yet were not removed from French territory, legalization opportunities in France are usually announced as part of a balanced effort by the government to curb illegal migration. Reinforcement of measures against illegal migration constitutes the stick and legalization the carrot. The parallels with the U.S. approach in 1986, of course, are striking.

The final article in the asylum/refugee section concerns Hong Kong. The influx of Vietnamese boat people to Hong Kong in the 1980s represented one of the crown colony's major foreign and domestic policy issues. The Hong Kong-based geographer Ronald Skeldon elucidates linkages between the Vietnamese influx and other migration issues. His analysis underscores the significance of homeland conditions and homeland governmental policies as factors influencing influxes of asylum seekers and refugees. While the dissuasive measures adopted by the colony's government clearly helped deter unwanted entry, the evolution of Vietnam's domestic economy and the reorientation of its foreign policy also played critical roles in the attenuation of the influx by 1993. The Hong Kong case study reflects the shift in conceptualization of international migration control strategies from an inward-looking preoccupation with domestic or internal measures to prevent unauthorized entry to a broader perspective inclusive of foreign policy, trade, and development assistance.

The next brace of articles involves case studies of national responses to the immigration control question common to all Western democracies. Robert Birrell's analysis of Australian control efforts, with frequent and telling comparisons made to the United States and Canada, seems to represent one extreme of the spectrum. Australia by and large has achieved an acceptable degree of control over international migration. Illegal migration is not widespread. Geography helps explain Australia's relative success, but other factors contribute as well. One of them is the strength of Australia's union movement, which, as elsewhere, is under duress. Birrell argues that measures undertaken by the Australian government since the late 1980s have diminished perceived problems like overstaying of visas.

The French immigration expert Claude-Valentin Marie analyzes the evolution of French governmental policy toward illegal labor and the underground economy. The growth of the informal or underground economy, what Germans call "*Schwarzarbeit*," is the context in which employment of aliens occurs. Illegal alien employment is a subset of all illegal practices by employers; it sometimes is equated and confused with a phenomenon that largely involves delinquency by citizens, not aliens. Marie emphasizes the importance of distinguishing between the broader socioeconomic delinquency and the role played in it by some aliens. His analysis is cogent and salutary in that it corrects the unwarranted equation of clandestine employment with aliens. At the same time, his analysis sounds a tocsin for those who advocate more stringent prevention of illegal migration. Many socioeconomic trends are rendering attainment of that goal more elusive. Marie details the remarkable governmental effort to curb illegal work, including unauthorized alien employment, since the mid-1980s and concludes that considerable progress has been made. He foresees closer cooperation on the European level in the future, although he bemoans the continuing focus on illegal alien employment as opposed to illegal work in many European states. His analysis deserves to be scrutinized carefully by Americans wondering how to make employer sanction enforcement here more credible and less controversial.

Hans van Amersfoort and Rinus Penninx's study of Dutch and, by extension, Western European immigration control efforts represents the other extreme. They argue that the Dutch government, beginning with its foreign labor recruitment policies of the 1960s, has failed to prevent international migration, which, they assert, is by and large opposed by the Dutch public and government. They argue that foreign worker settlement and the arrival of large numbers of Dutch citizens from overseas territories have created the basis for continuing arrivals, mainly in the form of family reunification, that the government is powerless to prevent. They note that Dutch governmental policies aimed at inducing repatriation had little effect, that large numbers of asylum seekers have entered, and that governmental efforts to prevent illegal alien entry and employment are allocated insufficient resources. In sum, they are very skeptical of any claim that the Dutch government is able to control international migration.

The final two articles examine questions pertinent to any international migration control strategy: the effects of regional integration on migration and the potential for development assistance, trade policy adjustments, and private investment to spur migration-abating development. During the debate over the North American Free Trade Agreement (NAFTA), explicit references frequently were made to the European Community, now the European Union (EU), as an example of how regional integration can, over time, abate international migration. The European Community model was cited in support of the notion that NAFTA would reduce immigration from Mexico in much the same way that Italian emigration declined after the signature of the Treaty of Rome, which created the European Economic Community in 1957.

In his contribution, Heinz Werner reviews the history of labor migration between EU member states. Despite a freedom-of-labor-mobility provision, relatively fewer EU workers opt to work abroad in another member state than might have been anticipated. One reason for this has been the tendency for workers from areas of low wages and high unemployment, say, the boot of Italy, to migrate internally, say, to Turin or Milan, instead of to Frankfurt or Paris. More important, however, the EU essentially has involved integration of economies at roughly equal levels of development. Even the recent inclusion of Greece, Portugal, and Spain within the European labor market will not lead to a sharp rise in intra-EU labor migration in Werner's eyes.

High-level and professional-level mobility have increased due to the Single European Act of the mid-1980s, which removed remaining barriers to labor mobility. But the trend is for decreasing migration of low-level manpower within the EU. This reflects the economic restructuring that has been ongoing since the 1970s, which has caused high unemployment of lesser-skilled, blue-collar workers. There are few vacancies for unskilled workers that are filled by such workers from elsewhere within the EU.

Werner's analysis reminds us that the EU is a very different creature from NAFTA. The EU involves a political project that, up to now, has not figured in discussions of North American regional integration. Moreover, regional integration in Western Europe involved, on the whole, similar economies, a quite different situation from that which exists between the United States and Mexico. Perhaps a more appropriate comparison would be between the EU's relationship with Turkey and the relationship between the United States and Mexico than with the Italy-Mexico comparison. Significantly, Turkey signed an association agreement with the EU in the early 1970s, but when it sought accession to full membership in recent years, its bid was rebuffed. Unofficially, it was feared that the grant of full membership to Turkey would lead to excessive migration, as a large developmental gap persists between Turkey and the EU as well as demographic disequilibria. NAFTA is likely to increase, not decrease, illegal migration from Mexico over the short to medium term. Over the long term, however, NAFTA should tend to decrease the developmental gap between North American states, and this will tend to decrease illegal migration of Mexicans.

The final word, appropriately, is had by W. R. Böhning, the International Labour Office's indefatigable migration specialist, who, over the past quarter century, has done more than anyone else to increase understanding of international migration. His concerns are trade expansion, foreign direct investment, and official development assistance as strategies to reduce international migration. Since 1989, these three questions have been revisited with a sense of urgency. His analysis of their potential for migration reduction is sobering and would seem to suggest that, however urgent improved and expanded international cooperation on migration issues is, individual states will not be able to forgo reliance on internal control strategies in the foreseeable future. The International Labour Office specialist outlines a strategy for cooperation between emigration countries, immigration countries, and multilateral organizations, a so-called bottoms-up approach that merits consideration and possibly emulation worldwide.

Collectively, the articles that constitute this volume sound an alarm. It is clear that much more will have to be done by many states if they are to keep international migration a positive factor in international comity rather than a source of tension and disorder. Several of the studies also point to a need for more intensive and systematic reflection on the normative and ethical dimensions of immigration and refugee policies.

At the same time, this volume suggests that governments do possess a limited capacity to prevent unwanted migration and that many recent reforms and policy initiatives have yielded measurable and desired results. There is little reason to think that governments are powerless to prevent unwanted migration or that sovereignty is an outmoded concept. For the primarily American audience of this journal, it is hoped that the present volume facilitates thoughtful and dispassionate analysis of the difficult challenge confronting the United States in the immigration policy realm. This volume underscores that the dilemma faced by the United States is shared by many of its closest allies and that cross-national learning is not only possible but imperative.

Twenty or thirty years from now, international migration will still be a historical constant. One suspects, though, that the decisions made concerning it in the meantime will do much to determine whether the post-Cold War period is one of renewed international order or a descent into disorder. Never before has the study of international migration appeared so central to statecraft. Yet the theories that most inform statecraft, namely, theories of international relations, scarcely address international migration. This cannot and will not endure.

An editorial note: as this volume was being finalized, the Treaty on European Union was ratified and went into effect, and what had been known as the European Community become the European Union. The articles in this issue might not reflect this change in terminology, however, due to the timing of events.

MARK J. MILLER

ANNALS, *AAPSS*, **534**, July 1994

Can Liberal States
Control Unwanted Migration?

By GARY P. FREEMAN

ABSTRACT: The commonly held view that liberal democracies cannot effectively control unwanted migration is unwarranted despite the intensification of migration pressures in recent years. To develop a more accurate position built on less sweeping generalizations, I disaggregate migration policy into four parts: managing legal immigration, controlling illegal migration, administering temporary worker programs, and processing asylum seekers and refugees. A review of the experiences of the liberal democracies with each of these migration challenges indicates that although there are numerous instances of policy failure, there is also considerable capacity to regulate migration. I argue that this capacity is certainly growing, not declining, over time, that some states possess more capacity than others, that the control capacities of particular states vary substantially across the four areas, and that these capacities fluctuate periodically in conjunction with contingent cycles of salience and effort.

Gary P. Freeman is a political scientist at the University of Texas at Austin. The author of Immigrant Labor and Racial Conflict in Industrial Societies: The French and British Experience, *he most recently cowrote and edited, with James Jupp,* Nations of Immigrants: Australia, the United States, and International Migration. *He is currently involved in a collaborative study of the nexus between trade and migration in the APEC region.*

THESE days one often hears assertions that liberal democracies cannot control immigration. A common view holds that push factors like population growth, poverty, and the irrepressible desire of individuals for economic advancement create such an ample supply of potential migrants from the poor countries that they defeat the attempts of rich states to resist. A second argument focuses on pull factors that derive from the material and moral economies of the advanced countries and are thought to stimulate global demand for migration. The structure of labor markets in the rich countries creates low-wage, low-skill jobs that, in the widely trafficked cliché, "the natives refuse to do."

Both push and pull theses deserve serious consideration. Supply-side pressures are strong and growing, and the role the receiving states play as magnets for immigration is a compelling topic. Taken together, these tendencies describe a global political economy that is becoming more integrated at a rapid pace and in which population movements are apt to be as important as movements of capital, goods, and services.[1]

This article will address the question of whether democratic states can mount effective policies to regulate migration for public purposes. Pessi-

mists argue that the laws, programs, and techniques employed by states to manage immigration are necessarily inadequate to the task. My premise is that such claims are exaggerated and unwarranted. A review of the immigration experiences of liberal states indicates neither that they have fundamentally failed to regulate and control population movements across their borders nor that it is impossible to exercise more control. The record is much more mixed. Any assessment of the control capacities of states must replace sweeping generalizations with more limited and specific claims.

I start by disaggregating migration policy, which is too broad a construct for our purposes. I discuss four distinct policy arenas that reflect the specific tasks and problems migration poses: (1) managing legal immigration through planning and migrant selection, (2) controlling illegal migration by patrolling the borders and enforcing visa requirements and employer sanctions, (3) administering temporary worker programs, and (4) processing asylum seekers and refugees and deterring frivolous claims. This list does not exhaust the dimensions of migration decisions. Dealing exclusively with control and regulation aspects of policy, it leaves such matters as integration, naturalization, and host-immigrant relations to the side.

I proceed with a brief and selective survey of the performance of liberal states with respect to these four aspects of immigration policy. The discussion is limited to those states that have liberal democratic institutions and processes. The argument would

---

1. Continuous Reporting System on Migration (SOPEMI), *Trends in International Migration* (Paris: Organization for Economic Cooperation and Development, 1992); Reginald T. Appleyard, *International Migration: Challenge for the Nineties* (Geneva: International Organization for Migration, 1991); Doris M. Meissner et al., *International Migration Challenges in a New Era* (New York: Trilateral Commission, 1993).

not extend to nonliberal states that are not bound by the same constitutional and political constraints. My review will show that democratic states operate under severe handicaps in the development and implementation of migration policies and experience frequent setbacks and failures. Nevertheless, they exhibit considerable capacity to regulate migration. I argue (1) that this capacity is certainly growing, not declining, over time; (2) that some states possess more capacity than others; (3) that the control capacities of particular states vary substantially across the four migration policy arenas; and (4) that these capacities fluctuate periodically in conjunction with cycles of salience and effort.

MANAGING LEGAL IMMIGRATION

The most basic migration policy tasks of states are to establish the terms under which persons may legally enter the national territory for long-term or permanent residence and to plan and manage inflows to contribute to national economic, social, demographic, and security objectives. This involves not only setting numerical targets but also determining the criteria by which migrants will be recruited or selected.

Canada, the United States, and Australia are the most important traditional countries of immigration. Among the West European states, only France and Belgium have promoted significant permanent immigration in the past. All the European democracies are under pressure to become immigration countries today, but they have only belatedly begun to develop frameworks for immigration planning.[2]

From a historical perspective, it is obvious that the settler societies enhanced their control and management capacities over the course of their national development. We have only to note that in the earliest days of European settlement, there were few if any restrictions on migration. These were built up gradually and, typically, after states adopted policies promoting and occasionally subsidizing immigration.[3] When exclusionary legislation was introduced, directed first at narrowly defined categories of individuals deemed undesirable, such as prostitutes and the insane, and then, more broadly, at Asians, it was undeniably effective.[4]

In one important respect, control capacity has begun to slip away in

2. On France, see Gary S. Cross, *Immigrant Workers in Industrial France: The Making of a New Laboring Class* (Philadelphia: Temple University Press, 1983). On the new countries of immigration, see Wayne A. Cornelius, "Controlling Illegal Immigration: Spain" (Paper delivered at the workshop "Controlling Illegal Immigration: A Global Perspective," Center for U.S.-Mexican Studies, University of California, San Diego, 18-20 March 1993); idem, "Controlling Illegal Immigration: The Case of Japan," ibid.; Kitty Calavita, "Italy and the New Immigration," ibid.

3. Robert Hughes, *The Fatal Shore* (New York: Random House, 1986); James Jupp, *Immigration* (Sydney: Sydney University Press, 1991); Thomas J. Archdeacon, *Becoming American: An Ethnic History* (New York: Free Press, 1983); Daniel Kubat, "Canada," in *The Politics of Migration Policies*, ed. Daniel Kubat (Staten Island, NY: Center for Migration Studies, 1979), pp. 22-23.

4. Charles A. Price, *The Great White Walls Are Built: Restrictive Immigration to North America and Australasia 1836-1888* (Canberra: Australian National University Press, 1974).

recent years. None of the liberal democracies, with the arguable exceptions of Great Britain and Japan, any longer indulges in selecting migrants according to ethnicity or national origins.[5] The new nondiscriminatory principles are a response to changes in both the domestic and international climates and, however welcome, represent a substantial constraint on national policies.

Otherwise, an examination of the contemporary structure of programs in the traditional immigration countries uncovers considerable variation in the capacity to select and recruit migrants and indications of a growing commitment to control. Australia, because of circumstances peculiar to its founding such as the need to attract migrants to a faraway and relatively expensive destination and the desire to preserve the European character of the population, has for a long time had a more formidable and interventionist state immigration apparatus than either Canada or the United States. One of the first acts of the new federal legislature in 1901 was the enactment of a comprehensive immigration law. Today Australia imposes a universal visa requirement that, combined with the special advantages of an island state, produces considerably more mastery

over entries than either Canada or the United States can achieve.[6]

Both Australia and Canada set annual intake targets in cabinet, and in both countries, governments have substantial discretion in the implementation of the targets. In Canada, the immigration ministry develops a five-year plan for intakes, but the government may alter the target if economic or other conditions suggest that it should.[7] Annual ceilings—not targets—for entry into the United States are legislated by Congress, and the executive has little flexibility to depart from them, except in the case of refugees whose numbers are determined annually by the State Department in consultation with Congress. Congress, in turn, alters annual ceilings infrequently and af-

5. Universalism was adopted in the United States in 1965, in Australia in 1973, in New Zealand in 1974, and in Canada in 1967. On Britain and Japan, see Zig Layton-Henry, *The Politics of Immigration: Immigration, "Race" and "Race" Relations in Post-War Britain* (Oxford: Basil Blackwell, 1992); *A Guide to Entry, Residence and Registration Procedures in Japan for Foreign Nationals* (Tokyo: Japan Immigration Association, 1990); Cornelius, "Controlling Illegal Immigration: The Case of Japan."

6. The only exception to the visa program is trans-Tasman migration under the Closer Economic Relations pact with New Zealand. See A. T. Yarwood, *Asian Migration to Australia* (London: Cambridge University Press, 1964); Gary P. Freeman, "From 'Populate or Perish' to 'Diversify or Decline': Immigration and Australian National Security," in *International Migration and Security*, ed. Myron Weiner (Boulder, CO: Westview Press, 1993), pp. 89-92; Kathryn Cronin, "A Culture of Control," in *The Politics of Australian Immigration*, ed. James Jupp and Marie Kabala (Canberra: Australian Government Printing Service, 1993), pp. 83-104.

7. Meyer Burstein, "Immigration Management: Control and Policy Concerns" (Paper delivered at the Conference on Immigration and Refugee Policy: The Australian and Canadian Experiences, York University, Toronto, 2-5 May 1992); Peter Lloyd, "The Political Economy of Immigration," in *Politics of Australian Immigration*, ed. Jupp and Kabala, pp. 59-82; Robert Holton and Judith Sloan, "Immigration Policy: Intake and Settlement Issues," in *Australian Immigration: A Survey of the Issues*, ed. Mark Wooden et al. (Canberra: Australian Government Printing Service, 1990), pp. 304-5.

ter lengthy and highly politicized legislative battles.[8]

How well do the three countries manage their numbers? The United States has experienced strong pressures that consistently fill its applicant pool to overflowing. In Australia, some critics describe policy in the 1970s and 1980s as a series of cave-ins and blowouts,[9] even though entries have sometimes fallen below planned targets. Canada failed to fall within its targeted range for new entries in any of the 12 years between 1980 and 1991, though the gap was small in some cases and the government was below as often as above the target.[10]

Both Canada and Australia implement immigrant selection through a points system that is designed to rate prospective entrants according to their qualifications, which in turn are linked in part to assessments of national labor market requirements. The points system is the most economically rational method of selection for permanent settlement, and its invention seemed to represent a

major step toward more systematic and comprehensive control over legal immigration. Points systems have serious deficiencies, however, and there are those who would argue that in their execution, both Australian and Canadian officials fall short of the mark. Either they fail to establish proper criteria for determining who desirable immigrants are by, for example, being unable to predict the types of skills that the economy will need or they fail to attract or select those who meet the criteria established.[11] Nevertheless, the creation of a points system denotes a state that seeks to tie immigration to the demands of the national labor market and is an expression of a strong planning instinct. It is the major alternative to a system dominated by the principle of family reunion.

No factor contributes more to the vitiation of state capacity to plan legal immigration than the norm of family reunification. The family category dominates the legal immigration statistics of all the immigration countries and is an important factor in transforming temporary worker programs into permanent immigration, as we shall see. Migration formally under the family category constitutes over two-thirds of total immigration in the United States and from one-half to two-thirds in Canada and Australia. It plays havoc with targeting overall numbers because governments cannot be sure how many persons with a claim for

8. Frank D. Bean and Michael Fix, "The Significance of Recent Immigration Policy Reforms in the United States," in *Nations of Immigrants: Australia, the United States, and International Migration*, ed. Gary P. Freeman and James Jupp (Melbourne and New York: Oxford University Press, 1992), pp. 41-55; Gary P. Freeman and Katharine Betts, "The Politics of Interests and Immigration Policymaking in Australia and the United States," in ibid., pp. 72-88.

9. See Katharine Betts, *Ideology and Immigration: Australia 1976 to 1987* (Melbourne: Melbourne University Press, 1988), pp. 120-56; Robert Birrell, "Problems of Immigration Control in Liberal Democracies: The Australian Experience," in *Nations of Immigrants*, ed. Freeman and Jupp, pp. 23-40.

10. Burstein, "Immigration Management Control and Policy Concerns," chart 1.

11. For a description of the points system in Canada, see Economic Council of Canada, *Economic and Social Impacts of Immigration* (Ottawa: Minister of Supply and Services, 1991), pp. 5-19.

immediate or preferential entry will present themselves in a given year. According to one Canadian official, this means that, in practice, planning annual intakes consists of estimating the number of persons who will enter the country through the family category—and also the refugee and humanitarian programs—and then expanding or contracting the independent or skills category to hit the target because it is the only segment over which the planners have direct control.[12] The 1990 Immigration Act in the United States institutes a modest skills component that moves in the direction of the Canadian and Australian systems but remains to demonstrate its effectiveness.[13] The actual impact of family considerations on migration flows is surely understated by official statistics. Lloyd has shown that for Australia in recent years, 85.6 percent of all entrants have had close family connections in the country.[14]

Looking broadly at the administration of legal programs in the traditional immigration countries, one concludes that the secular trend is clearly in the direction of more capacity, that control over absolute numbers is good though imperfect, but that migrant selection is highly problematic. Generally speaking, both Australia and Canada have more effective programs than the United States, though this is more a comment on the disrepair of the programs of the latter than an endorsement of the former.

CONTROLLING ILLEGAL MIGRATION

The apprehension of persons seeking to enter or remain in a country illegally is a problem every country confronts. It is in many respects more challenging than managing legal immigration because it has to do with individuals trying to evade detection or mislead the authorities. Moreover, there is evidence that those seeking clandestine entry and irregular status have become more ingenious in finding ways to skirt the law in recent years.[15] The presence of illegal immigrants indicates a failure of control mechanisms but should not be taken to mean that states cannot control their borders. Just as no country is willing to expend the resources and bear the costs necessary to reduce crime to near zero, neither would it be rational to try to establish impervious borders. We should assess the problem from the perspective of what a reasonable level of illegal immigration might be.

The two broad means of dealing with illegal migrants are (1) measures to prevent persons from entering the country without permission such as physical controls at frontiers and airports—what may be called external controls—and (2) the supervision of persons legally in the country to ensure that they leave when their visas expire and do not engage in illegal activities such as working

12. Burstein, "Immigration Management: Control and Policy Concerns."

13. Bean and Fix, "Significance of Recent Immigration Policy Reforms."

14. Lloyd, "Political Economy of Immigration," tab. 4.3, p. 77.

15. Employment and Immigration Canada, Managing Immigration: A Framework for the 1990s (Ottawa: Employment and Immigration Canada, 1992), pp. 6-8.

without permits—what may be called internal controls. A related response that is common is legalizing the status of long-term undocumented residents and their children. Although this essentially concedes defeat and is, in any case, a temporary measure, amnesties are usually undertaken in conjunction with renewed enforcement efforts.[16]

The effectiveness of external policies is highly dependent on the physical location of states. Australia has perhaps the least serious border control problem; the United States, undeniably the worst. Although individuals occasionally reach Australian shores through surreptitious means, the chief source of illegal immigrants involves persons overstaying their visas. In 1974-75, the government guessed that the numbers might be as high as 60,000, and a May 1990 estimate put the figure at 90,000. Various governments have dealt with the problem through a combination of additional compliance officers, expedited deportation procedures, and, in 1976 and 1980, amnesties.[17] Canadian officials estimated that there might be 50,000 illegals in the country in 1983, nearly a decade after a general amnesty had been declared in 1973. A policy of imposing visa requirements on countries

whose nationals show a tendency to become illegals has gradually resulted in most of the important source countries being covered.[18]

U.S. problems with illegal immigration eclipse those of other countries. The long, unfenced border with Mexico creates unique problems, but illegal entry is also common at airports and along thousands of miles of coastline. A 1980 government report concluded grimly that the Immigration and Naturalization Service (INS) "has not been able to adequately enforce immigration laws and . . . [it] has neither the legal means nor sufficient resources to stem the growing number of illegal aliens."[19] Estimates of the size of the illegal population in the 1970s and 1980s ranged from 3 to 12 million.[20] Growing concern about these matters culminated in the 1986 Immigration Reform and Control Act, the primary purpose of which was to stem illegal entries. The law resulted in amnesties being given to over 3 million persons, with provisions for the further entry of their families, but it had only a brief and limited effect on illegal movement across the southern border.[21] The widespread perception

16. For a comprehensive overview of the various sorts of illegal migration and the wide range of policy options available to deal with them, see David S. North, *Enforcing the Immigration Law: A Review of the Options* (Washington, DC: Center for Labor and Migration Studies, 1980).

17. Charles Price, "Australia: A New Multicultural Country?" in *The Politics of Migration Policies*, 2d ed., ed. Daniel Kubat (Staten Island, NY: Center for Migration Studies, 1993), p. 17.

18. Daniel Kubat, "Canada: Immigration's Humanitarian Challenge," in *The Politics of Migration Policies*, ed. Kubat.

19. U.S., General Accounting Office, *Prospects Dim for Effectively Enforcing Immigration Laws* (Washington, DC: General Accounting Office, 1980), p. i.

20. David Simcox, "Overview: A Time of Reform and Reappraisal," in *U.S. Immigration in the 1980s: Reappraisal and Reform*, ed. David Simcox (Boulder, CO: Westview Press, 1988), tab. 1.10, pp. 28-29.

21. Bean and Fix, "Significance of Recent Immigration Policy Reforms," pp. 44-47; Mark J. Miller, "Never Ending Story: The US

that this law has failed contributes to the consensus that serious border control is impossible. Spending on INS enforcement activities, especially the border patrol, has gone up markedly in the 1980s and received another substantial boost with the 1986 immigration act. But, as Simcox notes, "discounted for inflation, the INS budget had increased two and one half times in the twenty years following 1965, but the agency share of the overall federal budget had actually fallen by almost 2 percent in that period. Personnel growth also lagged behind work load and new responsibilities."[22]

Timid efforts to build a wall at heavy crossing points near San Diego seemed only to highlight the ineffectiveness of the authorities. Calls for a more forceful approach were either ridiculed as unrealistic or condemned as authoritarian. Some of this pessimism may need to be rethought in light of events in El Paso in the latter part of 1993. A new Border Patrol chief in the city imposed a strict enforcement policy called Operation Hold the Line and brought about dramatic reductions in the number of illegal crossings. Public opinion is strongly supportive, although immigrant advocate groups and some businesses have complained. The costs of the initiative make it unclear if it can be sustained in the long run, but its effectiveness is hard to deny.[23]

Illegal immigration in Europe is a complicated matter. It involves a variety of irregular statuses, and the sorts of problems experienced have changed rather dramatically over time with alterations in European migration policies. I will discuss European attempts to limit work by undocumented aliens through employer sanctions momentarily, but a word on more general efforts to control illegals is in order. As Europe has shut down many of the legal entry routes in recent years, there has been an upsurge in illegal entry or visa overstayers, and official attitudes have hardened. Enforcement is aided by the European practice of requiring national identity cards and by the extensive cooperation between European states on the matter. Against this must be set the difficulties arising from the movement toward the elimination of internal borders within the European Union.[24]

Employer sanctions are the most important internal control mechanism. Sanctions operate on the principle that, by removing the possibility of working, one removes the chief incentive for illegal migration. Sanctions were the most controversial aspect of the American immigration reform of 1986, and they have been, paradoxically, widely criticized as both ineffective and contributing to employer discrimination against minorities.[25] Comparative evidence from

Debate over Illegal Immigration," in *Nations of Immigrants*, ed. Freeman and Jupp, pp. 65-68.

22. Simcox, "Overview," p. 43.

23. *Austin American Statesman*, 26-28 Nov. 1993.

24. Didier Bigo, *L'Europe des polices et de la sécurité intérieure* (Paris: Editions Complexe, 1992); Mark J. Miller, *Employer Sanctions in Europe* (Staten Island, NY: Center for Migration Studies, 1987), pp. 19-23.

25. *Employer Sanctions and U.S. Labor Markets: First Report* (Washington, DC: Department of Labor, Bureau of International

Western Europe, however, suggests that sanctions are an essential component of any concerted effort to control illegal migration.

Although some European states have operated sanctions since the interwar era, most adopted them in the 1970s after the end to new labor recruitment made illegal immigration a salient issue. Within Western Europe the only major country without some form of employer sanctions is Britain.[26] Studies show that sanctions were not effective when they were initially introduced. Rather, after some early setbacks, most states revised their programs or enforced them with renewed vigor. Among the factors found to be vital to the success of sanctions are adequate resources for those charged with enforcement, a secure identification system, linkages to broader strategies for controlling illegal migration, and steps to deal with the possibility that sanctions will lead to discrimination.[27] The failure of American sanctions surely results from the absence of most of these prerequisites, especially secure modes of identification.

Labor Affairs, Division of Immigration Policy and Research, 1991); *Employer Sanctions and U.S. Labor Markets: Second Report* (Washington, DC: Department of Labor, Bureau of International Labor Affairs, Division of Immigration Policy and Research, 1991); *Immigration Reform: Employer Sanctions and the Question of Discrimination* (Washington, DC: General Accounting Office, 1990).

26. Miller, *Employer Sanctions in Western Europe*, p. 46.

27. See ibid.; idem, "Employer Sanctions in Europe: Deterrence without Discrimination," in *U.S. Immigration in the 1980s*, ed. Simcox, pp. 217-28; Malcolm R. Lovell, Jr., "Europe's Lessons for America," in ibid., pp. 229-44.

TEMPORARY WORKER PROGRAMS

For those countries that are unwilling to accept permanent new immigrants on a regular basis, temporary worker programs can seem an attractive alternative for dealing with labor shortages. They promise to produce what Straubhaar calls the "allocational" benefits of migration while avoiding the "distributional" costs.[28] The most notable examples of such efforts are those of the Western European states in the period after World War II, but the Bracero program, involving the United States and Mexico from 1942 to 1964, is also pertinent.[29]

The most important thing to understand about temporary worker programs is that they involve direct, active, and voluntary steps by states to stimulate and organize influxes of foreign workers and, often, their families. They may be a response to pressing labor market needs, but they are not thrust on states innocent of all responsibility. Despite their surface appeal, temporary worker programs are enormously complex and difficult to manage. In the most comprehensive overview of European temporary worker programs, Miller and Martin's general assessment is not so much negative as it is cautionary. They observe that the chief outcome of the European experience has

28. Thomas Straubhaar, "Allocational and Distributional Aspects of Future Immigration to Western Europe," *International Migration Review*, 26(2):462-83 (Summer 1992).

29. Richard B. Craig, *The Bracero Program: Interest Groups and Foreign Policy* (Austin: University of Texas Press, 1971); Kitty Calavita, *Inside the State: The Bracero Program, Immigration and the I.N.S.* (New York: Routledge, 1992).

been the creation of a large, permanent, non-European population in Europe and that this was wholly unanticipated and certainly undesired by those who introduced the programs. A close reading of their account shows, however, that the administration of these programs was a mammoth undertaking that must be seen in many respects as a significant accomplishment, unfortunate as the ultimate outcome may have been. Miller and Martin's basic advice is that a country wishing to create temporary worker programs should do so with its eyes open, without unrealistic expectations, and with the commitment to invest heavily in a multiplicity of complicated aspects of the process.[30]

As Miller and Martin note, the European states failed most completely in planning for and carrying out the return of migrants. It had been expected that migrants would go back home voluntarily once their immediate economic goals had been obtained, after they had worked for a period of years, or if poor economic conditions made them redundant. In fact, none of these expectations proved realistic. Even faced with widespread unemployment, the majority of migrants preferred to stay on. Moreover, many had children born or reared in the host country who were even less likely to return. Active efforts by governments to stimulate return through financial and other inducements were unsuccessful,[31] and governments' ability to coerce return was sharply constrained by diplomatic, legal, and political considerations.

Hollifield's recent study concludes that the German and French cases provide

tantalizing evidence of the difficulties that liberal states must face in their attempts to regulate international migration. . . . The inability of French and German governments to use immigration policy as a mechanism for regulating labor supply and for making employment policy is an indication of constraints on the autonomy of the administrative state.[32]

But as Miller has observed, his argument may be overstated.[33] Hollifield builds his case in part on two important claims: that European states, especially France, did not regulate temporary migration effectively during expansionary periods and that the labor-importing countries could not end new entries or reduce dramatically the foreign component of their labor forces after the immigration halts in the early 1970s. Miller raises a number of empirical and technical objections to this argument, but there are interpretive issues as well.

It is quite hard to know if the fact that most foreign workers in France arrived through irregular channels and were regularized by the government after the fact is evidence of administrative incapacity or deliberate, if cynical, policy choice. In the latter

30. See Mark J. Miller and Philip A. Martin, *Administering Foreign-Worker Programs* (Lexington, MA: Lexington Books, 1982), p. xv.

31. Ibid., pp. 88-90.

32. James F. Hollifield, *Immigrants, Markets, and States: The Political Economy of Postwar Europe* (Cambridge, MA: Harvard University Press, 1992), p. 94.

33. See his review of Hollifield's book in *French Politics and Society*, 11(2):95-102 (Spring 1993).

view, officials achieved exactly what they needed by turning a blind eye to the flagrant and widespread disregard of the law. Recourse to regularization may be less evidence of the state's weakness and its capitulation to employer interests than of its ability to acquire a labor force that met its needs precisely because it was unorganized and irregular. Likewise, the fact that, after immigration was halted in 1974, large numbers of foreigners continued to enter France via family reunion, seasonal worker programs, and illegal means is evidence of state incapacity only if one assumes that policymakers intended for all immigration to come to an end. Miller suggests that this cannot be assumed.[34] The most convincing argument about temporary worker programs is that they tend to produce permanent immigration. Exactly why this occurs and whether the European states could do nothing to prevent it is impossible to say given strong evidence that no all-out effort was undertaken.

REFUGEE SELECTION
AND SETTLEMENT

States typically have a good deal more control over the introduction of refugees than over their more general immigration policies. Refugees are normally outside the national territory, often in camps administered by the United Nations High Commission for Refugees, where they may be interviewed by officials before being given entry permits. An interesting indicator of the greater state capacity is that the politics of

refugee selection in most countries is characterized by criticism of government policies by refugee advocate groups who think the policies are too strict, which is just the opposite of the political dynamics that develop over immigration policy.[35]

Of course, states are not perfectly free in the choice of their refugee programs. Refugee selection takes place within the context of a well-articulated international regime of treaties and agreements, backed up by a small but influential bureaucracy located in the United Nations. International norms reduce the flexibility of states. Moreover, refugee policy is often put at the service of foreign policy and diplomacy. This does not represent a weakening of state capacity per se, but it does mean that individuals or groups may be admitted for *raisons d'état* who would otherwise have been denied. Finally, it is in the nature of refugee affairs that they are marked by crisis. States will from time to time find themselves confronted with an urgent situation that more or less compels operating outside normal channels.

34. Ibid., pp. 97-98.

35. See Howard Adelman, "Canadian Refugee Policy in the Postwar Period: An Analysis," in *Refugee Policy: Canada and the United States*, ed. Howard Adelman (Toronto: York Lanes Press, 1991), pp. 172-223; James C. Hathaway, "The Conundrum of Refugee Protection in Canada: From Control to Compliance to Collective Deterrence," in *Refugees and the Asylum Dilemma in the West*, ed. Gil Loescher (University Park: Pennsylvania State University Press, 1992), pp. 71-92; Gil Loescher and John Scanlon, *Calculated Kindness: Refugees and America's Half-Open Door* (New York: Free Press and Macmillan, 1986); Danièle Joly, *Refugees: Asylum in Europe?* (Boulder, CO: Westview Press, 1992).

Refugees are a phenomenon of the twentieth century; the international refugee regime finds its roots in the interwar period. National states have developed specific refugee policies in conjunction with and in reaction to the evolving international apparatus and the proliferating refugee crises of this century. As is the case with immigration control, then, the ability of states to manage refugee flows has undeniably been increasing since World War II. At the same time, however, as the number of refugees and refugee-generating conflicts and disasters has multiplied, the evolving policy mechanisms have barely kept pace with the expanding problem.

Contemporary discussion of immigration in Europe is dominated by questions of political asylum. The difference between asylees and refugees is that the former are either in the country where refuge is sought or are at the border asking to come in. Clearly, dealing with asylum seekers is much more challenging than with refugees proper. Since 1989, hundreds of thousands of persons have sought asylum in Western Europe but also in the United States, Canada, and Australia. By any fair assessment, the great majority of these persons, however desperate their plight, are economic rather than "convention" refugees.[36] Their num-

bers can be explained by numerous factors, especially the collapse of the Soviet Union, but perhaps the most important is that since the general immigration halt of 1973-74, asylum has been the only legal means for migrating to Western European states. For some observers, the sheer numbers made effective responses impossible and threatened to undermine the international refugee system.

For all the alarm these migratory movements have occasioned, there is reason to believe that the European states, along with the European Community, are taking the matter in hand. To be sure, the situation is still in flux and many of the steps taken to deal with it have been expansive and capitulatory. In a recent review, I argued that there are three basic objectives by which refugee and asylum policies must be judged: deterring persons with unfounded claims, dealing equitably with those in legitimate refugee situations, and removing those whose cases have been found wanting.[37] Writing in the summer of 1992, I concluded that none of these objectives is being satisfactorily met, but that the states in the region, the European Union, and other multilateral institutions are responding to the pressures with a redoubling of their efforts to establish stable control. Laws are being passed, programs launched, new asylum processors put

36. United Nations High Commissioner for Refugees, *The State of the World's Refugees: The Challenge of Protection* (New York: Penguin Books, 1993). A convention refugee is any person who, owing to well-founded fear of being persecuted for reasons of race, religion, nationality, membership of a particular social group or political opinion, is outside the country of his nationality and is unable to or, owing

to such fear, is unwilling to avail himself of the protection of that country. 1951 Convention and 1967 Protocol relating to the Status of Refugees.

37. Gary P. Freeman, "Migration Policy and Politics in the Receiving States," *International Migration Review* 26(4): 1144-67 (Winter 1992).

on payroll. The German government has recently amended its Basic Law to give it much more ability to deal with frivolous claims. Countries like Spain, Greece, and Italy that had no immigration policy to speak of before these events are rapidly developing them. The crisis is having the ironic effect of reinforcing both the principle of national prerogatives with respect to immigration and the distinction between economic and political refugees.[38]

CONCLUSION

Can the liberal democracies control migration? Posed so broadly, the question invites undisciplined speculation. I wish to advance four more specific conclusions. First, if we step back from the present crisis and take a longer view, there is no doubt that the democracies have more and better means to control their borders, monitor foreigners within their territory, and manage international flows than they did twenty, fifty, or one hundred years ago. The long-term trend is undeniably toward greater, not less, government effort and capacity to control international migration. This has to be qualified, of course, by recognition of rising pressures for migration around the world, advances in the technologies of travel and communication, and evolving domestic and international norms and rules that assert the individual human rights of migrants and refugees against the prerogatives of sovereign states. The political, legal, and social forces arrayed against strict regulation are growing stronger everyday; at present, they are outpacing corresponding state efforts to retain or regain command, but states nowhere show an inclination to concede defeat.

Second, immigration policy performance varies widely across states. While there is a striking convergence in the nature of the problems democracies face and in the kinds of policies they adopt, there is divergence in their capacity to manage migration overall. For example, the settler societies of traditional immigration, especially the United States, operate under constraints that have much less effect in Western Europe. Within Europe, Britain has more effectively curtailed immigration than its neighbors, while Germany is possibly the most vulnerable country on the continent. This variety alerts us to steer clear of facile claims that the democracies cannot cope with migration pressures and invites a serious attempt to identify the factors that account for greater or lesser capacity of individual states. We need particularly to distinguish those characteristics common to all liberal democracies, those specific to the traditional immigration countries, and those that may be limited to particular states.[39]

38. The German reforms had immediate effect, with numbers of applicants dropping by one-third to two-thirds over the first several months. See Judy Dempsey, "Refugees Entering Germany on Decline," *Financial Times*, 5 Nov. 1993.

39. Existing comparative studies, with a few notable exceptions, have not taken up this challenge. Two excellent summaries that argue that policies are converging are Tomas Hammar, "Comparative Analysis," in *European Immigration Policy: A Comparative Study*, ed. Tomas Hammar (Cambridge: Cambridge University Press, 1985), pp. 239-304; Sarah Collinson, *Europe and International Migration* (London: Pinter, 1993), pp. 109-38.

Third, specific states, whatever their general performance, can deal with certain types of migration better than others. The United States may perform poorly across all areas, but the government has traditionally practiced *realpolitik* in refugee affairs and has occasionally been surprisingly tough when confronted with undesired influxes, as from Haiti. Australia and the United Kingdom have more control over illegals than other states, while Germany, until very recently, had its hands tied with respect to asylum seekers. No state has run a successful temporary worker program, though Swiss governments have walked a tightrope with impressive skill between a hostile public and powerful employers.

Fourth, the evidence clearly indicates that the capacity of states varies over time in response to the waxing and waning of contingent factors—economic fluctuations, migration pressures—and issue salience. The politics of immigration is strongly cyclical. State policies are highly variable in terms of their objectives and intensity. Since 1989, public attention has been riveted on migration problems and states have been developing responses at a frenetic pace, but this is highly unusual. More commonly, states allow migration problems to accumulate and migration control policies to flounder until rising public pressure or some crisis makes action unavoidable.

ANNALS, *AAPSS*, **534**, July 1994

Employer Sanctions
and the Limits of Negotiation

By ROSANNA PEROTTI

ABSTRACT: This article provides an overview and assessment of the implementation of the Immigration Reform and Control Act (IRCA) of 1986, the major U.S. law intended to curb illegal migration. Enforcement of employer sanctions, protection against possible discrimination linked to employer sanctions, and legalization of alien workers are considered. IRCA should be viewed as a first step in coping with illegal immigration, but much more will have to be done to achieve an optimal balance between hospitality and control.

Rosanna Perotti is an assistant professor of political science at Hofstra University, Hempstead, New York. She is currently working on a manuscript dealing with the adoption of the Immigration Reform and Control Act of 1986. She has made several panel presentations on Congress and IRCA and has authored "IRCA's Antidiscrimination Provisions: What Went Wrong," International Migration Review *(Fall 1992).*

31

THE Immigration Reform and Control Act (IRCA) of 1986 was passed amid high hopes. It promised to stem illegal immigration to the United States by imposing penalties—employer sanctions—on employers who hire aliens ineligible to work. IRCA promised to legalize a large proportion of illegal aliens already living in the United States, including thousands of farm workers in a special, separate legalization. It promised to strengthen border enforcement while at the same time providing immigrants new protections against workplace discrimination.

Yet three of the major provisions of IRCA—employer sanctions, the antidiscrimination provisions, and the Special Agricultural Worker (SAW) legalization program—began to unravel in the implementation stage. Employer sanctions failed to significantly curb long-term illegal immigration to the United States. IRCA's employer eligibility verification requirements were found to have prompted new discrimination against the foreign born. Finally, a significant number of the 1.3 million SAW applications were fraudulent; the Immigration and Naturalization Service (INS) had been unable to meet the burden of proof necessary to deny benefits to those who abused the program.

Scholars and policy analysts were busy trying to document and pinpoint the sources of these implementation failures when events in 1992 and 1993 created more pressure for added enforcement. In January 1993 a nominee for Attorney General was rejected because of her confession that she had hired two illegal aliens in violation of IRCA.[1] Less than a month later, several foreign-born religious militants were charged in connection with the bombing of the World Trade Center in New York City. Not only were some of the suspects ineligible to remain in the United States, but several of them had applied for political asylum in order to avert deportation, a tactic now common in Europe and the United States.[2] Laxness in immigration control attracted particularly spirited criticism in light of the economic recession. In California, particularly hard hit by the economic downturn, Governor Pete Wilson, only recently an advocate of a broad temporary worker program, argued that immigrants were putting a drain on the state's welfare system.[3]

A new restrictionist mood surfaced in U.S. media and public opinion in 1993, as 60 percent of respondents to a *Newsweek* poll said they believed immigration is currently a bad thing for the country.[4] Amid flagrant

1. Holly Idelson, "Baird's Wrenching Withdrawal Mars the Inaugural Week," *Congressional Quarterly Weekly Report*, 23 Jan. 1993, pp. 179-81.

2. See Craig R. Whitney, "Europeans Look for Ways to Bar Door to Immigrants," *New York Times*, 29 Dec. 1991. In the United States, requesting political asylum serves to delay deportation proceedings, creating requirements for a separate hearing. Often, if arrivals to the United States request political asylum after flying to the United States on a commercial airline, they cannot be detained and are paroled until their hearing.

3. Robert Reinhold, "In California, New Talk of Limits on Immigrants," *New York Times*, 3 Dec. 1991.

4. The *Newsweek* poll asked first, "Was immigration a good thing or a bad thing for this country in the past?" and second, "Is immigration a good thing or a bad thing for this country

abuses of the immigration system, the failures of IRCA appeared directly responsible. *Newsweek* joined a chorus of popular journals in calling for measures beyond IRCA: "Illegal immigration is undeniably out of control. Congress tried to stop it in 1986 with a law called IRCA. . . . The act has failed. Despite the amnesty, the estimated number of illegals has once again risen to between 2 million and 4 million people."[5]

In response to pressures for tighter immigration control, the House and Senate Judiciary committees by summer 1993 were considering a broad array of proposals to tighten immigration enforcement in the face of IRCA's failures: narrowing the number of allowed work-eligibility documents from IRCA's 17 to 1 or 2, tightening immigration control at the border and in airports, curbing document fraud, and reducing abuse of the asylum adjudication process. President Clinton joined in the chorus on 27 July 1993 with a legislative proposal to increase border patrol re-

sources, issue machine-readable visas and passports, and expand pre-inspection at foreign airports. Clinton's proposal also promised to tighten the asylum application and adjudication process and to increase criminal penalties for alien smuggling.[6]

This article examines the assertion that, as *Newsweek* put it, IRCA "failed." First, I address key defects in the implementation of IRCA. Second, I return to the possible sources of these defects—in particular, whether they could have been prevented during the 15 years of negotiation that preceded the adoption of IRCA. IRCA, I will argue, was not intended by its framers to be a cure-all for illegal immigration. Rather, employer sanctions were thought to be an essential step toward controlling immigration. IRCA's implementation was marked by considerable success; some of the defects serve simply to identify areas for improved immigration control in the future.

DEFECTS IN THE IMPLEMENTATION OF IRCA

IRCA's framers hoped the law would deter illegal immigration without imposing new discrimination on lawful immigrants. Legislators also hoped that legalizing large numbers of undocumented aliens already in the United States would create a large enough documented workforce to crowd out the market for cheap undocumented labor. However, three types of failures frustrated legislators' intentions. First, employer sanctions apparently did

today?" Fifty-nine percent of respondents said immigration had been good in the past, but only 29 percent said it was a good thing today. On the contrary, 31 percent said immigration had been a bad thing in the past, compared with 60 percent responding that immigration was a bad thing today. Rich Thomas with Andrew Murr, "The Economic Cost of Immigration," *Newsweek*, 9 Aug. 1993, p. 19. In a June 1993 *New York Times*/CBS News poll, 61 percent of respondents said immigration to the United States should be decreased, up from 33 percent of respondents in 1965, 42 percent in 1977, and 43 percent in 1986. Seth Mydans, "Poll Finds Tide of Immigration Brings Hostility," *New York Times*, 27 June 1993.

    5. Tom Morgenthau, "America: Still a Melting Pot?" *Newsweek*, 9 Aug. 1993, p. 20. Copyright © 1993, Newsweek, Inc. All rights reserved. Reprinted by permission.

    6. "Fact Sheet: Initiatives to Curb Illegal Immigration" (U.S., Department of Justice, Aug. 1993).

TABLE 1
BORDER APPREHENSIONS, FISCAL YEARS 1986-91

	Border Apprehensions (millions)
FY 1986	1.7
FY 1987	1.2
FY 1988	0.97
FY 1989	0.89
FY 1990	1.11
FY 1991	1.13

SOURCE: U.S., Department of Labor, Bureau of International Labor Affairs, *Employer Sanctions and U.S. Labor Markets: First Report* (Washington, DC: Government Printing Office, 1991), p. 58; U.S., Department of Justice, Immigration and Naturalization Service, Statistics Division, *INS Factbook* (Washington, DC: Government Printing Office, 1993).

not stem the flow of illegal immigration to the United States. Second, in their anxiousness to exclude undocumented aliens from the workplace, many employers unlawfully excluded eligible workers—documented aliens and naturalized citizens—from their applicant pools, creating new workplace discrimination. Third, the special farm worker legalization program created by IRCA was plagued with fraudulent applications that escaped INS scrutiny. Moreover, the farm worker legalization failed to replace the western growers' large undocumented workforce with a documented one.

Employer sanctions:
Control of the border?

In the long run, IRCA does not appear to have impeded the flow of undocumented immigrants to the United States. Two types of research provide insight: research based on INS border apprehensions and research based on interviews in Mexican sending communities.

Apprehensions showed a sharp drop immediately following the passage of IRCA; however, apprehensions slowly began to creep up again to their pre-IRCA levels (see Table 1).

One must be cautious in evaluating apprehension data, however.[7] INS enforcement efforts and economic variables might have contributed to IRCA's effect on increasing apprehensions. Even so, Urban Institute and RAND Corporation studies taking such variables into consideration nevertheless attributed significant reductions in U.S.-Mexico border crossings to IRCA.[8]

7. Apprehension data fail to distinguish between those who stay in the United States and those who return to their native countries; fail to take into account repeat apprehensions; and rely on INS resources. See Jeffrey S. Passel, Frank D. Bean, and Barry Edmonston, "Assessing the Impact of Employer Sanctions on Undocumented Immigration to the United States," in *The Paper Curtain: Employer Sanctions' Implementation, Impact and Reform*, ed. Michael Fix (Washington, DC: Urban Institute Press, 1991), p. 200.

8. One study found that IRCA accounted for 30-44 percent of reductions in border crossings for fiscal years 1987 and 1988. Thomas J. Espenshade, "Undocumented Migration to the United States: Evidence from a Repeated Trials Model," in *Undocumented Migration to the United States: IRCA and the Experience of the 1980s*, ed. Frank D. Bean, Jeffrey S. Passel, and Barry Edmonston (Washington, DC: Ur-

During the first few years of implementation, then, analyses of apprehension data show that IRCA had a mild deterrent effect on the flow of undocumented immigration across the southern border. This initial drop in border apprehension figures was likely due to the removal of newly legalized individuals, especially SAW workers, who had been more likely to cross the border frequently than those legalized in the regular legalization program.[9]

Nonetheless, the effect of IRCA apparently was temporary. The subsequent decline in apprehensions was not fully attributable to increased border enforcement.[10] Spotty enforcement of employer sanctions, economic pressures in sending communities, and the availability of employment and false documents in the United States likely had begun eroding the deterrent effects of IRCA. Small firms and contractors, ethni-

cally owned companies, and non-union firms in certain areas were most likely to continue to recruit undocumented workers for low-wage and unskilled jobs.[11]

As a result, IRCA's employer sanctions provisions came to be seen in Mexican sending communities as an annoying but surmountable barrier to U.S. entry. Interview data in the Mexican sending communities provide a clearer picture. Donato, Durand, and Massey found no statistically reliable evidence that IRCA had had a significant effect in deterring undocumented migration from Mexico.[12] Migrants, the researchers found, were about equally as likely throughout the 1980s to make a first illegal trip to the United States. Repeat migration remained as likely as earlier in the 1980s. Similarly, Kossoudji found that "once a Mexican enters the migrant stream, the deterrent effect disappears and in fact becomes perverse; migrants return to the United States more quickly, and if not subsequently apprehended will stay here longer than if they had not been apprehended previously."[13]

International migration is a self-sustaining social process, these authors argued. Networks of immigrants establish economic and po-

ban Institute Press, 1990). A second study found that the law accounted for a 47 percent decline in apprehensions between November 1986 and September 1989, below the level that would have been anticipated in the absence of IRCA. Frank D. Bean et al., "Post-IRCA Changes in the Volume and Composition of Undocumented Migration to the United States," in ibid. A third study estimated that IRCA accounted for a 21 to 32 percent decline in apprehensions. Keith Crane et al., *The Effect of Employer Sanctions on the Flow of Undocumented Immigrants to the United States* (Santa Monica, CA: RAND, 1990). This research is summarized in Passel, Bean, and Edmonston, "Assessing the Impact of Employer Sanctions."

9. Bean et al., *Undocumented Migration*.

10. U.S., Department of Labor, Bureau of International Labor Affairs, *Employer Sanctions and U.S. Labor Markets: Second Report* (Washington, DC: Government Printing Office, 1991), p. 209.

11. U.S., Department of Labor, Bureau of International Labor Affairs, *Employer Sanctions and U.S. Labor Markets: First Report* (Washington, DC: Government Printing Office, 1991).

12. Katharine M. Donato, Jorge Durand, and Douglas S. Massey, "Stemming the Tide? Assessing the Deterrent Effects of the Immigration Reform and Control Act," *Demography*, 29(2):139-57 (May 1992).

13. Sherrie A. Kossoudji, "Playing Cat and Mouse at the U.S.-Mexican Border," *Demography*, 29(2):160-80 (May 1992).

litical relationships cemented by patterns of immigration that are difficult to reverse, even when the United States is in a recession. As border apprehension figures increased in the early 1990s, undocumented immigrants searching for employment in the United States simply reckoned with higher but still-bearable costs: more money to purchase fraudulent documents, more supportive informal social networks to sustain them during their employment search, and more time to find employment.[14] The result has been that IRCA has not yet worked "to protect the jobs of U.S. citizens" as many had hoped.

Within the United States, there was little evidence to indicate that employer sanctions had diminished the numbers of undocumented job applicants. With the exception of nannies and housekeepers hired by formal agencies, "new (undocumented) arrivals were showing up in about the same numbers as before the law was implemented," the Department of Labor found from field studies. "While an early response to the implementation of IRCA was reported in some areas . . . this effect was apparently temporary."[15]

Small and ethnically owned firms, especially in the low-wage and unskilled sectors, continued to hire undocumented workers. Many of these businesses, calculating their own risks, perceived little threat from employer sanctions. But the primary reason for continued employment of undocumented workers was IRCA's lack of a reliable means of identifying persons entitled to work in the United States. A market in fake identity cards quickly grew up to satisfy the needs of new arrivals searching to satisfy requirements for work authorization documents. In September 1991, for instance, INS agents arrested leaders of a Los Angeles counterfeiting ring believed to have supplied 1 million aliens with fake identification documents. Though street traffic in the documents appeared at first to decline, other counterfeiting operations quickly restored the availability of the documents.[16]

The antidiscrimination provisions

IRCA included two tools to combat national origin and citizenship discrimination against the foreign born. First, IRCA required employers to verify every worker's employment eligibility, limiting the possibility that employers would ask only foreign-looking or foreign-sounding applicants for documents. Second, IRCA created within the Justice Department an Office of Special Counsel for Immigration-Related Unfair Employment Practices (OSC) to investigate charges of national origin and citizenship status discrimination.

However, despite the verification and redress provisions, a March 1990 report by the General Accounting Office (GAO) to Congress argued that employer sanctions had prompted new discrimination in the workplace. Many employers had told the GAO

14. U.S., Department of Labor, *First Report*.
15. Ibid., p. 95.

16. Roberto Suro, "Boom in Fake Identity Cards for Aliens," *New York Times*, 19 Feb. 1992.

that they checked the documents of only those they suspected of being unauthorized aliens or that they had adopted exclusionary hiring practices since IRCA, rejecting persons on the basis of foreign appearance, accent, or birth.[17] Other studies support the GAO findings; a New York State task force found that 51 percent of employers did not know how to determine whether an unfamiliar work document was acceptable.[18]

Suggested remedies for discrimination came from many quarters. Edward Roybal (D., CA) in the U.S. House of Representatives and Edward Kennedy (D., MA) and Orrin Hatch (R., UT) in the Senate called for the repeal of sanctions. However, as the INS moved to reduce to two the number of available work-authorizing documents, most in Congress agreed that the twin goals of control and antidiscrimination would be served by narrowing the availability of other forms of identification: driver's licenses and social security cards often used as breeders for fraudulent documents. Alan K. Simpson (R., WY), taking the lead in the Senate, introduced legislation in March 1994 requiring the Clinton administration to develop "a secure system to verify the identification of persons who apply for work or for welfare benefits."[19]

The efforts to both tighten verification and shore up employer education assume that employer sanctions are a policy tool worth saving. By 1994, that assumption was being called into question not only by a growing chorus of advocacy groups but also by more detached analysts who had supported the concept in the first place.[20] For the United States to justify using employer sanctions to control illegal immigration, more resources would have to be dedicated to employer education and enforcement, more attention paid to discrimination, and more emphasis placed on evenhanded enforcement.

The SAW program

The SAW program ostensibly offered fruit and vegetable growers the opportunity to attract a legal workforce. Nevertheless, some of IRCA's worst implementation failures stemmed from the SAW provisions. The SAW legalization program, seen by immigrants as an easy way to gain

17. U.S., General Accounting Office, *Immigration Reform: Employer Sanctions and the Question of Discrimination, Report to the Congress* (Washington, DC: Government Printing Office, Mar. 1990).

18. Charles E. Schumer, "A Review of the Implementation of the Immigration Reform and Control Act of 1986, A Report of the Office of Congressman Charles E. Schumer," mimeographed (Washington, DC: Congress, House of Representatives, Mar. 1990).

19. See statement of Senator Alan K. Simpson, in U.S., Congress, Senate, *Congressional Record*, 103d Cong., 2nd sess., 2 Mar. 1994, p. S2290.

20. For instance, see Demetrios G. Papademetriou, "Introductory Remarks on Options for Improving the Current Employment Verification System," in U.S., Congress, Senate, Committee on the Judiciary, Subcommittee on Immigration and Refugee Affairs, *Options for an Improved Employment Verification System: A Staff Report Prepared for the Use of the Subcommittee on Immigration and Refugee Affairs*, S. Prt. 102-14, 102d Cong., 2d sess., Sept. 1992, p. xii. See also the discussion of repeal in Michael Fix, "Toward an Uncertain Future: The Repeal or Reform of Sanctions in the 1990s," in *Paper Curtain*, ed. Fix, pp. 316-25.

access to work eligibility, gave rise to massive numbers of fraudulent applications. Moreover, western growers do not appear to have hired a predominantly legal workforce as a result of IRCA's farm worker legalization. Rather, recently legalized SAWs have been joined by growing numbers of undocumented and fraudulently documented workers. These serve as a competing workforce with newly legalized SAWs, preventing improvements in agricultural wages and working conditions throughout.[21]

Fraudulent SAW applications. Despite growers' fears of an agricultural labor shortage, many more farm workers applied for legalization than expected. INS officials had expected 300,000 to 500,000 SAW applicants,[22] but by 15 August 1992, INS had approved 1.08 million SAW applications.

This was in keeping with the SAW program's design to make it as easy as possible to qualify for legalization. Farm workers are often paid in cash by an employer who does not maintain records; unlike applicants for IRCA's regular legalization, then, SAW applicants had to produce only minimal evidence to qualify for the program. They needed evidence of employment from which 90 days of qualifying work during 1985-86 could

be reasonably inferred. Both aggregate and anecdotal evidence suggests that many took advantage of the program's openness to gain residency fraudulently, producing what a reporter called "one of the most extensive immigration frauds ever perpetrated against the United States Government."[23] Using California unemployment insurance files, farm production data, and other sources, Philip Martin calculated that the SAW program in California generated three to four times as many applicants as there would have been even if all the state's farm workers employed in perishable commodities had been illegal aliens. One-half to two-thirds of the SAW applications in California might have been fraudulent, Martin suggests.[24]

At the anecdotal level, agricultural employers and farm labor contractors were reported to have sold false employment histories to applicants willing to pay the price. The SAW application process at the border opened the door wide for abuse as well. The border program allowed aliens to come to a U.S. port of entry, make a credible claim that they had done farm work in 1985-86, assert that the documentation supporting this claim was in the United States, and then be admitted to the United States for 90 days with work authorization. Martin writes:

---

21. See Commission on Agricultural Workers, *Report of the Commission on Agricultural Workers* (Washington, DC: Commission on Agricultural Workers, 1992).

22. Philip L. Martin and J. Edward Taylor, *The Initial Effects of Immigration Reform on Farm Labor in California* (Washington, DC: Urban Institute Press, Mar. 1990).

23. Roberto Suro, "False Migrant Claims: Fraud on a Huge Scale," *New York Times*, 12 Nov. 1989. Copyright © 1989 by The New York Times Company. Reprinted by permission.

24. Philip L. Martin, "Harvest of Confusion: Immigration Reform and California Agriculture," *International Migration Review*, 24(1):69-95 (Spring 1990).

As word of this border entry program spread, long lines formed at the U.S. ports of entry, as truck drivers, clerks, and others became aware of this low-cost program for a three-month work visa. INS inspectors reported that many of the border applicants knew little about farmwork; among those who claimed, for example, to have picked strawberries or watermelons in the United States were some who, when asked to describe what they did, said that they were given ladders to climb strawberry and watermelon trees.[25]

Many of the applications were suspicious on their face; while most harvesting activities last three to ten weeks, requiring legitimate SAW applicants to list more than one employer on their application, the typical SAW application listed only one 90-day activity with one employer.[26] Nonetheless, because of confidentiality requirements, insufficient resources, and a high burden of proof required of the INS to challenge an applicant's evidence, the INS was unable to deny many suspicious applications. As of 15 August 1992, 85 percent of the SAW applications processed had been approved, with 18,000 still pending.[27]

Continued illegal workforce. The SAW program itself also likely stimulated continued illegal immigration, according to the Commission on Agricultural Workers authorized by IRCA. The SAW program increased the number of "anchor" households in the United States for new immigrants, easing the transition for undocumented migrants into the U.S. labor force. In facilitating travel for SAWs, the program also reduced the travel costs for unauthorized workers who travel with them. The SAW legalization prompted reunification between newly documented farm workers and their undocumented spouses. Finally, the program "sent the message" that legal status may be obtained through illegal entry to the United States.[28] Growers continued to employ illegal workers as well, hiring more and more through farm labor contractors rather than directly.[29] Of the fieldworkers in perishable commodities who responded to the National Agricultural Worker Survey, 6 percent admitted to being unauthorized in 1989, while 12 percent did so in 1990. Case studies sponsored by the Commission on Agricultural Workers found up to 35 percent undocumented workers, depending on the region and commodity.[30]

All this worked to the disadvantage of SAW workers in the workplace. Employers were not forced to revise personnel policies to retain newly legalized SAWs. Rather, the new illegal agricultural workers glutted the agricultural labor market, causing displacement and internal migration among U.S. farm workers. Because of this labor market glut, the SAW legalization does not appear to

25. Ibid., p. 77.

26. Ibid., p. 84.

27. Commission on Agricultural Workers, *Report of the Commission*, p. 52. There were regional disparities in application approvals. In the Northeast, where 80 percent of the SAW applications were from ethnic groups other than Mexicans, only 50 percent of the SAW applications were approved.

28. Commission on Agricultural Workers, *Report of the Commission*, p. 52.

29. Martin and Taylor, *Initial Effects*. The data are taken from a survey of 300 California agricultural employers.

30. Commission on Agricultural Workers, *Report of the Commission*, p. 53.

have significantly improved agricultural wages or working conditions.[31] The SAW program's failures, then, could not help but lead to a backlash from pro-immigrant Hispanic and farm worker advocates as well as anti-immigrant groups concerned about the fraud issue.

SOURCES OF FAILURE

Did the failures of IRCA stem from poor implementation or from IRCA's having been a bad law, poorly fashioned in the first place? Arguments have been made for both propositions, and I will attempt to evaluate them briefly in this section.

Sanctions

Despite the INS's success in establishing the legitimacy of employer sanctions, its efforts to educate employers, and its expansion in the size and capability of the staff responsible for employer sanctions implementation, the INS spent less and less time enforcing sanctions between fiscal years 1988 and 1991. In many localities, sanctions took a back seat to the more urgent programs focusing on alien apprehension and criminal alien removal. The decentralization of the INS allowed local offices to place differing priorities on whether or not to enforce sanctions, what procedures to follow, what types of firms to target, and what types of fines to impose; many jurisdictions placed excessive emphasis on paperwork violations, for instance. In addition, there was little coordination between

the INS and the Border Patrol regarding enforcement of the sanctions provisions, so that similar firms were treated differently within some geographic regions. This opened up the possibility that firms would continue to be treated unequally.[32]

Difficulties in implementation do appear to have impeded the impact of sanctions. The question is whether implementation can be improved or whether, on the other hand, sanctions as a policy tool are ineffective. Often it is argued that sanctions have been successful in Europe, where officials believe illegal immigration would be higher without them. But the cost for this effectiveness appears too high from an American perspective; French and German officials have been willing to levy higher civil and criminal penalties on offending employers.[33] Moreover, tight residency and work permit systems—which make employment eligibility easier to verify—have failed to prevent widespread discrimination, particularly against North African immigrants in France.

In the United States, sanctions might be rendered a more effective deterrent if the INS in Washington gained more control over regional offices, and if more resources were devoted to the agency's investigations branch for sanctions work. Given increased demands on the agency in other areas, however, even these reforms will be difficult to achieve. Reducing document fraud to improve

31. Ibid., p. 54.

32. Michael Fix and Paul Hill, "Implementing Sanctions: Reports from the Field," in *Paper Curtain*, ed. Fix.

33. Fix, "Toward an Uncertain Future," p. 319.

sanctions' deterrent effect will be equally difficult. Anything approaching Simpson's proposed secure work permit system will continue to be politically impossible to adopt in the United States, even among the current popular demands for restricted immigration.

Antidiscrimination

Initially, implementation of IRCA's antidiscrimination provisions was hampered by the lack of secure employment-eligibility documents and by employers' confusion about IRCA's requirements. Clearly, the majority of charges from the Office of Special Counsel (OSC) continue to stem from employers' confusion about what documents are acceptable to verify work eligibility. Attacking both problems would require more money than IRCA originally had targeted for antidiscrimination efforts. Again, the question was whether methods for work verification and redress of discrimination could be improved or whether IRCA's enforcement and antidiscrimination missions were inherently contradictory.

Amid calls to repeal IRCA after the third GAO report, the Justice Department began a drive to narrow the number of INS work authorization documents. Congress, too, increased funding. The Immigration Act of 1990 set aside $10 million for employer and community education. The INS has continued to do employer education. In addition, it has worked with the OSC to underwrite a grant program for private organizations to spread information about IRCA's protections. The OSC is in the second year of a national advertising campaign to do the same.

It is difficult to determine whether these increased efforts at education have diminished the discrimination problem. The OSC's caseload increased from 1987 to 1993, but it is not clear whether the increase is due to more awareness on the part of workers or more frequent abuse on the part of employers.

While improving employer education has met little political opposition, further centralizing control of work authorization documents will be politically difficult, as mentioned previously. The effect of this political reality may be that discrimination based on employer confusion about IRCA's requirements may persist. However, there is no guarantee that a work permit system would not itself deepen discrimination against immigrants.

The SAW program

Like IRCA's other provisions, the SAW program may have suffered from being either ill conceived or poorly carried out. The program itself was an ingenious way to bridge the interests of western growers, who needed to be guaranteed a flexible and reliable workforce, and farm workers, who wanted workplace protections. All this had to be done in the context of applying the enforcement mission of IRCA to the area of agriculture. However, the SAW provisions themselves were vague and sometimes contradictory. The SAW provisions were inserted during the final year of the 15-year negotiation on IRCA. They were hammered out in relative haste—compared to the rest of the legislation—by a mediator, Representative Charles Schumer (D., NY), whose first goal was that of a broker: to get grower and farm worker advocates to agree. In such bargaining situations, the resulting agreement usually reflects the distribution of power among the parties. In this case, agriculture won a great deal in the long run; farm workers, even those who gained legal resident status, are not terribly better off as a result of IRCA's SAW provisions. Finally, the SAW program's liberal burden of proof to establish eligibility invited fraud. Even Schumer admitted that some of the implementation failure stemmed from the frailty of the original agreement.[34]

Because its framers did not anticipate some of its consequences, the SAW program also was difficult to implement. INS regulations had to further minimize impediments to establishing eligibility, allowing applicants, for example, to provide a single affidavit from a coworker. The agency was finally moved to accept SAW applications in Mexico, admitting farm laborers without the required evidence. Both these moves, intended to ease the application process for eligible workers, further eroded the enforcement goals of IRCA.

As in the case of sanctions, the INS also apparently applied the law inconsistently across regions. The Northeast, for instance, with the most sophisticated apparatus for detecting SAW fraud, also had the highest application denial rate. In addition, fines and the level of employer and immigrant education were in-

consistent across regions. Finally, INS fear of fraud led to some unjust denials of SAW applications, according to a report issued by Schumer's office.[35]

SHOULD IRCA BE REPEALED?

Immigration lawmaking is enormously complex and controversial; for this reason, it has historically been handled away from public view. IRCA dramatically changed that. The negotiations that produced IRCA brought diverse constituencies— from employers to immigrant advocacy groups to farm workers—to the legislative negotiating table to determine the direction of the nation's immigration policy. Throughout the implementation of the legislation, these groups remained active, vocal, and influential in policymaking—as should be the case in a democracy's decisions about its membership.

But because so many parties and so many issues were involved in IRCA's complex of agreements, the law itself was not the most efficient response to the illegal immigration problem. Employer sanctions have so far failed to stem the tide of illegal immigration. IRCA's antidiscrimination provisions may still be insufficient to curb citizenship-status and

---

34. Suro, "False Migrant Claims," p. 36.

35. Schumer, "Review of the Implementation." A 1991 GAO report also criticizes decentralization of the INS, citing the agency's "lack of control over politically appointed regional commissioners, who use their autonomy to thwart headquarters' efforts" to allocate funds and manage programs. U.S., General Accounting Office, *Immigration Management: Strong Leadership and Management Reforms Needed to Address Serious Problems* (Washington, DC: Government Printing Office, 1991).

national-origin discrimination. The farm worker legalization program helped foster in the immigrant community a widespread perception of the vulnerability of U.S. immigration enforcement.

Despite these failures, IRCA should be viewed as an initial step in coping with illegal immigration. Improvements in implementation should be given time to work. In addition, employer sanctions cannot be expected to be a cure-all. They should not be expected to work without adequate resources, proper management, and additional enforcement measures. They cannot work without continued employer education, attention to the underlying international economic reasons for illegal immigration, and continued attention to the fair and generous administration of other areas of immigration policy, such as legal immigration and refugee and asylum policy. IRCA prepared the nation to think more seriously about managing undocumented migration. But much more negotiation between key political groups will have to occur to achieve an optimum balance between hospitality and control.

ANNALS, *AAPSS*, **534**, July 1994

Good Intentions Gone Awry: IRCA and U.S. Agriculture

By PHILIP L. MARTIN

ABSTRACT: Agriculture has been the major side door and backdoor through which unskilled immigrants have entered the United States for the past half century. If the 1980s' immigration patterns continue in the 1990s, up to one-fourth of the working-aged U.S. immigrants who arrive during the decade may have their initial U.S. employment in fruit and vegetable agriculture. Immigration reform was expected to reform agriculture's revolving-door labor market. By legalizing the farm workforce, it was hoped that legal workers who did not have to compete with a continuing influx of illegal aliens could force farmers to improve wages and working conditions. Farmers, in turn, would stop planting labor-intensive crops in remote areas and expect the U.S. government to admit or tolerate the entry of immigrant workers to harvest them. The immigration reforms have proven to be a case of good intentions gone awry. Instead of a legal farm workforce, 20-40 percent of today's farm workers are unauthorized. Most farm employers did not make adjustments to retain newly legalized farm workers; instead, more farmers sought newly arrived and often unauthorized immigrant workers.

Philip L. Martin is a professor of agricultural economics at the University of California, Davis. He is the author of books and articles on European guestworker programs, U.S. farm workers, and the relationship between migration and development in Turkey, Mexico, and Egypt. He was a member of the Commission on Agricultural Workers (1989-93).

U.S. agriculture provides a case study of how an industry can frustrate effective immigration control. There are many reasons why agriculture receives special treatment in immigration matters: it is considered a crown jewel of the U.S. economy; it is an old and dispersed industry with formidable political clout; and its need for unskilled seasonal workers has meshed neatly with the need of small farmers in Mexico for supplemental jobs. Politicians have embraced the contradictory goals of protecting the industry by making immigrant workers available, and then trying to help farm workers by speeding their movement into the nonfarm labor market. As a result, agriculture opens the most convenient door to the U.S. labor market for unskilled Mexican immigrants.

Special treatment for agriculture in immigration and labor matters is a leitmotiv of American history. Slavery in the southern colonies and states seemed necessary to the farmers of the time to keep a seasonal farm workforce available to fill seasonal jobs on cotton and tobacco plantations when free land was available to non-slave farm workers in the west. When irrigation and the transcontinental railroad made it profitable to grow labor-intensive fruit crops for eastern U.S. markets in the 1870s, California farmers looked for an " 'un-American' " supply of labor. The leading farm magazine of the time asked, " 'Where shall the laborers be found . . . to become the working men' " on the state's farms? Farm work was described as " 'the work of the slave,' " and the magazine repeated its question and offered a solution: " 'Then where shall the laborers be found? The Chinese! . . . those great walls of China are to be broken down and that population are to be to California what the African has been to the South.' "[1]

The same American farming system that is often considered a crown jewel of the U.S. economy for its ability to supply both American and foreign consumers with food and fiber is also the major magnet for Mexican immigrants. It is hard to change immigration exceptions and labor practices in an industry that is considered a success story: Americans devote only 12 percent of their expenditures for personal consumption to food and beverages, versus 15 to 20 percent in Western Europe, 42 percent in Japan, and over 50 percent in India.[2] Anything that might threaten this bountiful supply of cheap food, such as a reduced availability of immigrant workers, must jump over the high hurdles of farmer resistance and fears that fewer immigrants might mean higher food prices.

1. *The California Farmer* (1854), quoted in Varden Fuller, *Hired Hands in California's Farm Fields* (Berkeley, CA: Giannini Foundation, 1991), p. 7. A California farm spokesman in 1872 observed that hiring seasonal Chinese workers who housed themselves and then " 'melted away' " when they were not needed made them " 'more efficient . . . than negro labor in the South [because] it [Chinese labor] is only employed when actually needed, and is, therefore, less expensive' " than slavery. Quoted in Fuller, *The Supply of Agricultural Labor as a Factor in the Evolution of Farm Organization in California*, in U.S., Congress, Senate, Committee on Education and Labor (LaFollette Committee), 1940, pt. 54, p. 19809.

2. U.S., Department of Commerce, Bureau of the Census, *Statistical Abstract of the United States*, 1992, p. 833. Data are for 1988.

Agriculture is a frequently misunderstood industry. A handful of large farms produce most of the nation's food and fiber; the largest 5 percent of all farms, each a significant business, account for over half of the nation's farm output, while the smallest two-thirds of the nation's farms account for 5 percent of all farm output and they, on average, lose money farming.[3] Most American farms are family farms—defined by the U.S. Department of Agriculture as those that can operate with less than the equivalent of one and one-half year-round hired hands—and it is these livestock and grain operations that wrote the American agricultural success story.

The subsector of U.S. agriculture that is most closely associated with the U.S. demand-pull for Mexican immigrants are the 75,000 U.S. farms that hire workers to produce fruits, vegetables, and horticultural specialties (FVH) such as flowers and nursery products. Even the 75,000 number is deceptive, because the largest 10 percent of these FVH farms account for 80 percent of U.S. fruit and vegetable production and employment. It is true that most U.S. farms, as well as most fruit and vegetable operations, are small family-run operations, but seasonal factories in the fields account for most of

U.S. farm worker employment, and it is their efforts that have led to immigration exceptions for agriculture.

Immigration policy and immigrants are linked to fruit and vegetable agriculture because immigrants constitute almost two-thirds of the industry's current workforce and nearly all the entrants to the seasonal fruit and vegetable workforce.[4] Among the 140 million Americans who have paid employment sometime during a typical year, only 2 percent do farm work, and many of these farm workers are teenage hired hands on midwestern family farms. But of the almost 6 million immigrant workers who were in the United States legally by the end of the 1980s, up to 1.5 million, or 25 percent, did at least some farm work, reflecting the enormous appetite of seasonal farm factories for new workers.[5] If the immigration patterns of the 1980s continue in the 1990s, up

4. Farm worker data are notoriously unreliable. Seasonal fruit and vegetable agriculture appears to employ between 1 and 2 million workers annually, and almost all of the 200,000 to 300,000 new workforce entrants each year are immigrants. There are some U.S. citizen children of immigrant farm workers who also enter the farm workforce, but most are farm workers only as teenagers.

5. About 600,000 legal immigrants entered the United States annually during the 1980s, and 50 percent, or 300,000, joined the labor force, including about 5 percent (150,000 of 3 million) with farming occupations. *The Effects of Immigrants on the U.S. Economy and Labor Market* (Washington, DC: Department of Labor, International Labor Affairs Bureau, 1989), pp. 25 and 27. About 80 percent of the 1.8 million general legalization applicants were in the labor force (1.44 million), including 80,000 farm workers (5 percent). All of the 1.3 million applicants under the Special Agricultural Worker (SAW) program should have done farm work in the mid-1980s. The Immigration and

3. Ibid., p. 649. There were 2.1 million farms with a gross cash income of $186 billion in 1990. The largest 107,000 farms each sold farm products worth $250,000 or more, and they accounted for 56 percent of gross cash income. The smallest 1.3 million farms each sold farm products worth $20,000 or less, and they accounted for 5 percent of gross cash income. These small farms lost $500 million farming.

to one quarter of the working-aged U.S. immigrants who arrive during the decade may be Mexicans whose initial U.S. employment is in fruit and vegetable agriculture.

IMMIGRATION REFORM

When the congressional hearings that eventually culminated in the Immigration Reform and Control Act (IRCA) of 1986 began in 1981, the positions of farm worker and farmer advocates were not well developed. United Farm Workers (UFW) representative Stephanie Bower, for example, testified on 30 September 1981 that the UFW supported "imposing sanctions on employers who hire illegal aliens . . . [but since] laws covering farm workers have been rarely enforced . . . we strongly urge that a large budget for staff and operations be allocated to enforce sanctions."[6] The UFW also supported issuing counterfeit-proof social security cards to all workers, including farm workers, to verify their legal right to work in the United States.

The National Council of Agricultural Employers (NCAE) testified that it had not yet developed a position on employer sanctions, but that if there were to be a sanctions law, "we [agriculture] must have some means to offset a worker shortfall if there are not enough U.S. workers to fill the needs of agricultural employers." The council offered two reasons why sanctions might lead to farm labor shortages: "they [illegal alien

farm workers] will move to other jobs where they may get 12 months out of the year employment" and many of "those people" (illegal aliens) "do not want amnesty," so if they must "choose amnesty" in order to work in the United States, "they may just opt [to go] back to Mexico."[7]

When the Simpson-Mazzoli immigration reform bill was introduced in 1982, it included sanctions on U.S. employers who knowingly hired illegal aliens, an amnesty for aliens in the United States illegally since 1978, and a streamlined H-2 program that allowed temporary farm workers to fill temporary U.S. jobs if American workers were unavailable at government-set wage and working conditions. Western farm employers were not satisfied with the prospect of a government certification process standing between them and the Mexican workers to whom they had become accustomed. They argued that they could not plan their need for seasonal labor because they produced perishable commodities, that they lacked the free housing that was required to obtain H-2 workers, and that unions might urge the government not to approve their requests for alien workers on the grounds that U.S. workers were available.

In January 1983, representatives of most U.S. farm employers met in Dallas, Texas, to decide whether to press for further changes in the H-2 program to accommodate western growers or to seek a new foreign worker program. The decision was made to seek a new foreign worker program. The Farm Labor Alliance (FLA), a coalition of about 22 farm

Naturalization Service indicated in March 1991 that it would approve only 910,000, or 71 percent, of these SAW applications.

6. U.S., Senate, Congress, Serial J-97-61, 1981, p. 78.

7. Ibid., p. 125.

organizations, was created to press for such a program in Congress.[8] The FLA decided to work through Tony Coelho (D., CA), then the number-three person in the Democratic hierarchy of the House of Representatives.

The FLA wanted a flexible guestworker program under which legal nonimmigrant workers would be confined while in the United States to farm jobs, and U.S. farmers would not be required to go through a certification process to employ them. Both Senator Simpson and Representative Mazzoli opposed such a free-agent guestworker program, arguing that such a program was hard to justify in legislation designed to reassert control over immigration. Free-agent guestworkers, they argued, would be difficult to regulate in a manner that would not undermine the wages and working conditions of U.S. farm workers.

Representatives Panetta (D., CA) and Morrison (R., WA) introduced the FLA's P-visa guestworker program as an amendment to the Simpson-Mazzoli bill in the House in 1984. To the surprise of many observers, the House approved the Panetta-Morrison guestworker program in June 1984, producing what the *New York Times* described as one of the year's top 10 political stories. In the Senate, Simpson tried to appease the FLA with a streamlined H-2 program for agriculture, a three-year transition

program under which farmers—and only farmers—could use 100, 66, and 33 percent of their base year's employment of illegal aliens, and a Commission on Agricultural Workers to study farm labor issues further. However, the FLA got Senator Wilson (R., CA) to offer another version of the Panetta-Morrison program in 1985 as an amendment to the immigration reform bill and, after Wilson agreed to cap the number of guestworkers at 350,000, the amendment passed.

When the House considered immigration reform in 1986, Representative Rodino (D., NJ) asserted that he would try to block legislation that included a Panetta-Morrison-type or Wilson-type guestworker program for agriculture. During the summer of 1986, Representative Schumer (D., NY) negotiated a compromise legalization program with Representative Panetta, representing employer interests, and Representative Berman (D., CA), representing worker interests, and this so-called Schumer compromise was a key element in permitting IRCA to be enacted.

IRCA created the Special Agricultural Worker (SAW) and Replenishment Agricultural Worker (RAW) programs: SAW to legalize and stabilize the current illegal alien workforce, and RAW to admit probationary immigrant farm workers if newly legalized SAWs quit doing farm work and their exit led to farm labor shortages. Worker advocates agreed to this SAW-RAW compromise because the SAWs were free to leave agriculture; these advocates were concerned primarily about H-2-type workers who were dependent on their U.S.

8. The FLA included 22 farm organizations, from the CA Grape and Tree Fruit League to the Washington Asparagus Growers. Many farm employers on whose behalf the FLA lobbied belonged to 2 or more of the organizations that in turn constituted the FLA.

farm employers to stay employed in the United States. SAWs, they reasoned, would have the power to say no to unfair wages and working conditions and, after illegal immigration stopped, the power to negotiate higher farm wages. Farmers won assurances that the relatively easy requirement for SAW legalization would permit them to continue to employ their current workers, and then RAWs could enter the United States if labor shortages developed.

IRCA'S AGRICULTURAL PROVISIONS

IRCA included three major agricultural provisions: deferred sanctions enforcement and search warrants, the SAW legalization program, and the H-2A and the RAW foreign worker programs. Each provision had anticipated and unanticipated consequences.

IRCA also made significant changes in agricultural enforcement practices. Before IRCA, the Immigration and Naturalization Service (INS) enforced immigration laws in agriculture by having the Border Patrol drive into fields and apprehend aliens who tried to run away. Farmers pointed out that the INS was required to obtain search warrants before inspecting factories for illegal aliens, and they argued that the INS should similarly be obliged to show evidence that illegal aliens were employed on a farm before raiding it. IRCA extended the requirement that the INS have a search warrant before raiding a workplace for illegal aliens from nonfarm to agricultural workplaces.

This search warrant provision was won by the farmers' argument that farms should be treated like factory workplaces. The similarity stopped there: farmers argued that farms, unlike factories, were extraordinarily dependent on unauthorized aliens and that sanctions should not be enforced while the legalization program for farm workers was under way. Sanctions enforcement was thus deferred in most crop agriculture until 1 December 1988.

IRCA created two legalization programs: a general (I-687) program, which granted legal status to illegal aliens if they had continuously resided in the United States since 1982, and the SAW farm worker (I-700) program, which granted legal status to illegal aliens who did at least 90 days of farm work in 1985-86. Because farmers and farm worker advocates testified that many illegal alien workers were paid in cash, it was much easier for illegal alien farm workers to satisfy this work requirement than it was for nonfarm aliens to satisfy the residence requirement.[9]

No one knew how many illegal aliens were employed in U.S. agriculture in the mid-1980s. Most farmers and farm worker advocates accepted a U.S. Department of Agriculture estimate that there were 350,000 illegal aliens employed in agriculture, and this number became the maxi-

9. A SAW applicant, for example, could have entered the United States illegally in early 1986, left after doing 90 days of farm work, and then applied for SAW status from abroad. An applicant was permitted to apply for the SAW program with only an affidavit from an employer asserting that the worker named in the letter had done 90 days of work in virtually any crop. The burden of proof then shifted to the INS to disprove the alien's claimed employment.

TABLE 1
LEGALIZATION APPLICANTS

Characteristic	LAW*	SAW†
Median age at entry	23	24
Age 15 to 44 (percent)	80	93
Male (percent)	57	82
Married (percent)	41	42
From Mexico (percent)	70	82
Applied in California (percent)	54	52
Total applicants	1,759,705	1,272,143

SOURCE: U.S., Department of Justice, Immigration and Naturalization Service, *Statistical Yearbook 1991* (Washington, DC: Immigration and Naturalization Service, 1992).

*Persons filing I-687 legalization applications.

†Persons filing I-700 legalization applications. An additional 80,000 farm workers received legal status under the general or pre-1982 legalization program.

mum number of Group I SAWs.[10] However, the major surprise of the SAW program was that 1.3 million aliens applied for SAW status, or almost three-fourths as many as applied for the general legalization program, even though it was widely asserted that only 15 to 20 percent of the undocumented workers in the United States in the mid-1980s were employed in agriculture.

SAW applicants turned out to be mostly young Mexican men (Table 1). Their median age was 24, and half were between 20 and 29. Since SAWs had to be employed in 1985-86 to qualify, there were few SAWs under 15, compared to 7 percent of the general legalization applicants. Over 80 percent of all SAW applicants were male, and 42 percent were married.

10. Group I SAWs did at least 90 days of Seasonal Agricultural Services (SAS) work in each of the years ending in 1 May 1984, 1985, and 1986. Group II SAWs, by contrast, did 90 days of SAS work only in the year ending 1 May 1986. Over 90 percent of all SAW applicants were in the Group II category.

In a few limited surveys, it was found that SAWs who had an average of 5 years of education earned between $30 and $35 daily for 100 days of farm work in 1985-86.

By early 1992, the INS had adjudicated 93 percent of the SAW applications. The INS approved 88 percent of the applications on which it had completed its work, which means that just over 1 million illegal aliens have become immigrants through the SAW program. There may be additional SAWs approved, but the INS has recommended that many of the remaining 235,000 applications for legal status be denied.

Some SAWs did leave agriculture, but the major reason that so few SAWs are reported to be still working in agriculture is that many of the people who applied and were legalized under IRCA's provisions for agricultural workers were not farm workers at all. Employer-generated data in California, for example, suggest that there should have been fewer than 200,000 legitimate SAW applications in the state, but 700,000 were submitted.[11] Surveys report that legitimate SAWs and other farm workers are not leaving the farm workforce: a national survey of farm workers found that over 90 percent of the persons doing farm work when interviewed in 1989 were still doing farm work in 1990, largely because lack of English-language skills, other skills, and contacts kept them in the farm workforce.

If two-thirds of the mid-1980s' unauthorized farm workers had really left agriculture, frequent complaints of farm labor shortages might be expected.[12] But there have been far more reports of farm labor surpluses than shortages. Ample supplies of labor encouraged expansion: if there were profits to be made by expanding fruit and vegetable production, U.S. growers expanded; IRCA did not signal U.S. growers that in the future, immigrant harvest labor would be scarce or more expensive.

Before IRCA, illegal alien farm workers were often called undocumented workers because they did not have documents that authorized them to work in the United States.

IRCA changed many of these undocumented workers into documented SAWs, and those who continue to arrive in the United States into "documented illegal aliens." Today's "documented illegals" have the work authorization documents—usually an I-551 green card and a driver's license—needed to be employed legally in the United States, although these documents are generally purchased at weekend flea markets for $30 to $50, not issued by the U.S. government.

Neither the RAW nor the H-2A program has admitted any additional legal foreign workers since IRCA. RAW program admissions depend on national calculations of farm labor need and supply made by the Secretaries of Labor and Agriculture,[13] while H-2A admissions require employers to initiate a request for alien workers. RAW labor shortage calculations indicated that no RAW visas should be issued in fiscal years 1990-93, that is, national calculations of farm labor needs and farm worker availability did not produce the necessary prediction of a labor shortage to justify the issuance of RAW visas, and the RAW program expired on 30 September 1993. The H-2A program has shrunk since IRCA.

IRCA'S EFFECTS

The effects of the SAW-RAW compromise on U.S. farmers and farm workers were not debated extensively in Congress, although the pos-

---

11. Philip Martin, Edward Taylor, and Philip Hardiman, "California Farm Workers and the SAW Legalization Program," *California Agriculture*, 42(6):4-6 (Nov.-Dec. 1988).

12. There were newspaper reports of labor shortages and rising wages in the wake of IRCA, but they turned out to be isolated exceptions. For example, a story in the *Wall Street Journal* noted that growers complained of too few strawberry pickers in California and too few cucumber pickers in North Carolina, and a U.S. Department of Agriculture representative attributed instances of wage increases to the problem of finding adequate labor. "Labor Letter," *Wall Street Journal*, 5 Sept. 1989.

13. These calculations are described in Philip Martin, "The Outlook for Agricultural Labor in the 1990s," *UC Davis Law Review*, 23(3): 499-523 (Spring 1990).

sible effects of other immigration reforms on agriculture had been discussed throughout the early 1980s. It is possible to discern a range of expected IRCA effects on farmers and farm workers, but most suggest that IRCA should have had at least two effects in agriculture: farm workers should be legal U.S. workers, and farmers should have raised wages somewhat and improved employment practices in order to retain newly legalized SAW workers.

IRCA has not had these hoped-for effects in agriculture. There are several reasons, including a continued influx of unauthorized workers and less rather than more effective enforcement of immigration and labor laws in agriculture.

One of the most dramatic changes in the farm labor market due to IRCA is the switch from undocumented workers to falsely documented workers. Illegal immigrants who do farm work are usually among the poorest and least sophisticated of such workers in the United States. IRCA may well be remembered as a stimulus to illegal immigration for spreading work authorization documents and knowledge about them to very poor and unsophisticated rural Mexicans and Central Americans, encouraging first-time entrants from these areas.

In the early 1990s, pre-IRCA legal farm workers, newly legalized SAWs, and a continued influx of illegal aliens have produced an ample supply of seasonal workers, giving farmers little incentive to improve wages and working conditions. Study after study confirms the fact that most farmers have not raised wages, improved working conditions or housing, or otherwise made adjustments to recruit and retain legal workers. Instead, the IRCA-wrought influx of workers has, in some cases, encouraged reductions in wages and farm worker earnings.[14]

Most farm workers have been paid the same per hour worked or unit of work done since the late 1980s, but farm worker earnings have nonetheless declined in many instances because, with more workers, each does fewer hours of work. Farm worker profiles indicate that a typical seasonal worker is available for farm work about 40 weeks per year, finds work during 20 to 25 weeks, or 700 to 1000 hours, so that, at $5 hourly, farm work generates $3500 to $5000 annually.[15]

Seasonal farm workers have also been affected by the post-IRCA tendency of farm operators to hire more seasonal workers through farm labor contractors (FLCs). In California, the market share of FLCs appears to

14. These studies are summarized in Commission on Agricultural Workers, *Final Report* (Washington, DC: Government Printing Office, 1992).

15. The Department of Labor's National Agricultural Worker Survey (NAWS), which probably includes a disproportionate share of the long-season and year-round workers who do most of the days of farmwork done by hired workers, reports that median earnings in 1989 were $7500 for 37 weeks of work. These SAS workers were young (median age 30), male (three-quarters), foreign-born (three-quarters), and poorly educated (median of six years of education; three-quarters could not read English well). SAWs are about 40 percent of the NAWS sample, and post-IRCA "documented illegals" are about 10 percent. *Findings from the NAWS: A Demographic and Employment Profile of Perishable Crop Farm Workers* (Washington, DC: Department of Labor, July 1991).

have risen from about one-third of all job matches in the early 1980s to over half in the early 1990s. Employees of FLCs are worse off in several ways, including the tendency of FLCs to pay lower wages to recently arrived immigrants. Many FLCs condition employment on worker acceptance of housing away from the work site, and then they charge workers for both housing and rides to work. Housing away from the farm, usually in barracks-style accommodations, costs each worker $25 to $35 weekly, and then the private rural taxis that provide rides to work sites typically charge each worker $3 to $5 daily. A worker getting $200 weekly (40 hours at $5 per hour), often has $50, or 25 percent, less take-home pay if he or she is employed by an FLC because of these housing and taxi charges.

Hiring documented illegal workers through FLCs means that few farmers have planned for a future of fewer and better-paid legal workers. Unlike the U.S. manufacturing industries that shrank in the face of lower-wage competition during the 1980s, labor-intensive U.S. agriculture expanded, usually in ways that guarantee farm labor shortages in the 1990s. In state after state, the story is similar: Washington apple acreage is up 25 percent since IRCA; 3000 acres of citrus have been planted in remote areas of California since the mid-1980s; thousand-acre blocks of orange trees have been planted in southern Florida. When asked about the labor assumptions that went into these plantings, many of which will not need harvest workers until the mid-1990s, the farmers

sheepishly admit that they did not think about labor or that they assumed seasonal labor would be available at the minimum wage, "as it always has been."

REFORM RECOMMENDATIONS

There was a great deal of uncertainty about IRCA's effects on farmers and farm workers. This uncertainty, as well as the four-year life of the RAW program, gave the IRCA-created Commission on Agricultural Workers its mandate to review the effects of IRCA and especially its SAW provisions on the farm labor market.

The commission was charged with "reviewing" nine questions and conducting "an overall evaluation of the special agricultural provisions"[16] of IRCA. On the basis of case-study research and hearings, the commission made three types of findings. First, in its overall evaluation of the SAW program, it concluded that the majority of SAW-eligible undocumented workers gained legal status, but through such a flawed worker- and industry-specific legalization program that Robert Suro in the New York Times described the SAW program as "one of the most extensive immigration frauds ever perpetrated against the United States Government."[17]

Second, the commission found that, although the SAW program legalized many undocumented farm workers, the continued influx of illegal workers prevented newly legal-

16. Immigration Reform and Control Act (1986).
17. Roberto Suro, "False Migrant Claims: Fraud on a Huge Scale," New York Times, 12 Nov. 1989. Copyright © 1989 by the New York Times Company. Reprinted by permission.

ized SAWs from obtaining improvements in wages and benefits from farmers. Third, the commission reported that the farm labor market continues to leave the average farm worker with below-poverty-level earnings.

The commission recommended that federal and state governments should take steps to develop a legal farm workforce, to improve social services for farm workers and their families, and to improve the enforcement of labor laws. In response to IRCA's failure to reduce illegal immigration, the commission recommended more enforcement and a fraud-proof work authorization card. To combat declining real wages, the absence of benefits like health insurance, and the exclusion of some farm workers from federal and state programs that would make them eligible for unemployment insurance benefits and workers' compensation, the commission recommended that the federal government provide more services to farm workers and their children and that farm workers be covered under protective labor laws. Finally, the commission recognized that federal and state agencies today have only a limited ability to enforce farm labor laws, and it recommended that enforcement efforts should be better coordinated and targeted.

The commission also made several recommendations that may undermine some of these efforts to reduce farm worker poverty. For example, it recommended that the same regulations govern the importation of nonimmigrant farm and nonfarm workers. This recommendation was made in the spirit of ending agricul-tural exceptionalism, the practice of exempting farmers from labor laws under the theory that family farmers should not be burdened by excessive formal regulation. However, the employer certification and worker protections in the agricultural H-2A program are there because of past problems. While the commission developed no evidence that the nonfarm H-2B program needs these extra procedures and protections, it heard considerable testimony that current protections in the H-2A program are inadequate. Thus the intent of this recommendation can only be to substitute weaker H-2B procedures for stronger H-2A rules, and this flies in the face of the evidence that was developed. The H-2A program may need to be reviewed, but probably not with the goal of substituting H-2B criteria for H-2A criteria.

THE UNFINISHED AGENDA

Most of the commission's consensus recommendations are a useful step in the right direction, but they fail to deal with the root causes of the farm labor problem and the legacies of IRCA's agricultural provisions. The federal government has permitted immigration to be a subsidy for the labor-intensive fruit and vegetable subsector of U.S. agriculture. This immigrant labor subsidy encourages the expansion of an industry in which the majority of workers earn below-poverty-level incomes. This farm worker poverty is widely recognized, but there is unlikely to be an effective solution to reduce it until the question of who is responsible for the farm worker's plight is confronted.

It is often argued that poor farm workers are the price that must be paid for cheap food. But the relationship between cheap farm workers and cheap food has not been studied. The numbers seem to belie this conventional wisdom. Two-thirds of the nation's farm work is done by farmers and their families. Hired workers do only one-third of the nation's farm work. Immigrant farm workers, the poorest hired workers, do about two-thirds of the work done by hired workers. This means that, if there were no immigrant farm workers, almost 80 percent of the nation's farm work would be done without them. In other words, holding down the wages of seasonal farm workers, while it impoverishes more than 1 million American workers, holds down the average family's food bill only a little. Even in the case of the fruits and vegetables that immigrant workers harvest, farm wages typically account for less than 10 percent of the retail price of a head of lettuce or a pound of apples. Doubling farm wages, and thus practically eliminating farm worker poverty, would raise retail food prices by less than 10 percent.

Retail food prices may not even increase if the U.S. government aimed to increase rather than depress farm wages. The farmers who relied on Mexican Bracero workers in the early 1960s argued that "the use of braceros is absolutely essential to the survival of the tomato industry."[18] What happened when they nonetheless disappeared? The termination of the

18. California, Senate, Senate Fact Finding Committee on Labor and Welfare, *California's Farm Labor Problems: Part 1*, 1961, p. 105.

Bracero program in 1964 accelerated the mechanization of the harvest in a manner that quadrupled production to 10 million tons between 1960 and 1990. Cheaper tomatoes permitted the price of ketchup and similar products to drop, helping to fuel the expansion of the fast-food industry.

Not only is it inefficient to hold down food prices by holding down farm worker wages; it is also morally wrong. Why should immigration exceptions hold down the wages of farm workers, who average $5000 annually, in order to lower food prices for nonfarm workers, whose average earnings are $25,000 per year? The federal government should collect data and conduct studies on the true costs of cheap farm workers. These costs are significant, and as the farm workforce includes more and poorer immigrants, the cost will rise.

Second, the government will have to deal with the new dynamic element that is gradually reducing its ability to regulate the farm labor market: farm labor contractors. FLCs are the intermediaries who, for a fee, recruit, transport, and supervise farm workers. Since IRCA was enacted in 1986, the share of all seasonal job matches made by FLCs has increased. Today it exceeds 50 percent in many harvest labor markets. Worker, farmer, and agency testimony as well as research suggests that FLCs are practically a proxy for the employment of undocumented workers and egregious or subtle violations of labor laws.

Given ineffective immigration controls and insufficient farmer-provided and public services, such as housing for newly arrived immigrants, FLCs have privatized important parts of both immigration policy and immigrant services. As they play the role of nineteenth-century ship captains in recruiting, transporting, and employing new arrivals, their activities promise to bring into rural communities some of the neediest immigrants—relative to the average American—that have ever arrived in the United States.

The increase in FLC activities has been driven by several factors, including farmer efforts to minimize enforcement risk, the arrival of more diverse immigrant workers, and the legalization of people with the requisite experience to get into the game. IRCA's employer sanctions increased the potential cost of hiring illegal alien workers, so growers rationally tried to shift these risks to FLCs, since they, under IRCA, are employers in their own right. Second, the "new-new" immigrants arriving since IRCA have in many cases needed nontraditional intermediaries for language, recruitment, or social service reasons—farmers used to dealing with Mexicans from the Central Highlands are not necessarily capable of dealing with the Mixtecs and Guatemalan Indians arriving today. Third, the SAW program legalized more persons, who could be FLCs; FLC registration usually requires legal status, and some newly legalized SAWs became FLCs.

FLCs, immigrants, and labor standards seem to be mutually incompatible. A contractor operates between a farmer and a farm worker, but the power of the two over the contractor is very different. Farmers typically know what the going overhead or commission is, and thus FLCs are unlikely to extract an extra-high fee from them. Newly arrived immigrants, on the other hand, may not know the minimum wage, so FLCs can turn what appears to be a money-losing deal with farmers into a profit-making deal by extracting money from workers. As the U.S. Industrial Commission observed in 1901, "the position of the contractor . . . is peculiarly that of an organizer and employer of immigrants. . . . He holds his own mainly because of his ability to get cheap labor . . . [he] succeeds because he lives among the poorest class of people, knows them personally, knows their circumstances, and can drive the hardest kind of bargain with them."[19] The United States may have to follow the German practice and prohibit labor contracting in industries in which contracting has proven difficult to regulate.

The third item on the unfinished farm labor agenda may be IRCA's most important legacy: the foundation it has laid for a new wave of rural poverty in the United States. The rural poverty that many thought was reduced when millions of small white and black farmers left agriculture in the 1950s and 1960s may be recreated through immigration in the 1990s.

The SAW program legalized mostly young Mexican men who were working illegally in U.S. agriculture. By legalizing only these working men, some hoped that they would be encouraged to continue to return to

19. U.S., Industrial Commission, *Reports* (Washington, DC: Government Printing Office, 1901), vol. 15, pt. 3, pp. 320-21.

their families each winter. Many continue to commute between the United States and Mexico, but many others are bringing their families to the United States. These mixed families—mixed in terms of the legal status of family members—need education, health, and social services if they and their children are to succeed in the United States. However, their settlement in rural America and their mixed legal status make it difficult to provide them with the social services that they need.

CONCLUSION

Immigration reform in U.S. agriculture was a case of good intentions gone awry. Instead of ending a century of immigration and labor law exceptions, IRCA has reinforced them: immigrant workers continue to act as a subsidy that encourages the expansion of a subsector of the U.S. economy in a manner that leaves the majority of its workers in poverty. Cheap farm workers do not provide consumers with cheap food, but they do act as a regressive tax on some of the poorest American workers. Furthermore, fruit and vegetable agriculture does not employ seasonal farm workers for a lifetime; when they leave through agriculture's revolving-door labor market, they increasingly become the neediest residents in American towns and cities.

Americans want a prosperous farm economy that can provide them with an abundant supply of food. But the fruit and vegetable subsector of American agriculture is expanding in a manner that requires all taxpayers to alleviate the human suffering it produces. Making the fundamental changes in the immigration policy and enforcement that are necessary in order to reduce or eliminate farm worker poverty, instead of merely mitigating it, is the economically and morally right thing to do.

Farm workers and their families remain near the bottom of the socioeconomic ladder because the federal government has been more willing to help individuals escape from the farm labor market than to control immigration so that farm workers can help themselves. Farm workers and their children who find nonfarm jobs often obtain higher incomes, but if they are replaced in agriculture by even more desperate immigrants, the United States is condemned to a Sisyphean task in its quest to reduce farm worker poverty.

ANNALS, *AAPSS*, **534**, July 1994

Enforcing the Minimum Wage and Employer Sanctions

By DAVID S. NORTH

ABSTRACT: This article examines the interaction between the enforcement of the minimum wage and of employer sanctions—fining employers for hiring illegal aliens—in Los Angeles County. Los Angeles was selected because there is, proportionately, more immigration, legal and illegal, there than in any other urban county in the nation, and work in the secondary labor market has become progressively less well paid with the passage of time, two trends said to be intertwined. The roles of four groups of agencies are examined: unions, community-based organizations, employment standards agencies, and the Immigration and Naturalization Service. The expected interagency cooperation to raise wages for those at the bottom of the labor market was not found. Further, resources for enforcing the minimum wage turned out to be minimal, with social service agencies and foundations much more interested in a more fashionable, if less pervasive, labor market problem, namely, sanction-caused discrimination against foreign-appearing workers.

David S. North holds a B.A. in political science from Princeton University and an M.A. (N.Z.) from Victoria University College, Wellington, New Zealand, where he was a Fulbright scholar. After service in the New Jersey Department of Labor and Industry, he was an assistant to the U.S. Secretary of Labor. For the last 25 years he has conducted immigration and labor market research. He is affiliated with the New TransCentury Foundation, Arlington, Virginia.

NOTE: This article is based on a study funded by the U.S. Department of Labor: David S. North, *IRCA Did Not Do Much to the Labor Market: A Los Angeles County Case Study*, Immigration Policy and Research Working Paper 10 (Washington, DC: Department of Labor, 1991).

IF lots of immigrants are good for the economy, which is the Ben Wattenberg-Julian Simon thesis,[1] then Los Angeles must be booming. There are more immigrants, legal and illegal, in Los Angeles County per thousand residents than any other urban county in the nation. An examination of Immigration and Naturalization Service (INS) and census data for legal immigration in the period 1984-90, for example, shows that Los Angeles County in those years had 56.0 arriving immigrants per thousand residents, compared to 42.7 for California as a whole and 17.5 for the nation. Thus the county absorbed proportionately three times as many immigrants as the nation as a whole.

In order to obtain roughly comparable numbers about the extent to which illegal immigrants were attracted to LA County, one can look at the volume of applicants for legalization under the Immigration Reform and Control Act (IRCA) of 1986.[2] Here we find that the incidence of illegals was eight times greater in LA County than in the nation as a whole. There were 94.5 legalization applicants for every 1000 residents of LA County (about 1 in 11) compared to 12.4 applicants per thousand in the nation generally.[3]

1. See, for example, Julian L. Simon, *The Economic Consequences of Immigration* (New York: Basil Blackwell, 1989).
2. It is generally conceded that the geographical distribution of all undocumented aliens in the country was roughly similar to the distribution of the segment of that population seeking legalization.
3. For the geographical distribution of immigrants, see U.S., Department of Justice, Immigration and Naturalization Service, *1991 Statistical Yearbook of the Immigration and*

But Los Angeles is not booming. More specifically, Los Angeles is a particularly bad place in which to be one of the working poor, and this statement has become progressively truer with the passage of time.

One can quote grim statistics endlessly on this point; for example, between 1969 and 1987 the number of jobs grew more slowly in LA County (at a rate of 38.4 percent) than in the nation as a whole (45.1 percent). While LA County had 11.0 percent of its people below the poverty line in 1969—a percentage point better than the nation—by 1987 it had 15.6 percent of the population below the poverty level, two points worse than the nation.

Similarly, Paul Ong, a student of poverty in Los Angeles, has shown that, when income distribution is examined, the gap between the rich and the poor widened between 1969 and 1986-87 (see Table 1).

When the low stratum for 1986-87 is disaggregated, we find that 8.7 percent of the Anglo workers and 8.8 percent of the blacks were in the low stratum, while the comparable figure for U.S.-born Chicanos was 18.0 percent. In other words, the latter group has taken more of the brunt of the immigrant competition than blacks or whites. The group with the highest percentage in the lowest stratum, of course, were the foreign-born Latinos, with 44.6 percent of them in the bottom category.[4]

Naturalization Service (Washington, DC: Department of Justice, 1992), tab. 18 and predecessor tables. For the distribution of legalization applicants, see ibid., tab. 23.
4. Data in these three paragraphs are largely from the Bureau of Labor Statistics and

TABLE 1
INCOME DISTRIBUTION IN LOS ANGELES, 1969 AND 1986-87

	Income Range	Distribution (percentage)	
		1969	1986-87
Low stratum	< $11,202	8.2	17.5
Middle stratum	$11,202-$44,404	86.1	71.1
High stratum	> $44,404	9.7	11.4

SOURCE: Paul Ong, *The Widening Divide: Income Inequality and Poverty in Los Angeles* (Los Angeles: University of California at Los Angeles, Research Group on the Los Angeles Economy, 1989), p. 47.

NOTE: Figures are in constant 1986 dollars.

Moving from the statistical evidence of the depressed LA County labor market to some of the underlying trends, we find, to summarize quickly, the following:

— high-wage manufacturing activity—planes, automobiles—in recent years was decreasing;
— low-wage manufacturing—for example, garments—was increasing;
— government employment, with its solid wages, was not increasing—LA is neither a state capital nor a federal regional city—and LA County was setting records for the privatization of work previously done by civil servants;
— some industries, notably building maintenance, were using pro-management federal, state, and local regulatory environments to break unions and to hire low-wage immigrants, legal and illegal, in preference to the blacks and other citizen

workers who had formerly dominated this business.[5]

Meanwhile, and presumably to some extent as a consequence of all of the foregoing, Muller and Espenshade point out that 134,000 resident blue-collar workers left California for other states between 1970 and 1983, and 372,000 resident workers left Los Angeles County for other parts of California and for other places in the United States between 1970 and 1980. Muller concludes later in the book, "These data suggest that there is a positive relationship between the influx of low-skill, low-wage immigrant labor in California, and the out-

can be found in Paul Ong, *The Widening Divide: Income Inequality and Poverty in Los Angeles* (Los Angeles: University of California at Los Angeles, Research Group on the Los Angeles Economy, 1989).

5. Commenting on this point, Steven T. Nutter, Western Regional Director and Vice President of the International Ladies Garment Workers Union (AFL-CIO), wrote to me on 30 Sept. 1991, "The City Attorney and County District Attorney essentially ignore criminal violations of the state labor code, which they are charged with enforcing. The City Fire Department does not conduct systematic inspections of large decaying buildings in the garment district of Los Angeles that house most of the contractors. The State has continued to reduce the staffing and budget of the state agencies which are charged with enforcing the law, while continually adding additional duties to their charge."

flow of native workers with similar characteristics from California to other regions of the United States."[6]

Clearly, LA's secondary labor market has become less rewarding to low-skilled workers at the same time that LA has remained attractive to immigrants. The latter are often drawn to the county, despite the evidence just presented, because of the stark contrast between wage rates at home and those in California and by the family networks that often facilitate immigration, both legal and illegal, even when times are hard in the First World destination.

BACKGROUND: IRCA

Federal policymakers sought to do something about labor markets flooded by desperate illegal immigrants. After a decade and a half of debate, in 1986 Congress passed IRCA with its two principal provisions: legal status for many of the then illegals, provided they met the statutory requirements, paid a fee, and applied; and employer sanctions, that is, fines for employers who hired undocumented workers. Legalization was designed to take care of much of the then current generation of illegals, while employer sanctions were supposed to discourage future influxes of the undocumented by removing the magnet of jobs in the American economy.

While many of the supporters of IRCA voted for it primarily as a matter of law enforcement, to "give us

back the control of our borders," in the words of Reagan's first Attorney General, William French Smith, it would not have passed without the active support of the American Federation of Labor and Congress of Industrial Organizations (AFL-CIO). The unions, at the national level, wanted to slow down illegal migration because of the way it tended to depress wages and working conditions in those parts of the labor market where the undocumented clustered.

Given all of the preceding, LA County was a logical place to study the impact of IRCA on the secondary labor market. If employer sanctions could make a difference, it would be more easily visible here than anywhere in the nation.

ENFORCING SANCTIONS AND THE MINIMUM WAGE

Our fieldwork in 1991 carried us into what we regarded as a familiar field, the decentralized operations of the INS.[7] It also took us into a brand-new field, the enforcement of the minimum wage law, a topic, incidentally, that has been the subject of very little scholarly activity.

We thought, naively, that there might be close cooperation between four sets of agencies, all interested in

6. Thomas Muller and Thomas J. Espenshade, *The Fourth Wave: California's Newest Immigrants* (Washington, DC: Urban Institute Press, 1985), pp. 53, 148.

7. See, for example, David S. North and Anna Mary Portz, *The U.S. Alien Legalization Program* (Washington, DC: TransCentury Development Associates, 1989); David S. North, *The Long Grey Welcome: The Naturalization Process in the United States* (Washington, DC: National Association of Latino Elected and Appointed Officials, 1985); idem, *The Border Crossers: People Who Live in Mexico and Work in the United States* (Washington, DC: National Technical Information Service, 1970).

bringing about change in the secondary labor market. These were, in our eyes, the following: state and federal operations enforcing the various minimum wage laws; the unions; community-based organizations working with low-income populations; and the INS, charged with penalizing employers hiring illegal aliens. The first three sets of organizations would, we thought, pay some attention to lifting wages in the secondary labor market and would regard the INS effort to remove illegal aliens as a way of tightening the labor market, thus nudging up wages.

We could not have been more wrong. Each of the four groups had its own agenda, and there was next to no cooperation between them on this matter.

Thumbnail sketches of the players and their relationships to each other may be helpful.

*The minimum
    wage enforcers*

While the federal government in the United States has a monopoly on immigration policy, this is not the case in the field of labor standards. Both the state of California's Department of Industrial Relations and the U.S. Department of Labor have separate, different, and overlapping roles to play in the arena; this is often, but not always, the case elsewhere in the United States as well. California employers have to follow the higher of the two standards in specific instances; usually the state program is more protective of the worker than the federal program is.

Without getting into the fascinating details of the two systems, it is useful to make these distinctions:

1. The California minimum wage is set differently from the way the federal minimum wage is set, and in some years it has been higher.

2. The California rules on overtime are tougher than the federal ones.

3. The California labor standards enforcement program is broader than that of the federal agency, in that more laws are enforced.

4. The focus of the federal effort is to secure the payment of legal wages to all workers in a given plant; much of the focus of the state program is to secure the wages to which an individual complainant is entitled.

5. Under some circumstances, with federal contractors or with agricultural employers, the federal agency has more power than the state one.

Regardless of the rigor of the law, or the vigor of its enforcers, the number of enforcers is a key factor. There are only 18 federal employees enforcing the minimum wage law in the LA area, or about one for every quarter of a million workers. There are several times as many state employees in the same general field.

The federal agents, who are with the Employment Standards Administration (ESA), look after the federal minimum wage ($4.25 an hour) and several other labor standards laws and help INS with the enforcement of employer sanctions. The ESA role in the latter situation is quite narrow: it examines employer records to see if the IRCA-stipulated paperwork requirements are met; if they are not met, it so reports to the district INS office. IRCA requires employers to maintain in their own files a hiring-related form, the I-9, which indicates the worker's legal presence in the nation and the nature of the supporting documentation provided by that worker.

The state enforcers, who work for the Bureau of Field Enforcement (BOFE), have no immigration-related tasks. They enforce a series of state labor laws, not just the state minimum wage. Many of them are engaged in efforts to see to it that individual, complaining workers are paid what is owed to them; this is the wage claims operation.

BOFE has good relations with the unions and carefully avoids any contact with INS. BOFE and ESA speak to each other frequently and manage to stay out of each other's way. ESA feeds information to INS, but, in LA at least, gets little feedback from INS.

The unions

If anyone should be interested in wages in the secondary labor market, it would be the unions. Nationally, the AFL-CIO—but not all of its affiliates—supported IRCA; it wanted both employer sanctions and legalization because it thought that this would lead to tighter labor markets in cities where the previously undocumented concentrated. Los Angeles was just such a city.

But, as the first part of its name indicates, organized labor is a federation, and in a federal system there is much room for independent action by the component parts. While the construction trades in Los Angeles support IRCA, the representatives of every other union organization we encountered in LA were opposed to sanctions. The local Building and Construction Trades Council reported that it had tried to reach out to the Immigration Service with leads on illegal alien workers but had had trouble getting its phone calls returned.

To sum up a number of long conversations, the union representatives, other than those in construction, argued that IRCA had been used by employers to break up organizing efforts and that there was no major change in the flow of newly arrived illegal aliens, so the promised benefit of a tighter labor market was a will-o'-the-wisp. I often heard them say, "We represent all our workers, not just the legal ones."

Beyond the legalization program, in which there were some contacts, the union officials said that they rarely talked with INS, and when they did so, it was usually in an argument. There was no concept of using INS and sanctions to tighten the labor market, no one mentioned the fact that most INS employees are members of the American Federation of Government Employees, and no one knew any INS official by name.

The unions not only shun INS, but they also tend to steer clear—without acrimony, however—of ESA, on the grounds that ESA is in touch with INS and that it checks I-9 files for that agency.

The community agencies

These organizations, such as the Mexican American Legal Defense and Education Fund, the American Civil Liberties Union, and the Coalition for Human Immigrant Rights of Los Angeles, to name a few, are resolutely opposed to employer sanctions, and though each has some interest in low-wage workers as a group, none will defend the use of employer sanctions to assist legal low-wage workers to secure higher wages. As a result, they never cooperate with INS and rarely are in touch with ESA.

We identified exactly one small community agency that dealt with the minimum wage. Funded by the Legal Aid Foundation of Los Angeles, the Employment Law Office is a small, if spirited, agency that helps low-income workers with employment standards matters.[8] It works with unions, prefers the state to the federal labor standards enforcement system, and has nothing to do with INS.

The INS

The immigration service, at least in LA, has little interest in the labor market, no contacts with unions, and rarely uses the I-9 leads provided to it by ESA. It does not see itself as playing a role in improving labor standards. It also spends relatively little staff time on enforcing employer sanctions.

What INS does see as its duty is to win convictions against employers who violate IRCA. To win the maximum percentage of cases, it uses as its

8. I am indebted to its ranking attorney, Anthony Mischel, for a thorough explanation of the different powers and patterns of the federal and state employment standards agencies discussed in this article.

principal leads labor certification applications filed with the U.S. Department of Labor by employers seeking to convert illegal alien workers into legal ones. The attraction to INS of this approach is that it has a document in its hands, signed by an employer, admitting the employment of the undocumented alien in question.

While, from a batting-average point of view, this approach is a sure winner, from a public policy viewpoint it is largely useless. Employers filing such documents tend to have few illegal aliens on their payrolls, and they are generally trying to do the right thing by them. INS could better channel its energies at the large and exploitive garment industry in LA, where employer sanctions could be used simultaneously to penalize employers who hire the undocumented, and employers who are highly likely to violate a range of labor and tax laws, as well as the immigration law. But INS, at least in LA, does not think like that.

A distraction

While the number of ill-paid and illegally ill-paid workers is legion, and while a disproportionately large number of these workers are immigrants, the immigrant-rights groups pay relatively little attention to such matters. Instead they pay a great deal of attention to a public policy problem that touches what I am sure is a much smaller population, the problem of employer-sanction-caused discrimination against foreign-looking job applicants. Aided by foundation grants and federal funds, these agencies have set up, in Los

Angeles and elsewhere, outreach organizations designed to alert workers to the dangers of this specialized form of discrimination and to organize attacks against it.

One wonders about the priorities of these organizations. Why devote substantial resources to a lesser problem, and lesser resources or none to a greater problem?[9] There are several answers, suggested Anthony Mischel, who has devoted his life to fighting the good fight for ill-paid workers. First, there are no breakthroughs, no precedents to be made in the labor standards field. Rather, it is a repetitious series of similar battles as one worker, or one small group of workers, is assisted toward economic justice.

Second, if the lawyer does secure a back-wage claim for a worker or a group of workers, there is a one-dimensional quality to it, but if the same lawyer wins an IRCA-caused discrimination case, maybe he or she can do some damage to a program—employer sanctions—with which the lawyer disagrees. Third, the battles over IRCA-caused discrimination take place in a new and interesting legal setting, which makes them more satisfying to the attorney than minimum wage cases. Finally, there is the question of funding. "The work that nonprofits do is shaped to some extent by what the funders want done," we were told. Foundations, it appears, are much more interested in pro-immigrant projects than they are in pro-working-poor projects.

9. At this point, one reviewer of an earlier version of this article remarked, "The public interest bar has a sure instinct for the capillary."

If I may draw a rather distant comparison, I see a parallel between the fascination in Los Angeles immigrant-rights agencies with IRCA-caused discrimination and the fascination in the migrant farm worker legal agencies in the Northeast with cases involving the H-2A program. This is the program that brings in nonimmigrant workers for seasonal work; in the Northeast, they are used primarily in the apple harvest.

In each case, there is a body of massive, dull problems out there—illegal wages and working conditions in the garment industry in Los Angeles, and illegal wages and working conditions in vegetable harvesting in the Northeast. In each case, bright, largely young, always dedicated public service lawyers pay more attention to an attractive, lesser issue than to drab, greater issues.

In the Northeast, the migrant legal action people seem to spend more time and energy on minor problems with the H-2A program and the apple growers—a relatively prosperous and enlightened group of employers —than they do with the vegetable growers, many of whom have very bad records in wages, housing, access to camps, and the like. They do this because they think, as I do, that the H-2A program is not necessary and that it deprives U.S. workers of jobs. But because of this predilection the migrants really needing their help—such as those pulling onions—do not get it or do not get as much as they would otherwise.

What is ironic here is that while the patterns are similar, and both groups of lawyers are unhappy about an aspect of the immigration law, those in Los Angeles want to make international migration easier while their counterparts in New York and West Virginia want to make it harder.[10]

RECOMMENDATIONS

The following recommendations are organized into four categories: the financing of labor standards enforcement, the statutory powers of the relevant agencies, suggested administrative actions of government agencies, and suggested actions by the private sector.

Funding enforcement operations

Based on the staffing levels for the federal wage-hour and the state BOFE operations in the Los Angeles area, both could appropriately use substantially more resources, perhaps an early doubling and a later tripling of staff levels. With each federal staffer producing about $180,000 in paid back wages, and each BOFE staff member doing even more, increased staffing would be a cost-effective way of bringing more income to some of southern California's working poor. Similarly, INS needs not only to refocus its efforts in the employer sanctions field, but it needs more investigators in the field.

In order to secure long-term funding for labor standards enforcement, the labor market agencies should adopt some of the fund-raising techniques used by other enforcement agencies: it should collect from the users and the abusers, and it should use these resources in addition to budgeted support.

BOFE collects a substantial body of fines from exploitive employers, such as the $100 fine it levies for each absence of a timecard. These fines, in a roundabout, partial way, help fund some of its activities. A tighter system should be created, along the lines of the INS Adjudications Fund,[11] which would provide a growing body of resources for the federal and state labor standards agencies. The fines could be called abuser fees.

The labor standards enforcement agencies might also consider levying a 2-3 percent surcharge on back wages on both the laggard employer and the lucky employee. This would produce for the Los Angeles ESA office, at its fiscal year 1990 collection rates, 4-6 percent of the gross back wages collected, or about $130,000 to $195,000 a year to help support the work of the office.

Needed statutory changes

Currently most of the work that ESA does on employer sanctions goes to waste; it makes detailed reports to INS, which, at least in Los Angeles,

10. For more on this, see David S. North and James S. Holt, "The Apple Industry in New York and Pennsylvania," in *Appendix I: Case Studies and Research Reports Prepared for the Commission on Agricultural Workers 1989-1993 to Accompany the Report of the Commission,* by Commission on Agricultural Workers (Washington, DC: Commission on Agricultural Workers, 1993.) Dr. Holt and I have a friendly disagreement on the utility of the H-2A program; Dr. Holt supports it.

11. This fund is supported by fees paid by those seeking decisions—naturalizations, petitions, legalization—from INS, and it is used to support these decision-making activities.

ignores them. Sooner or later employers will learn about this practice. ESA should be given statutory authority to enforce the paperwork requirements of IRCA, and it should be allowed to use the fines to support agency operations, as suggested previously in another connection. ESA, presumably, would be reluctant to interview workers as to their legal status in this country, but it could enforce the I-9 paperwork regulations without talking to any workers.

The enforcement of employer sanctions would be far more effective if the Congress amended IRCA to require a secure, database-related universal work permit to be issued to all legally present U.S. workers. Such workers would be allowed to carry the permit only when seeking employment or unemployment insurance benefits; the card would be banned for all other uses. This is, however, unlikely to happen soon.

State and perhaps federal legislation should be enacted to prevent the major economic interests in the garment industry from shucking off their obligations as employers. (The major economic forces in garments are the manufacturers—the Ralph Laurens and Liz Claibornes of the world—not the individual contractors who actually hire the workers.) Much forward movement along these lines has taken place in agriculture, against much more powerful interests than the garment industry, the notion being that the crew leader is no more the real employer than the garment contractor. Legislation to this end was passed in the California Legislature, only to be vetoed by then Governor Deukmejian.

Congress and the California state legislature, in addition to creating a system of fines, could take a leaf from the drug enforcement book and give labor standards agencies the power to seize goods and machinery in particularly flagrant labor standards cases; the goods and machinery could be sold, if need be, to pay back wages and agency fines.

It would also be helpful if both state and federal labor standards statutes were amended to give incentives—as well as protection—to workers who successfully blow the whistle on employers who have violated the law. Further, the laws should be amended to provide an incentive for the private bar to become involved, such as the availability, under certain circumstances, of double or triple damages for workers who were underpaid. Lawyers could take these cases on speculation against a predetermined portion of the damages to be awarded.[12]

Administrative reforms

INS should place more emphasis, nationally and in the Los Angeles area, on employer sanctions, and it should redesign its program operations to place its emphasis on exploitive employers who hire illegal workers.

In that vein, INS should, as a matter of policy, work with all other governmental and nongovernmental agencies that are concerned about exploitive employers. More specifically,

12. This suggestion, certain to encounter substantial resistance from management, is part of the International Ladies Garment Workers Union legislative package on labor standards.

INS should work closely with the Internal Revenue Service and ESA to crack down noisily and publicly on the worst of such employers; the Los Angeles garment industry would be a good place to start.

Perhaps the best long-term manner to persuade INS to act appropriately in the labor market would be to undo Franklin D. Roosevelt's World War II decision of taking the agency out of the Department of Labor and assigning it, for wartime reasons, to the Department of Justice. World War II ended 49 years ago.

ESA should make use of its fairly new hot-goods seizure powers as a leverage device to meet the goal mentioned earlier, namely, to move the level of corporate accountability in the garment industry to the level where the profits reside. While the scenario I have in mind might take both some careful timing and intelligence work, I think it could be effective. The notion would be to bar specific, valuable collections of hot goods from interstate commerce after the goods had become the property of the manufacturer and before they left the state of California. Other, perhaps less deftly timed uses of these powers would be helpful as well.

Another way to make ESA more effective would be for the U.S. Department of Labor to confer with the California Department of Industrial Relations regarding the possible cross-accreditation of ESA and BOFE investigators, so that they could enforce each other's laws and collect each other's fees, as suggested previously. Neither agency could possi-

bly collect all the $100 no-time-cards fines available in California, for example, and therefore they should not be in competition with each other.

The private sector

Advocacy organizations that purport to seek a better life for the disadvantaged should take a look at how few resources they devote to labor standards matters regarding all U.S. workers, legal and illegal, and at how much they devote to illegal residents. Without changing their position on the repeal of one segment of IRCA— employer sanctions—they could devote some of their energies and idealism to securing a better break for the working poor.

Similarly, the foundations that have been extensively funding research, outreach, and advocacy, largely along the lines described in the preceding paragraph, might consider investing some money in the dull but valuable task of helping enforce the minimum wage. There appears to be virtually no research, no conferences, no demonstration programs in this field supported by either the public or the private sector. While various immigration-oriented entities are numerous and often well funded, I did not encounter a journal, a newsletter, or an academic specializing in the field. In Los Angeles, filled with disadvantaged workers, there is, as mentioned, only one small, game nonprofit agency working on this subject.

Some foundation could take the lead in this neglected field and do a lot of good for a lot of silent people.

ANNALS, *AAPSS*, **534**, July 1994

U.S. Policy toward Haitian Boat People, 1972-93

By CHRISTOPHER MITCHELL

ABSTRACT: In the early 1970s, Haitians began migrating by sea to south Florida without authorization. Influential economic and social elites in that region pressed for federal action to deter this population stream. Until 1981, arriving Haitian boat people were detained in Florida, and most were deported as rapidly as possible. Since 1981, the U.S. government has used the Coast Guard to intercept boats laden with Haitian migrants. Since May 1992, "interdicted" Haitian vessels have been escorted back to Haiti, without affording passengers an opportunity to request political asylum in the United States. Although this policy has aroused condemnation from many observers as inhumane and discriminatory, the U.S. government arguably has the administrative, legal, and political ability to uphold it. Political criticism of the interception policy has helped induce the U.S. government to act in favor of a democratic regime in Haiti. Such a political trend would undercut the argument that Haitian boat people are fleeing political persecution and would bolster the policy of repatriation. As both U.S. political leaders and the general public become more restrictionist, the policy of returning Haitian boat people may, unfortunately, come to seem normal rather than anomalous.

Christopher Mitchell is professor of politics at New York University. He is the author of The Legacy of Populism: Bolivia: From the MNR to Military Rule *(1977) and the editor of* Changing Perspectives in Latin American Studies: Insights from Six Disciplines *(1988) and, most recently,* Western Hemisphere Immigration and United States Foreign Policy *(1992).*

MODERN migration from Haiti to the United States began in the 1950s. It was modest in size, and for the most part it brought migrants who enjoyed at least middle-class status in Haiti to the New York metropolitan area. Between fiscal years 1951 and 1960, legal immigration from Haiti totaled 4442. During the following ten years, 34,499 Haitians migrated legally; this migrant wave included many members of Haiti's urban working class. These population streams raised few political problems. Although Haitian immigrants to New York often experienced great difficulties in adapting to reduced social status in a society with harsh and unfamiliar racial attitudes,[1] neither the sending nor the receiving governments paid great attention to this immigrant group.

After 1970, however, migration from Haiti became politically problematic both for Washington and for the regime in Port-au-Prince. The size of the migratory stream increased considerably; in the 1970s, 56,335 Haitians migrated legally, followed by 185,425 between 1981 and 1991.[2] These migrants tended to come from poorer classes in Haiti, and the legal migrants were supplemented by thousands of Haitians holding visitors' visas who overstayed their allotted time in the United States. New York was still the preferred destination, and by the 1990s the Haitian community there numbered approximately 400,000.

Besides this airplane migration to the U.S. Northeast, thousands of Haitians also began in the early 1970s to try migrating without authorization to south Florida by sea. From 1972 through 1979, 7837 undocumented Haitians arrived by this route in small or moderate-sized vessels; in 1980, fully 24,530 reached U.S. shores. About 28,000 were intercepted in the same attempt during the following ten years, and in 1991-92 at least 37,000 undertook the perilous 600-mile sea voyage.

This article will focus on U.S. policy toward undocumented Haitian migrants to south Florida during the past twenty years. Beginning in the early 1970s, influential economic and political leaders in south Florida pressed for federal action to stop the migration of Haitians by sea; Washington responded by detaining most boat people from Haiti in Florida camps, returning them to Port-au-Prince as rapidly as possible.[3] A key watershed in policy toward Haiti's boat people occurred in 1980 and 1981. In 1980, a "migration crisis" took place, during which about 125,000 Cuban migrants came to the United States by boat from the port of Mariel, just as 25,000 Haitians ar-

---

1. Cf. Susan Buchanan Stafford, "The Haitians: The Cultural Meaning of Race and Ethnicity," in *New Immigrants in New York*, ed. Nancy Foner (New York: Columbia University Press, 1987).

2. Immigration data in this and the preceding paragraph are drawn from U.S., Immigration and Naturalization Service, *1991 Statistical Yearbook*, tab. 2, pp. 29-30.

3. Florida groups urging action to slow migration by sea argued "that the boat people were a disruptive force, destroying the community and draining public resources." Alex Stepick, "Unintended Consequences: Rejecting Haitian Boat People and Destabilizing Duvalier," in *Western Hemisphere Immigration and United States Foreign Policy*, ed. Christopher Mitchell (University Park, PA: Penn State Press, 1992), pp. 133-35.

rived by sea as well. A new status was invented by the Carter administration—"Cuban-Haitian Entrant"— that permitted most of the 1980 boat people from both Mariel and Haiti to remain in the United States. Once the crisis—and the U.S. presidential election—were over, however, a new and harsher official course of action was instituted toward Haitians. The United States began to intercept Haitian migrants on the high seas, returning most of them to Haiti on Coast Guard vessels. Sometimes a hearing to establish potential eligibility for political asylum has been accorded these Haitians and sometimes not. This policy is still in effect.

Despite many observers' aversion to the interception policy as discriminatory and inhumane, from the record I will recount it can be asserted that the United States has the legal, technical, and political means to prevent unwanted seaborne migration from Haiti. The interdiction policy takes advantage of the fact that Haiti is an island sharing no easily crossed land border with the United States. Under routine conditions, the policy does not consume many U.S. administrative resources, and it has been approved emphatically by U.S. courts. The policy has been continued under three U.S. presidents, representing both major parties.

Politically, interdiction has certain costs within the United States, most notably the vigorous opposition of civil liberties groups, the Congressional Black Caucus, and, recently, even some elected officials in Florida. During periods when large numbers of Haitian boat people try to reach the United States, the interception policy also strains the U.S. government's funds and heightens friction between the public agencies involved. These costs have influenced the details of U.S. immigration actions and have affected U.S. foreign policy toward Haiti itself in interesting ways. The political expenses of intercepting Haitian migrants, however, have not been so high as to change the policy. Indeed, as restrictionism on immigration issues has risen in the past few years both among rank-and-file Americans and among the U.S. political elite, the political penalties implied by the Haitian repatriation policy have probably diminished.

I will examine, in turn, two key aspects of the U.S. government's policy toward unauthorized migration from Haiti. I will first explore legal and technical issues, before turning to the political implications of intercepting unauthorized Haitian migrants at sea. Finally, I will discuss whether the post-1980 treatment of Haitian migrants is an exceptional case in U.S. immigration policy.

LEGAL AND TECHNICAL
ASPECTS OF PREVENTING
UNWANTED MIGRATION
FROM HAITI

U.S. law makes a firm distinction between persons who are viewed as political migrants and those considered to be economic migrants. Refugees and asylum claimants are considered as political migrants, and policy toward them is governed by the Refugee Act of 1980 and by a series of court decisions, especially on matters of asylum.[4] The refugee sys-

4. On the Refugee Act, see U.S., Congress, House, Committee on the Judiciary, *Immigra-*

tem is basically geared to consider applicants who are abroad, whether in their home nation or another country. The executive branch and Congress annually agree on the number of refugee visas that will be made available and the world regions that will receive them. In the 13 years since this program was instituted, the Western Hemisphere has received very few of these refugee "numbers."

Procedures for handling asylum petitions, which are too haphazard to be called a system, deal with the claims of migrants who arrive in the United States and ask to remain, in the words of the Refugee Act of 1980, due to "persecution or a well-founded fear of persecution on account of race, religion, nationality, membership in a particular social group, or political opinion" in their home nation. From the late 1970s until 1990, asylum adjudications were blatantly affected by U.S. foreign policy interests; petitioners fleeing repressive regimes friendly to the United States tended to be denied, while those seeking shelter from left-wing governments usually had a greater chance of receiving asylum. A new and more impartial system for considering asylum claims, offering a considerably greater chance for applications to be approved, was instituted in 1990 to settle a class action suit on behalf of Salvadorans and Guatemalans.[5]

One requirement of U.S. asylum policy has proven to be crucial for Haitians: a claimant must be within U.S. territory in order to request safe haven. Litigation on behalf of Haitians has, in fact, done much to solidify the law on this point. Being in U.S. custody but outside the United States itself does not grant eligibility to claim asylum, and public interest groups in the United States have been ruled ineligible to bring actions on behalf of Haitians who are situated outside U.S. borders.

Economic migrants, to win legal entry to the United States, must accord with the provisions of the Immigration and Nationality Act of 1952, which was most recently amended in 1990. That law gives advantages to applicants who have close relatives already in the United States or who possess scarce labor skills or would bring significant amounts of capital with them. A large though undetermined number of migrants also enter the United States on visitors' visas and abuse their provisions by staying longer than the time allowed—sometimes permanently.

The U.S. policy opposing unauthorized migration by sea from Haiti is based on the assertion that the great majority of Haitians who attempt to come to the United States by this means are economic migrants. Conditions endured by the poor in the Western Hemisphere's lowest-income nation,[6] the U.S. gov-

tion and Nationality Act, with Amendments and Notes on Related Laws, 7th ed. (Washington, DC: Government Printing Office, 1980).

5. See Sarah Ignatius, An Interim Assessment of the Asylum Process of the Immigration and Naturalization Service (Cambridge, MA: Harvard Law School, National Asylum Study Project, 1992).

6. The United Nations Development Programme has devised a Human Development Index (HDI) for nations, combining indicators of real purchasing power, education, and health. Haiti stands at number 137 out of 173 nations in the HDI ranking; its neighbor, the Dominican Republic, is number 97; Venezuela

ernment contends, strongly motivate some of them to undertake even a dangerous ocean voyage to U.S. shores. Most Haitian unauthorized migrants, for their part, contend that they are politically motivated, and they file asylum claims if they are able to cross U.S. frontiers. U.S. officials view many of these claims as fraudulent, intended simply to prolong the applicant's time in the United States—sometimes at liberty, but often not—while the request is processed and available appeals are made.[7] Many observers have argued that the especially stringent U.S. policy toward Haitians is based on racial considerations;[8] that is energetically denied by the policy's proponents and administrators.

At all events, the U.S. government's goal has been to prevent seaborne Haitians from reaching U.S. territory and the jurisdiction of U.S. courts. The U.S. Coast Guard began to patrol near Haiti's shores in 1981, and a routine developed that lasted

fully ten years. Any Haitian vessel that appeared to be carrying migrants was boarded, and its occupants were transferred to a Coast Guard cutter. There they were interviewed by a team including representatives of the State Department, the Immigration and Naturalization Service (INS—a section of the Justice Department), and a Haitian Creole interpreter. If a passenger appeared able to substantiate a "well-founded fear of persecution," he or she was to be transported to the United States (but in ten years only 28 migrants out of 25,000 intercepted were not deemed to be economic migrants). The Haitian vessel was then burned, and the remaining passengers were returned to Haiti.

This procedure was backed up by an agreement reached in 1981 between the U.S. and Haitian governments under which the latter undertook to permit the U.S. patrols, to restrain emigration by prosecuting smugglers, and to accept migrants returned by the United States without reprisals.[9] This agreement has never been repudiated by the government of Haiti, although the dictatorship of President Jean-Claude Duvalier, which had first negotiated the accord, was overthrown in 1986. Numerous coups and abortive elections took place before the Reverend Jean-Bertrand Aristide was chosen president with massive popular backing in 1990.

The costs of the U.S. interdiction program were manageable though not trivial: one Coast Guard cutter was usually assigned, and the pro-

---

is number 50; and the United States is number 6. Haitian gross domestic product per capita in 1990 stood at $933, while for the United States the same variable was $21,449. See United Nations Development Programme, *Human Development Report 1993* (New York: Oxford University Press, 1993), pp. 135-37, tab. 1.

7. There is a good case to be made that these stark alternatives distort the reality of mixed motivations for population movement. Migrants' motives are especially likely to be both economic and political in Haiti, where for many decades the state and its repressive capacity have been the principal sources of an economic surplus for elites. See Michel-Rolph Trouillot, *Haiti: State against Nation* (New York: Monthly Review Press, 1990).

8. See, for example, Randall Robinson and Benjamin Hooks, "Haitians: Locked Out Because They're Black," *Washington Post*, 24 Aug. 1992.

9. Stepick, "Unintended Consequences," pp. 144-47.

gram cost an average of $30 million yearly during the 1980s. The deterrent effect was considerable. In 1980 alone, 24,530 undocumented Haitian migrants—mainly boat people—were arrested in south Florida; over the succeeding eight years, a total of only 21,906 were apprehended there.

U.S. immigration policy toward Haiti was placed under notable stress following the overthrow of President Aristide by the military on 30 September 1991. The army and other repressive groups attacked many of Father Aristide's supporters, killing approximately 1500.[10] In October, a massive outflow of boat people began, and by 18 November the Coast Guard had intercepted at least 1800. A refugee flotilla of this size had to be handled in a new way. Political violence in Haiti seemed palpable enough that the policy of quick return might draw great public criticism in the United States, and there were too many migrants to be housed, as was tried at first, on the decks of Coast Guard cutters. Instead, a tent camp was hurriedly erected at the U.S. naval base at Guantánamo Bay in Cuba to house as many as 12,000 Haitian emigrants.

At Guantánamo, more extensive asylum interviews were conducted, and a much higher percentage of Haitians were judged to have claims with sufficient plausibility to warrant transportation to the U.S. mainland. In all, 32.6 percent of Haitians who had reached the U.S. base in Cuba by the end of February 1992 were permitted to apply for asylum.[11] Opponents of the interdiction policy sought through the courts and through congressional lobbying to oblige the executive branch to bring all intercepted Haitians to the U.S. mainland, but they did not prevail. In January 1992, court injunctions were lifted and the Coast Guard began to return to Haiti those Guantánamo internees who were considered by the government as economic migrants.

The government faced a new challenge when the number of intercepted Haitians surged to more than 10,000 during the month of May 1992; Haitians sought to flee what Amnesty International termed pervasive lawlessness in Haiti.[12] After internal debate, the Bush administration decided to begin escorting detained boats back to Haiti without affording any asylum review at all; the Guantánamo camp was closed, partly on the grounds that, as Richard Boucher of the State Department stated, "it was increasingly clear that [the camp] was acting as a magnet and causing more Haitians to get on boats in the hopes of getting there."[13]

Advocates for the Haitians and for human rights were scathing in their criticism. "This is as wrong as it gets in terms of international refugee law," commented Arthur C. Helton, director of the refugee project of the Lawyers Committee for Human Rights.

10. Amnesty International, *Haiti: The Human Rights Tragedy—Human Rights Violations since the Coup* (New York: Amnesty International, 1992).

11. Barbara Crosette, "House Passes Bill to Let Haitians Stay at Guantánamo for 6 Months," *New York Times*, 28 Feb. 1992.

12. Amnesty International, *Haiti: Human Rights Held at Ransom* (London: Amnesty International, 1992).

13. Barbara Crosette, "U.S. to Close Refugee Camp at Guantánamo to Haitians," *New York Times*, 29 May 1992.

Democratic presidential aspirant Governor Bill Clinton of Arkansas later termed the Bush stance a "cruel policy of returning Haitian refugees to a brutal dictatorship without an asylum hearing."[14] Nonetheless, the new U.S. policy effectively discouraged boat people. By 5 June, the seaborne exodus had virtually stopped.

As Clinton's inauguration approached following his electoral defeat of Bush, his advisers became concerned that a new rush of migration by sea from Haiti might be encouraged by the President-Elect's position, expressed on 12 November, that the United States "should have a process in which these Haitians get a chance to make their case." In early January 1993, Clinton announced that he would reverse his position and maintain the Bush policy. "The practice of returning those who flee Haiti by boat will continue, for the time being, after I become President," he stated in a broadcast to Haiti and to Haitians in the United States. "Leaving by boat is not the route to freedom."[15] No increase in refugee shipping was noted following this announcement.

The 1991-92 policy of interning large numbers of Haitians on U.S. ships and at Guantánamo was notably more costly than U.S. efforts over the preceding decade. At the height of the crisis, 15 Coast Guard cutters were assigned to the Haitian patrol, out of 33 available for the whole eastern seaboard of the United States.[16] During the first seven months after President Aristide's overthrow, combined U.S. costs were estimated at $60 million, an annual spending rate nearly four times that of the 1980s.

Tensions and disagreements also surfaced among U.S. agencies after September 1991. The Defense Department was unhappy at having the Guantánamo base used for refugees, asserting that it might provoke the Cuban government to inundate the facility with a Mariel-style exodus of Cubans; State Department officials criticized the INS for allowing such a high proportion of Haitians to apply for asylum, arguing that human rights conditions were not that bad in Haiti; both State and INS faulted the Coast Guard for sending so many ships near Haiti that they might actually encourage emigration.[17]

The U.S. court system offered an important forum for advocates of Haitian migrants who had made it to U.S. territory. Through an arduous course of litigation beginning in the late 1970s, supporters of the Haitians contested the government's inclination to detain Haitians for long periods of time, and the conditions and location of that detention. They

14. Michael Wines, "Switching Policy, U.S. Will Return Refugees to Haiti," *New York Times*, 25 May 1992.

15. Elaine Sciolino, "Clinton Says U.S. Will Continue Ban on Haitian Exodus," *New York Times*, 15 Jan. 1993.

16. Testimony of Rear Admiral William P. Leahy, Jr., Chief, Office of Law Enforcement and Defense Operations, U.S. Coast Guard, in U.S., Congress, House, Judiciary Committee, Subcommmittee on International Law, Immigration, and Refugees, *Cuban and Haitian Immigration*, Hearing, 102d Cong., 1st sess., 20 Nov. 1991, p. 92.

17. Howard W. French, "Flight of Haitians Suddenly Resumes," *New York Times*, 16 May 1992.

achieved some hard-won and partial victories.[18]

The government position, however, prevailed resoundingly in legal tests of the interception policy; the key decision came in June 1993 in *Sale* v. *Haitian Centers Council*. Following a series of conflicting decisions in lower courts, the United States Supreme Court ruled 8 to 1 in favor of the government. The Refugee Act of 1980 states that the Attorney General "shall not deport or return any alien" to a nation "if the Attorney General determines that such alien's life or freedom would be threatened" there. Justice John Paul Stevens, writing for the Court's majority, stated that neither the Refugee Act nor the United States' 1968 accession to the United Nations Protocol Relating to the Status of Refugees barred the government from returning aliens outside U.S. borders to any destination it chose. The law's guarantees, in the majority's view, applied only to migrants within U.S. territory. In a bitter dissent, Justice Blackmun stated:

I believe that the duty of nonreturn expressed in both the Protocol and the statute is clear. The majority finds it "extraordinary" that Congress would have intended the ban on returning "any alien" to apply to aliens at sea. That Congress would have meant what it said is not remarkable. What is extraordinary in this case is that the Executive, in disregard of the law, would take to the seas to intercept fleeing refugees and force them back to their persecutors and that the Court would strain to sanction that conduct.[19]

POLITICAL ASPECTS OF
PREVENTING UNAUTHORIZED
MIGRATION FROM HAITI

Funds, administrative mechanisms, and legal approval are not enough to sustain a highly visible governmental policy on an issue of active public concern. The balance of political forces in the domestic arena must also be favorable for the policy to endure. Throughout its existence, the policy of intercepting Haitian migrants at sea has been vigorously attacked by groups concerned with civil and human rights, by Haitians resident in the United States, and by African American politicians and civic leaders. Since Aristide's overthrow, these opponents have been especially mobilized and passionate. In November 1991, Congressman Charles B. Rangel (D., NY), for example, interrogated INS Commissioner Gene McNary:

Rangel: I hope I'm making it loud and clear that I think the policy is racist. And I would like to just ask you, Mr. McNary, is there any question in your mind that if the people on these boats came from Ireland, that we would exercise the same policy, notwithstanding the law? And if the situation existed in Ireland with this ragtag, crooked, violent group of gangsters who call themselves soldiers, do you think for one minute that the United States of America would return these Irish people to Ireland?

McNary: Congressman, that is even an offensive question. We return anyone who is supposed to be returned under the laws of the United States of America.[20]

In September 1992, a widely publicized rally protesting the repatria-

18. Cf. Stepick, "Unintended Consequences," pp. 137-40.

19. Excerpts from the opinion appeared in *New York Times*, 22 June 1993.

20. U.S., Congress, *Cuban and Haitian Immigration*, p. 107.

tion policy for Haitians was held by about 650 activists in front of the White House. Tennis star Arthur Ashe, less than a year before his death, was among those arrested for blocking traffic; also present was 82-year-old African American dancer and choreographer Katherine Dunham, who had conducted a hunger strike during the preceding winter to protest U.S. actions. Ashe stated, "I'm outraged. [Haitian refugees] are entitled to a fair hearing just to see if they are indeed political refugees."[21] The repatriation policy was also the subject of vivid photographs throughout the crisis, carrying—probably inevitably —a generally critical message to newspaper readers nationwide. Particularly striking were images of unwilling Haitian returnees being carried ashore by Coast Guard sailors in Port-au-Prince and of fearful migrants waiting to be interrogated by officials of the government they had fled.[22]

The weight of political influence, however, has consistently stood on the other side of the balance, in favor of the interception policy. Influential political and economic forces in south Florida steadily backed the policy during the 1980s. Their concerns found a ready echo in the INS district office in Miami, whose director, Perry Rivkind, told a reporter in 1985: "Asylum is a legitimate need for people escaping political troubles. It ought to be confined to persecuted

people, not a whole country who want [sic] a better life."[23]

In 1991 and 1992, both public and elite opinion in Dade County did become more favorable toward granting safe haven to Haitians. A public opinion survey found that 57 percent of respondents in Florida supported allowing Haitians to remain in the U.S. temporarily, and Miami Mayor Xavier Suarez stated, "I think the old distinction between political and economic refugees just doesn't wash any more. The Haitians come here with a lot of good strong societal values and just want an opportunity. We should give it to them."[24] The *Miami Herald* dubbed Bush's repatriation policy "Operation Racist Shield."[25] However, members of Congress from south Florida were divided on a bill to suspend the return of Haitians.[26]

Presidential policy not to admit Haitians was also affected by public opinion at the national level and by national political calculations. During the 1980s, restrictive immigration policies became notably more popular than in preceding decades. For example, 49 percent of a national sample in 1986 supported a decrease in immigration, while only 7 percent backed an increase. The idea of legislation to penalize employers of unauthorized migrants was endorsed by 70 percent, though a smaller majority was willing to permit law-abid-

21. Gary Lee and Molly Sinclair, "Refugee Policy Protested," *Washington Post*, 10 Sept. 1992.

22. See, for example, a front-page color photograph in the latter vein published under the headline "An Uncertain Future for Thousands of Haitians," *Gannett Suburban Newspapers* (Westchester County, NY), 4 Feb. 1992.

23. Barry Bearak, "Bedeviled Haitian Boatlift Resumes," *Los Angeles Times*, 2 Mar. 1985.

24. Larry Rohter, "Haven for Haitians Backed in Miami," *New York Times*, 5 Feb. 1992. Copyright © 1992 by the New York Times Company. Reprinted by permission.

25. *Miami Herald*, 1 Feb. 1992.

26. See the vote recorded in U.S., Congress, *Congressional Record*, 27 Feb. 1992, p. H824.

ing undocumented aliens to remain if they had lived in the United States for several years.[27]

At least as important as these figures has been the interpretation placed on them by presidential advisers for more than ten years: that a powerful restrictionist current of public opinion would emerge to punish any president who was perceived as permitting a weak immigration policy that did not safeguard the nation's frontiers. It became axiomatic that President Jimmy Carter had been gravely wounded when his administration had proven unable to stop the influx of Cuban and Haitian boat people in 1980. Neither Reagan, Bush, nor Clinton has wished to incur the same political penalties.

Opposition to the government's hostile stance against Haitian boat people did have a major impact on U.S. policy not toward Haitian migrants but toward Haitian internal politics. Both advocates for Haitian migrants and, in principle, the executive branch could agree on making efforts to improve the Haitian government's observance of human rights and civil liberties. If such pressures were successful, political violence might be diminished in Haiti, and—of importance to the executive—the claim of political motivations for emigration would be severely undercut. As Representative Major Owens (D., NY), whose district includes many Haitian American voters, stated in 1991, "The best way not to have the problem that has been placed on our doorstep by this current wave of Haitians trying to leave is to have a policy where we support unequivocally democracy and the democratic process in Haiti."[28]

Congress started down this road in 1982 when it passed the Mica Amendment, which conditioned economic aid to Haiti on the Haitian regime's efforts to restrain emigration and to advance democratic development and civic guarantees. These strictures against the Duvalier government may have helped to undermine it.[29] After receiving mainly lip service while a series of military governments ran Haiti in the late 1980s, this U.S. course of action was strongly renewed following President Aristide's ouster, and it now dominates U.S. policy toward Haiti.

The Clinton administration has cooperated very closely with initiatives of the Organization of American States and the United Nations, the latter of which produced in July 1993 a commitment on the part of Haiti's ruling military and civilian elite to reinstate President Aristide by the end of October of that year. The issue of migration has come to shape U.S. foreign policy toward Haiti; Washington wishes to help establish a government in Port-au-Prince that will be arguably democratic, in large part so that the policy of repatriating migrants may be continued without effective political challenge.

27. Robert Pear, "New Restrictions on Immigration Gain Public Support, Poll Shows," *New York Times*, 1 July 1986. See also Edwin Harwood, "Alienation: American Attitudes toward Immigration," *Public Opinion*, pp. 50-51 (June-July 1983).

28. U.S., Congress, *Cuban and Haitian Immigration*, p. 44.

29. Stepick, "Unwanted Consequences."

IS HAITI AN EXCEPTIONAL CASE?

The U.S. policy I have reviewed is on balance a discreditable affair. Under "interdiction," one of the world's most powerful and wealthiest nations selects some of the Western Hemisphere's poorest people, who are almost invariably black, for summary—or near-summary—return to grinding poverty and a repressive and often violent political atmosphere. U.S. officials regularly present some arguable justifications for the policy, most notably the concern that many boat people would drown on their journey north if their often rickety boats were not stopped by the Coast Guard. However, the predominant official motivations are probably a concern at the presidential level that U.S. immigration policy not appear weak or out of control and an anxiety not to have thousands of additional black migrants from Haiti added to the population of south Florida.

In concluding, we may ask whether this policy is an exceptional one. An important issue throughout the U.S. debate on policy toward Haitian boat people has been whether Haitians are being treated differently from other similar migrants. By and large, for years it was evident that the answer was yes, especially in comparison with Cubans. Unauthorized migrants from Cuba enjoyed both the benefits of the Cuban Adjustment Act of 1966, permitting them to avoid detention in the United States and return to Cuba, and the active sympathy of the INS district office in Miami. The claims of succeeding U.S. administrations that they were "only applying the law"

rang hollow when it was noted that Haiti was the only country with which Washington had a repatriation agreement.

As we move further into the 1990s, however, Haiti is becoming less of an exceptional case. Beginning in late 1992, small ships laden with migrants from mainland China began to arrive off the shores of Hawaii and California, and in June 1993 a similar vessel, the *Golden Venture*, ran aground in New York City with scores of Chinese aboard; 11 were killed in the wreck. This episode combined in the public's mind with the image of lax immigration control conveyed by the admission to the United States of alleged participants in the February 1993 World Trade Center bombing in New York. National opinion surveys showed a marked increase in restrictionist sentiment, and even large majorities of Hispanic respondents agreed with the proposition that "there are too many immigrants coming to the United States."[30]

The Clinton administration responded both by indirectly repatriating hundreds of Chinese boat people and by seeking broad new legal powers for excluding asylum claimants. In mid-July, the United States—with difficulty—persuaded Mexico to land and immediately return to China more than 650 migrants aboard three ships that had been detained in inter-

30. For the results of a national poll and findings of a survey of Hispanics in the United States, see, respectively, Seth Mydans, "Poll Finds Tide of Immigration Brings Hostility," *New York Times*, 27 June 1993, and Rodolfo O. de la Garza, et al., "Attitudes toward U.S. Immigration Policy: The Case of Mexicans, Puerto Ricans and Cubans," *Migration World*, 21(2-3):13-16 (1993).

national waters by the U.S. Coast Guard before they could reach California.[31] Two weeks later, Clinton requested new legislative authority to adjudicate rapidly asylum claims by migrants who reach U.S. territory and to limit the petitioners' rights of appeal prior to deportation.[32]

Governor Pete Wilson of California was the most vocal among a host of national politicians calling for stronger immigration control. He sent an open letter to President Clinton proposing that children of illegal migrants should be denied public education and, if born in the United States, U.S. citizenship. He also called for a tamper-proof system of immigrant identification and the denial of emergency medical care to illegal migrants.[33] By August 1993, advocates for international migrants were announcing campaigns "to beat back nativism."[34] It is too soon to tell whether the pluralistic U.S. policy-making process will approve or fund the sort of broad authority for near-summary exclusion requested by the executive branch. However, U.S. policy toward Haitian boat people may well come to be considered, for better or worse, as exemplary rather than anomalous.

31. Tim Golden, "Mexico, in Switch, Decides to Return Stranded Chinese," *New York Times*, 15 July 1993.

32. Thomas L. Friedman, "Clinton Seeks More Powers to Stem Illegal Immigration," *New York Times*, 28 July 1993.

33. See the editorial "Denying the American Birthright," *Chicago Tribune*, 15 Aug. 1993.

34. "Plan of Action to Combat Anti-Immigrant Backlash" (Memorandum to members, National Immigration, Refugee, and Citizenship Forum, 8 Aug. 1993).

ANNALS, *AAPSS*, **534**, July 1994

The French Response to the
Asylum Seeker Influx, 1980-93

By CATHERINE WIHTOL DE WENDEN

ABSTRACT: This article analyzes the evolution of the asylum situation in France, the untoward effects of rigor, and the humanitarian price paid for French efforts to curb possible abuse of asylum. French asylum policy reforms in recent years have significantly reduced asylum applications, attesting to a certain, if limited, governmental capacity to prevent unwanted migration.

Catherine Wihtol de Wenden is research director at the National Center for Scientific Research and a member of the Center for the Study of International Relations in Paris. She has written and edited several books: Les immigrés dans la cité *(1978);* Les immigrés et la politique: Cent-cinquante ans d'évolution *(1988);* Citoyenneté, nationalité et immigration *(1987);* La citoyenneté *(1988), and* Les immigrés dans la cité: Expériences européennes *(1993). She is also the author of many articles on immigration to France and Europe.*

THE adoption, in 1951, of the Geneva agreement on refugees led to the creation of the United Nations High Commissioner for Refugees (UNHCR) in the context of the Cold War, when the refugee was an individual very different from a migrant worker and was usually a victim of the Eastern European political situation. During the following years, the regime protecting refugees adapted itself to a series of unforeseen circumstances, and it was only in 1967 that the New York convention on refugees extended the definition of refugee to southern areas with other types of asylum seekers. Today, Africa, Central America, and Asia are the scenes of the major refugee problems. In Europe, the lessons from Yugoslavia are also showing that, as the UNHCR's Mrs. Ogata stated at a conference at Graz in May 1992, "movements of people are likely to become both a major and security issue in the near future. An issue that cannot be dealt with through charity. An issue that requires political vision, leadership and statesmanship. . ."[1]

Faced with such pressures, democratic states can curb asylum seeker inflows but at a cost to democratic values and without solving a worldwide problem. Moreover, these states encounter pressures from quarters with contradictory and conflicting viewpoints and positions: respect for human rights, public opinion in support of law and order, movements agitating in favor of the defense of asylum seekers, and the logic of the European framework. Increasingly,

there is an awareness that Europe has reached a turning point concerning immigration.

Europe is relatively much less affected by refugees than are Third World countries, which produce but also welcome most of the world's 17 million asylum seekers, 3 million quasi refugees, and 23 million displaced persons, a total of 43 million people who scarcely meet the spirit of the criteria laid down at Geneva in 1951.[2] But the refugee flows are not equally distributed among the European countries. For instance, since 1945, Germany alone has welcomed half of all the applicants for asylum in Europe—438,000 in 1992. There are different legal and administrative situations among European countries because of differences in the interpretation of asylum law, the criteria used, the constitutional or legal rights to asylum, and the like. The geopolitical situation also varies from one receiving country to the next. For example, there are differences with regard to the degree of permeability of national borders in relation to the South, proximity to countries affected by serious political crises, traditions of migratory flows, cultural areas of exchange, involvement with ethnic populations, the existence or lack of colonial links, the democratic and/or prosperous image of the destination countries, and so on.

Nonetheless, the countries of Europe are moving toward a common asylum policy, as witnessed by the agreement signed in Dublin in 1990,

1. "Refugees in Europe," an international conference, Academy of Graz, Austria, May 1992.

2. Aristide Zolberg, Astri Suhrke, and Sergio Aguayo, Escape from Violence: Conflict and the Refugee Crisis in the Developing World (New York: Oxford University Press, 1989).

and toward a shared control of their continent's external frontier. Europe is now confronting a new situation characterized by this dual imperative.

Measures to address this situation include, first, reasserting protection of asylum seekers by respecting humanitarian methods when repatriating unsuccessful applicants, by legalizing those refused refugee status who have effectively settled in the receiving country, and by avoiding treating asylum only in security terms. Second, a common European immigration policy linked with asylum policy must be adopted in order to avoid a disjunction between immigration and asylum policies. The absence of legal opportunities for economic migrants, the inflexibility of migration policies, and the difficulty of effectively policing borders lead to a confusion, in the mind of the public, between illegals and asylum seekers, because nondemocratic countries often are also poor countries. In many circumstances, law is contradicted by facts and one can wonder about the legitimacy of refugee offices whose role consists mainly of transferring 90 percent of the demands for asylum to appeals commissions.

A new type of asylum seeker is thus emerging. Instead of a single male who applies for asylum due to physical threats against him as a result of his political ideas, there is a trend toward collective asylum seekers, that is, a group of people who are in danger because of ethnic, cultural, or religious associations. These asylum seekers are not far removed from economic migrants, and they sometimes find it difficult to prove the threats they face.

Third, it is necessary to study seriously the alternatives to migration. There must be a real medium- and long-term analysis of the opportunities for repatriation, development, and cooperation. The public must be informed of the findings.

Fourth, it is necessary to promote human rights by establishing sanctions against countries that generate flows of refugees and by regularly reviewing a list of the countries considered as politically safe.

In the absence of a generous and humanitarian policy toward asylum seekers, the Europe of nation-states will be in conflict with the Europe of human rights.[3]

In order to avoid the growing gap between North and South, East and West, Europe has to take into account global changes such as the end of the East-West struggle; the evolution of the situation in Third World countries; changes in the competence of the nation-state, whose powers with regard to border controls, asylum rights, and migration policies are being progressively transferred to the international European level; and transnational actors who try to influence the European-level decision-making processes by acting as so many pressure groups.[4]

NUMBER AND CHARACTERISTICS
OF ASYLUM SEEKERS
IN FRANCE, 1980-93

The Schengen group, created in 1985, has sought to harmonize and

3. Catherine Wihtol de Wenden, "Migrations et droits de l'homme en Europe," *Etudes internationales*, 24(1) (Mar. 1993).

4. Catherine Wihtol de Wenden, "Réfugié politique: Une notion en crise?" *Esprit*, pp. 73-86 (May 1990).

TABLE 1
ASYLUM SEEKERS ACCORDED REFUGEE STATUS, 1956-60

	Number of Asylum Seekers
1956	19,212
1957	28,813
1959	16,457
1960	9,119

SOURCE: France, Office for the Protection of Refugees and Stateless Persons (OFPRA).

coordinate policies toward immigration by fostering common policing of frontiers between the nine group members: France, Germany, Benelux, Italy, Spain, Portugal, and Greece. In a parallel fashion, the Trevi group, consisting of the 12 European Community countries, prepared the Dublin agreement of 1990, which, among other provisions, committed governments to accept as definitive most adjudication outcomes. One might think, then, that the responses of the European countries to the asylum situation would be roughly similar. In fact, this is not so. In spite of some convergence, each country tends to have its own policy, although they all are enmeshed in an international and European corpus of constraints. As for the French case, the years 1980-93 have witnessed dramatic changes in refugee flows and in policies.

The flows

France has a long tradition of offering asylum. Until 1960, an average of 15,000 applicants per year sought asylum (see Table 1), and refusals were rare, about 200 yearly.

Most of the applicants during this period were Europeans, and their welcome was facilitated by a policy of assistance and integration. Perhaps because of the low number of applicants, the number of applicants who were granted refugee status was much higher than now. By 1956, 384,000 refugees had registered at the OFPRA, the French Office for the Protection of Refugees and Stateless Persons, created in 1952 to implement the Geneva agreement of 1951. In addition, there were 190,000 persons registered with the International Office for Refugees, a former office of the United Nations, located in France. In all, there was a total of 578,600 refugees with or without formal status, according to estimates of the OFPRA. In 1962, there were still 252,000 refugees in France and, in 1964, 174,000.

The rise in requests for asylum occurred in the middle of the 1970s. The turning point came in 1973-74, when recruitment of most foreign workers stopped while the situation in the Third World was deteriorating. Before 1974, many potential asylum candidates probably entered as foreign workers or came illegally, while after 1974, some who were unable to enter as immigrants asked for asylum. Asylum seekers from Eastern Europe gave way increasingly to Third World flows: Latin Americans, Vietnamese, black Africans fleeing

TABLE 2
ASYLUM SEEKER FLOWS, 1980-92

	Number of Asylum Seekers
1980	20,000
1987	27,000
1988	34,000
1989	61,000
1990	54,000
1991	46,800
1992	27,500

SOURCE: OFPRA.

civil wars, and new groups of relatively poor people who were fleeing persecution in countries such as Turkey and Sri Lanka but who were unable to assemble proof of their persecution. The increase in the number and diversity of asylum seekers prompted a change in the orientation of French policy toward them. There was now a much more suspicious attitude: the selective welcome of asylum seekers was replaced by dissuasive procedures.

Between 1973 and 1989, the number of asylum seekers grew from 1620, of whom 1237 were accorded refugee status, to 61,000. The Indochinese dominated in 1975-76; other Third World applicants dominated in 1984-85, mainly from Africa—Zaire, Ghana—and then, in 1989, there was a new surge of applicants from Africa—Zaire, Mali, Angola—and from Turkey, Sri Lanka, and the Indian subcontinent. France experienced a continuous increase in asylum seekers until 1990 (see Table 2). At the same time, the rate of refusals rose from 4 percent in 1976 to 85 percent in 1990.

From 1979 to 1989, the demand for asylum tripled. This increase took place in two stages. Circa 1985, requests by Africans multiplied rapidly and continued to increase during the following years. Today Africa accounts for one-third of all asylum applications. Then, circa 1989, a new upsurge of requests by Africans occurred, coupled with a large increase in requests by Europeans, principally Turks and Romanians. Since 1989, the number of requests for asylum has decreased, as seen in Table 3.

The more the demand for asylum grew, the less asylum was granted. From a 77.7 percent acceptance rate for those seeking refugee status in 1981, the rate decreased to 15.5 percent in 1990, with the number of favorable decisions stabilizing in absolute terms at around 15,000 per year.

The refugee recognition rate of 29 percent in 1992 is higher than in many other European countries. At the frontier, those whose application is considered by the police to have an insufficient basis have an initial rejection rate of 50 percent. But one can observe strong disparities according to the country of origin of the applicants: chances are much better for an Asian than for an African to obtain refugee status. Moreover, the Refugee Appeals Commission tends to confirm the OFPRA refusals.

TABLE 3
ASYLUM ADJUDICATIONS, REFUGEES RECOGNIZED,
AND RECOGNITION RATE, 1981-92

	Number of Cases Adjudicated	Refugees Recognized	Recognition Rate (percentage)
1981	18,767	14,586	77.72
1982	21,210	15,670	73.88
1983	20,860	14,608	70.03
1984	21,928	14,314	65.28
1985	26,662	11,539	43.28
1986	27,274	10,645	39.03
1987	26,628	8,704	32.69
1988	25,425	8,794	34.59
1989	31,170	8,770	28.14
1990	87,352	13,486	15.44
1991	78,442	15,467	19.72
1992	37,202	10,819	29.08

SOURCE: OFPRA

In 1992, applications by asylum seekers rapidly decreased, falling to 28,000 from 61,000 in 1989. The recent decrease in applications has been accompanied by an increase in the recognition rate, now up to 29 percent. But it is difficult to explain this relationship. It is possible that recent deterrence measures have, in fact, deterred frivolous applications.

Currently, the asylum procedure is completed in six months. As for the displaced persons coming from the former Yugoslavia, a dispensation allows them to be granted a provisional residence permit of 3 to 6 months with a work permit. There were 10,000 persons with this status in early 1993. For most of them, France refuses to admit that their situation is definitive, as this would represent recognition of the enduring consequences of ethnic cleansing.

The refugee and asylum seeking population also varies in age. In 1991, the average age of Eastern European asylum seekers was 30

years; that of refugees, 57 years. African asylum seekers and Latin American asylum seekers had an average age of 29 years, and refugees, 37 years. Asian refugees averaged 38 years old.

While today there are 140,000 people with refugee status, thirty years ago, in 1962, there were 252,000.[5]

THE EVOLUTION OF
FRENCH POLICIES:
TOWARD GREATER RIGOR

The asylum right is mentioned in the preface of the French Constitution of 1946 and of 1958 (Fifth Republic) as being "among the principles particularly necessary to our period," inspired by the Declaration of Human Rights of 1789: "Every man per-

5. Luc Legoux, "Statistiques des flux de réfugiés depuis la création de l'OFPRA," in Les réfugiés en France et en Europe: Quarante ans d'application de la Convention de Genève 1952-1992 (Paris: Primavera-Quotidienne, 1993), pp. 389-405.

secuted because of his action in favor of freedom has the right to asylum on the territory of the Republic." There is, thus, a right to territorial asylum, independent of the granting of the refugee status. It is not necessary to be a statutory refugee to benefit from asylum.

Following signature of the agreement for international protection of refugees embodied in the Geneva treaty of 28 July 1951, the law of 25 July 1952 created the OFPRA, which grants juridical and administrative protection to bona fide refugees and stateless persons and implements the international agreements related to this protection. The head of the OFPRA has to make a decision concerning the grant of refugee status in the four months following an asylum seeker's application. If the application is accepted, the asylum seeker becomes a registered refugee. He or she receives the right to stay, through a ten-year freely renewable residents' card, and the right to work and is welcome in specialized integration centers. If the application is rejected, an appeal is possible before an appeals board during the month following the notification of the negative decision of the OFPRA. In practice, however, due to the sheer numbers of asylum seekers, the procedure often is protracted, and many asylum seekers encounter difficulties dealing with the authorities in a climate of suspicion.

The French response to the upsurge in applications was an increased demand for proof and measures to avoid fraud, as if the policy toward refugees was an instrument to control immigration flows. In 1989, the OFPRA decided to reform its structure.

The reform includes a shortening of the decision-making process concerning refugee status. Before 1989, cases were often in adjudication for several years, which gave the applicant time to find a job, to establish a family, and so to settle in France. Since 1989, applications have been dealt with in 55 days, which is called by the defenders of human rights a "T.G.V. procedure"—as rapid as the French "train à grande vitesse." The applicant must appeal a negative decision within four months.

Another new measure is the taking of fingerprints. Each applicant must be fingerprinted; the prints are then computerized. This permits authorities to identify possible multiple applications made by one person. It has dissuaded asylum seekers from making more than one application.

Other measures include an increase in the financial support and in the number of civil servants granted to the OFPRA, together with improvements in efficiency. But one might wonder about the aims of such a reform, when some cases have very little chance of being heard. Only half of the applicants benefit from an oral hearing with the OFPRA, although such an interview is considered more or less essential if an OFPRA officer is to be persuaded to grant refugee status.

During the years 1990-92, new restrictive measures were added, sometimes because of the pressure of the European context.[6] First, the notion

6. Danièle Joly and Robin Cohen, *Reluctant Host: Europe and Its Refugees* (Aldershot: Gower Press, 1989).

of manifestly unfounded requests developed. These requests are linked to proof of persecution, which is at the center of the debate over the granting of refugee status. The OFPRA case officer has to be convinced by evidence given by associations, embassies, and consulates of the asylum seekers' country of origin. If the pieces of evidence are convergent and compelling, refugee status is granted.

Second, sanctions were imposed against transporters. Air companies are fined if they agree to carry undocumented passengers. The law of February 1992 sanctions transporters carrying illegal immigrants. If such individuals seek asylum and their demand has no documented basis, then sanctions are applicable in principle. Transporters have to pay a fine and to lodge and eventually repatriate the illegals. There are worries about the legality of transporter sanctions, however, as they give transporters the right to assess by themselves the nature of asylum applications.

Third, agreements on readmission were adopted at the European level—by France, Germany, Austria, Switzerland, and Spain—that allowed states to send denied asylum applicants home. Responsibility for multiple asylum applicants is borne by the state that granted a visa for the longest period. If a visa is not requested, the responsible state is the one that the applicant enters first, according to the Dublin agreement.

Fourth, international areas where the Geneva agreement is not implemented—*zones de transit*—were established at entry points such as airports. The government now has the right to assess and to refuse manifestly unfounded requests when applicants enter the country and to detain those foreigners in areas of transit. This innovation is highly controversial in the eyes of associations working in defense of asylum seekers.[7]

Fifth, the government stopped authorizing asylum applicants to work from 1 October 1991, the same time that Germany restored access to employment. The evolution of this policy is significant. In 1975, employment of asylum applicants was permitted, and in 1981, they did not even have to ask for work permits, as they had an automatic right to work. Applicants even obtained the possibility of legalization if they found employment, and they could receive housing assistance and help with integration. In 1991, this automatic right to work was abolished, and employment authorization for asylum applicants has since depended on the state of the labor market.

Sixth, measures to deal with asylum seekers at the moment of their application were given priority over longer-term integration measures. Reception Centers for Asylum Seekers were established in 1991 to carry out the new measures.

All these reforms—in addition to the effects of more restrictive access to the national territory resulting from the Pasqua Law, and the more rapid processing of cases, with resulting shorter stays in French territory

7. Groupe d'Information et de Soutien aux Travailleurs Immigrés, "Droit d'asile: Suite et . . . fin?" *Plein Droit*, no. 18-19 (Oct. 1992).

—may explain the decline in asylum applications in 1993. If we consider in addition that the country an applicant chooses for asylum is limited by the chances he has of receiving asylum according to his geographical area of origin, we observe that the right to asylum is strongly restricted. A source of further restriction can be found when an applicant requests asylum in various countries. A state receiving such a request may, since the Edinburgh resolution of 1992, send the applicant to the country of first asylum.

THE UNTOWARD EFFECTS OF RIGOR AND ITS MORAL PRICE

An asylum seeker now has more chances to be refused (*débouté*) than to be granted the status of refugee, and many asylum decisions may be dissuasive, more to respond to the anti-immigrant mood both in France and internationally than to supply a long-term solution to the flows of asylum seekers and displaced persons. Fifteen thousand refugees are officially recognized as such each year in France, but there are very few family reunifications.

Such a policy may lead to unclear situations for those whose request for asylum has been refused but who nevertheless remain in France. Two years ago, it provoked a campaign advocating refugee status for 100,000 people who had been refused asylum. In 1991, hunger strikes developed and prompted the adoption, on 23 July 1991, of an exceptional circular requiring prefects, senior civil servants in charge of the administration of departments (the major French administrative units), to legalize the refused applicants if they were successfully integrated and employed. The situation of these applicants was reexamined, and roughly 13,500 of 50,000 were legalized. This legalization brings some discredit to the initial criteria of selection of refugees because it makes them appear very unpredictable. Since a decision of 2 February 1992, the right to asylum has been a principle of French constitutional law, as in many other European countries. But the right to ask for asylum and to benefit from territorial asylum is now granted in a very limited fashion. What credibility can the asylum procedures have when private associations have to fight constantly to protect the human rights involved from deteriorating?

A policy that is too dissuasive may also lead applicants to enter and remain in the country illegally instead of asking for asylum and being thereby threatened with expulsion from the territory. Illegal residence would become a reward for clandestineness. At the same time, there is a policy of refugee integration, and help is given to asylum seekers. Refugees are placed in provisional housing for six months; roughly 3000 refugees a year are welcomed after a stay of two weeks in a transit center. Asylum seekers waiting for a decision on their status are hosted in specialized centers. Refugees learn the French language, are helped to locate housing, and are given pocket money and professional training. Many refugees and asylum seekers, however, do not utilize government services, and they find housing and employment through their own networks. They

TABLE 4
ASYLUM APPLICATIONS BY CONTINENT, 1981-92

	Africa		North and South America		Asia		Europe		Stateless Persons		Total
	Number	%	Number	%	Number	%	Number	%	Number	%	Number
1981	3,583	18.04	1,685	8.48	11,842	59.62	2,658	13.38	95	0.5	19,863
1982	3,733	16.59	1,252	5.56	13,858	61.58	3,628	16.12	34	0.2	22,505
1983	4,590	20.54	1,684	7.53	12,816	57.34	3,195	14.30	65	0.3	22,350
1984	4,043	18.62	1,518	6.99	13,197	60.78	2,866	13.20	90	0.4	21,714
1985	9,984	34.52	1,110	3.84	14,136	48.87	3,579	12.37	116	0.4	28,925
1986	10,708	40.73	1,057	4.02	9,795	37.26	4,636	17.63	94	0.4	26,290
1987	10,478	37.86	1,247	4.51	8,934	32.29	6,909	24.97	104	0.4	27,672
1988	14,725	42.87	2,236	6.51	8,377	24.39	8,915	25.94	99	0.3	34,352
1989	23,456	38.19	3,352	5.46	13,950	22.71	20,614	33.56	50	0.1	61,422
1990	22,122	40.36	1,712	3.12	13,333	24.32	17,543	32.01	103	0.2	54,813
1991	16,494	34.82	1,091	2.30	14,730	31.10	14,968	31.60	91	0.2	47,374
1992	9,392	32.53	923	3.20	11,092	38.42	7,159	24.79	307	1.1	28,873

SOURCE: OFPRA.

also have access to a grant of money to help them integrate into society.

In the summer of 1993, the debate on asylum seekers and their human rights was renewed. The Constitutional Court ruled that certain provisions of recent governmental policies were unconstitutional, and the new conservative government requested revision of the Constitution. The French Constitution was amended to adopt European rules concerning asylum on 19 November 1993. Many opponents of the new conservative government denounced the revision as incompatible with the fundamental republican ideals of France.

CONCLUSION

The Geneva Convention of 1951 was conceived as a tool of remedy for political phenomena different from those that we have today (see Table 4). The expatriation of the middle classes that had no hope of promotion in their home countries, exile due to poverty and authoritarian regimes, and collective demands by ethnic groups instead of individual requests for asylum by well-known persons all constitute challenges to the international regime for refugees. The problem can be summarized in the question, Why should asylum seekers from the South not have the same legitimacy as those from the East? This is a very controversial question in France.

ANNALS, *AAPSS*, **534**, July 1994

Hong Kong's Response to the Indochinese Influx, 1975-93

By RONALD SKELDON

ABSTRACT: The changing nature of the population flows from Vietnam to Hong Kong between 1975 and mid-1993 is examined in this article. Hong Kong's population is largely a product of refugee movements from China. Over the period under discussion, official policy toward all arrivals, whether from China or from Vietnam, became much more restrictive. The first wave of Vietnamese to Hong Kong mostly consisted of ethnic Chinese. These were relatively quickly recognized as refugees and resettled. The later waves of ethnic Vietnamese have been held in closed camps; those arriving after 1988 have been subject to screening to determine their refugee status. Those screened out are repatriated either voluntarily or forcibly to Vietnam. The outflows from Vietnam can be fully understood only after a comprehensive analysis of the nature of the origin and destination economies and societies. An economic dimension is usually present in supposedly political flows.

Ronald Skeldon is a reader in the Department of Geography and Geology at the University of Hong Kong. He was educated at Glasgow and Toronto and has worked for the Australian National University and for various agencies of the United Nations. He is author of Population Mobility in Developing Countries: A Reinterpretation *(1990) and* Reluctant Exiles? Migration from Hong Kong and the New Overseas Chinese *(1994).*

NOTE: I am grateful for the assistance of Brian Bresnihan, Refugee Coordinator, Hong Kong Government Secretariat, and Kaiser Zaman, Deputy Chief of Mission, United Nations High Commissioner for Refugees, Hong Kong, who both supplied information. Neither should be held responsible for the interpretations drawn from that information.

AS the South Vietnamese cities fell to the advance of the Northern armies in March and April 1975, there was a mass panic exodus to American evacuation planes and ships, many people fleeing in small boats to American ships waiting offshore. Over 132,000 people left within a very short time, mainly directly for the United States,[1] and the majority of these were ethnic Vietnamese who had been in the army or the bureaucracy or had otherwise worked with the Americans. Large numbers were Catholics. A hiatus followed until 1978, when a flood of people began fleeing in boats from Vietnam to countries in Southeast Asia and to Hong Kong. In 1977, just over 1000 people arrived in Hong Kong directly in small boats or were rescued from small boats by ocean-going vessels en route to Hong Kong. Most of these were quickly resettled in the United States. In 1978, this number had increased to almost 6000, excluding the 3318 who arrived on the freighter *Huey Fong* on 23 December 1978, which brought to the attention of authorities in Hong Kong, and overseas, the potential magnitude of the crisis. During 1979, 68,748 Vietnamese arrived in Hong Kong. During one day in May, 1700 arrived, while only one departed for resettlement.[2]

The exodus at this time cannot be understood without taking into consideration three important factors: first, that Hong Kong itself is largely the product of refugee migrations; second, the power and influence of the overseas Chinese community in Vietnam and its linkages with Hong Kong; third, the state of the Vietnamese economy. I will briefly examine each of these factors in turn.

HONG KONG AS A CITY OF REFUGEES

Hong Kong emerged from World War II with much of its infrastructure and economy destroyed. Its population was about 650,000 in May 1945, down from 1.44 million in 1941, although that population was much swollen by refugees from the war in China. By February 1946, its population had surpassed 1 million; it reached 1.8 million in 1949 and 2.1 million in 1951. Over one-half of a sample of heads of household who had come into Hong Kong during this period cited "political reasons" for fleeing China; 37.2 percent gave "purely economic reasons."[3] Among those who fled were wealthy entrepreneurs from Shanghai, which until the war had been the center of capi-

---

1. The waves of migration and subsequent settlement are described in Paul James Rutledge, *The Vietnamese Experience in America* (Bloomington: Indiana University Press, 1992). See also Keith St. Cartmail, *Exodus Indochina* (Auckland: Heinemann, 1983).

2. The figures for 1977 and 1978 come from the official yearbooks published by the Hong Kong government. All figures for 1979 come from the government's *Monthly Statistical Re-*

ports on Vietnamese (Arrivals and Departures). To give an idea of the importance accorded the influx of the late 1970s, see the official yearbook *Hong Kong 1980: A Review of 1979* (Hong Kong: Government Printer, 1980), in which the first chapter is "The Boat Refugees from Vietnam."

3. The most important work on this topic at the time is Edvard Hambro, *The Problem of Chinese Refugees in Hong Kong* (Leydon: A. W. Sijthoff, 1955). The results of the sample survey referred to here are in ibid., p. 23.

talist activity in China. Their capital and expertise were important in the later establishment of Hong Kong as an industrial economy, following the Korean War, which laid the basis for the modern developed economy of today. It is argued that there is a "refugee mentality" in Hong Kong that "actually creates a spirit of enterprise and engenders economic dynamism."[4] If this argument is valid, the refugee element has been critical to Hong Kong's development.

The waves of refugees into Hong Kong after World War II were followed by two subsequent waves of migration from China. The first was in 1962, when up to 120,000 entered, fleeing from the famine and disruption in China following the Great Leap Forward. Over 60,000 of these were arrested and deported back to China, but the balance remained. The second wave occurred at precisely the time of the Vietnamese influx in the late 1970s. During this period, 125,000 people arrived legally in Hong Kong from China, 160,000 illegal migrants managed to evade border controls and reach the urban areas to claim Hong Kong residence status, and another 200,000 were caught and repatriated. Hence, when Hong Kong was dealing with an influx by sea from Vietnam, it was also dealing with a much bigger influx over land and coastal waters from China.

THE OVERSEAS CHINESE CONNECTION

The second of the factors identified is the role of the Chinese community in Vietnam and its linkages with Hong Kong. Vietnam, in common with the other countries in Southeast Asia, has a substantial Chinese minority, built up mainly during the first half of this century through migration from southern China. In the mid-1970s, estimates of the Chinese population of Vietnam varied between 1 and 2 million, with the vast majority, or about 84 percent, located in the south.[5] Some 60 percent of the Chinese in Vietnam were Cantonese. As in the case of other Southeast Asian countries, they played a prominent role in local business, with possible investment in what was then South Vietnam of close to US$2 billion.[6]

Given the large number of Cantonese, it is hardly surprising that there were close kinship relationships between Hong Kong and Vietnam, and substantial numbers of Hong Kong residents lived in Vietnam. After the fall of Saigon, many were stranded, so many, in fact, that a special task force was set up in Hong Kong to deal with the 34,000 applications received by the authorities. While it was clear that there was widespread forging of documents, substantial numbers of

4. Wong Siu-lun, "Emigration and Stability in Hong Kong," *Asian Survey*, 32(10):931 (1992). For a discussion of the role of Shanghainese in Hong Kong, see idem, *Emigrant Entrepreneurs: Shanghai Industrialists in Hong Kong* (Hong Kong: Oxford University Press, 1988).

5. The range of estimates will be found in Yuan-li Wu and Chun-hsi Wu, *Economic Development in Southeast Asia: The Chinese Dimension* (Stanford, CA: Hoover Institution Press, 1980), p. 84. See also Pao-min Chang, *Beijing, Hanoi and the Overseas Chinese*, China Research Monograph, no. 24 (Berkeley: University of California, Institute of East Asian Studies, 1982), p. 9.

6. Wu and Wu, *Economic Development in Southeast Asia*, p. 86.

cases were genuine, and in 1978 and 1979 the Immigration Department organized some 53 charter flights to Ho Chi Minh City to bring over 8000 people back to Hong Kong.[7] Thus, until December 1978, more people had come from Vietnam to Hong Kong as part of this government-sponsored program than had arrived on boats.

The main characteristic of the pronounced exodus of boat people from Vietnam to Hong Kong in 1979 was that it was made up of ethnic Chinese. Over 80 percent of the people arriving were classified as Chinese, with two-thirds of these coming from North Vietnam (Table 1). Hong Kong was clearly not the only target of the exodus at this time, but it received more people than any other country—68,748 in 1979 alone, compared with 53,996 by Malaysia, 48,651 by Indonesia, 11,928 by Thailand, 7281 by the Philippines, and 5451 by Singapore.

THE VIETNAMESE ECONOMY

The third background factor was the state of the Vietnamese economy. From 1976 through 1978, Vietnam faced severe economic problems. There were substantial food deficits in terms of grain production in 1976 and 1977, and 1978 saw the gravest food crisis in the country's history, with a disastrous paddy harvest, widespread flooding, and one-fifth of the cattle destroyed. In the south of the country, 1978 saw greater attempts to socialize the economy and society, with petty trading banned

7. The information is contained in the yearbooks for Hong Kong for 1977 and 1978.

and the introduction of a new currency, which in effect eroded the wealth of many of the rich and middle classes. Those who found these policies ideologically incompatible and could not be easily integrated into the new system were allowed, encouraged, or forced to leave. It can be claimed that these policies were universal and affected all equally; in practice, they hit the Chinese particularly hard. With their economic base undermined, the Chinese were faced with several bleak alternatives: to move to New Economic Zones in isolated rural areas or to join the army to fight against the Cambodians. For an essentially urban population, neither of those alternatives was acceptable; the real choice was flight.

Relations between Vietnam and China progressively deteriorated during 1978. Chinese were being encouraged to leave Vietnam for China through a curious information and disinformation campaign as China was becoming increasingly concerned at what it perceived to be discriminating policies against the ethnic Chinese.[8] Huge numbers went to China, with over 200,000 moving when the border between China and Vietnam was opened up in mid-1978 and an additional 40,000 crossing after the border was closed. With the Vietnamese invasion of Cambodia at the end of 1978 and the subsequent

8. A useful summary of this whole period can be found in Aristide Zolberg, Astri Suhrke, and Sergio Aguayo, *Escape from Violence: Conflict and the Refugee Crisis in the Developing World* (New York: Oxford University Press, 1989), pp. 164-65. See also Ramses Amer, *The Ethnic Chinese in Vietnam and Sino-Vietnamese Relations* (Kuala Lumpur: Forum, 1991).

attack by China on Vietnam in February and March 1979, the situation of the Chinese in Vietnam further deteriorated, increasing pressure on ethnic Chinese to leave, particularly from the urban areas. It was at this time that the movement to Hong Kong became prominent. The exodus was handled as a business, and Chinese and ethnic Vietnamese who wished to leave had to pay—the payment to be made in gold. Estimates of the cost vary between US$1500 and US$3000 for an adult; children were half-price.[9] The overall impact on the economy at a time of difficulty was significant indeed. For example, in April 1979 alone, a total of US$242 million was remitted through Hong Kong to Ho Chi Minh City from overseas Chinese sources to facilitate the escape of friends and relatives in Vietnam; by June, the refugee business had become the country's main source of foreign exchange, with an estimated value of US$3 billion.[10]

In Hong Kong, the authorities opposed the landing of freighters bringing thousands of Vietnamese. The *Huey Fong* and the *Skyluck* were left outside Hong Kong for weeks, in the first case, and months, in the second. Their captains were charged with illegal shipment of passengers, and, in the case of the *Huey Fong*, the full extent of the people-smuggling rackets became established.[11] Here was a dilemma. While there were undoubtedly cases of persecution in Vietnam,

the whole exodus of the Chinese, and also of the Vietnamese who were leaving at this time, was being organized as a business that probably went to senior levels of government in Vietnam, and understandably so, given the state of the economy at the time. Those who could escape were the better-off, those with contacts, and those with wealthy relatives outside the country. Clearly, there is no association of refugee status with any particular level of wealth, but the sudden influx of tens of thousands of people in what was apparently a migration industry raises several important questions about refugee status. How many had really been persecuted? How many were fleeing the parlous state of the Vietnamese economy? How many fled because they could afford to leave? There are, as yet, no clear answers to these questions and perhaps there never will be, but when this phase of the exodus from Vietnam was over—relatively few Chinese left after September 1979, mainly because it became much more difficult to do so—there was still a substantial Chinese community in Vietnam of over 900,000. As subsequent developments would show, those who stayed were able to play an important role in Vietnam's reconstruction as the reforms got under way almost ten years later.

THE CREATION OF REFUGEES

The outcome of this exodus was clear; there were hundreds of thousands of Vietnamese waiting for resettlement in camps in Hong Kong and throughout Southeast Asia. The

9. See Amer, *Ethnic Chinese*, p. 86, for an account of the amounts of money involved.

10. The figures are cited in Chang, *Beijing, Hanoi and the Overseas Chinese*, pp. 56-57.

11. These are recounted in Barry Wain, *The Refused: The Agony of the Indochina Refugees* (New York: Simon & Schuster, 1981).

Southeast Asian countries refused to allow the migrants to remain in their countries indefinitely and became unwilling to accept further migrants without clear guarantees that they could move on somewhere else. Significantly, Vietnam refused to discuss the possibility of repatriation "except in the context of normalization of relations with the United States."[12] This the Americans were unwilling to do. Even at this early stage, the Vietnamese migrants could be seen as a bargaining chip in the geopolitical arena. The magnitude of the crisis caused by the buildup of Vietnamese throughout the region culminated in a meeting of foreign ministers in Geneva in July 1979, when it was decided that Hong Kong and Southeast Asian countries would provide first asylum for all leavers from Vietnam while they awaited final resettlement in the developed countries of the West. Highly significant from a more long-term perspective was that the meeting agreed that all those leaving Vietnam would automatically be deemed refugees and hence eligible both for first asylum and for resettlement in the West. In the words of the director of Oxfam, Hong Kong, in the late 1980s, "It was an extraordinary decision, and it is hardly surprising that for the next ten years the Vietnamese people took up this open invitation."[13]

In the aftermath of the Geneva meeting, the rate of resettlement from Hong Kong was high, with

12. Zolberg, Suhrke, and Aguayo, *Escape from Violence*, p. 165.

13. Chris Bale, "Vietnamese Boat People," in *The Other Hong Kong Report 1990*, ed. Richard Y. C. Wong and Joseph Y. S. Cheng (Hong Kong: Chinese University Press, 1990), p. 160.

24,377 resettled in 1979, another 37,468 resettled in 1980, the peak year for resettlement, and 17,818 resettled during 1981. Over 40,000 of those resettled from Hong Kong during those three years went directly to the United States. Some 13,400 went to Canada and almost 11,750 to Britain. Hong Kong itself accepted only 276, but this must be balanced against those thousands of Hong Kong residents and close relatives of Hong Kong residents brought from Vietnam by the Immigration Department in 1978 and 1979. The number of refugees awaiting resettlement in Hong Kong dropped to 12,940 at the end of 1981, but there was only a gradual decline after that until 1988, when the influx to Hong Kong again began in earnest.

THE CLOSING OF THE BORDERS

The first influx of Vietnamese was virtually over by late 1979, and the year 1980 saw a major change. No longer were the boat people primarily ethnic Chinese; over 95 percent of those arriving were Vietnamese, the majority from what had been South Vietnam. In October 1980, faced with continuous migration from China, Hong Kong abandoned the touch-base policy and essentially closed the border to migration. The number of illegal immigrants dropped dramatically, from 150,089 in 1980 to 9220 in 1981. All Chinese illegal immigrants caught were repatriated almost immediately to China. The implementation of this policy toward the Chinese immediately introduced a fundamental contradiction with the Vietnamese. Before 1980, Hong Kong had pursued a much more open policy toward Chinese illegal migrants. Before 1980, as we have seen, the vast majority of those arriving from Vietnam were ethnic Chinese fleeing the imposition of a Communist system that bore similarities, in Hong Kong eyes, with their own history of fleeing from Shanghai and other places in China before the establishment of the People's Republic of China in 1949.

After October 1980, Hong Kong was operating a very restrictive immigration policy toward movement from China; the vast majority of arrivals from Vietnam, although in much reduced numbers compared with 1979, were ethnic Vietnamese. It was a contradiction to allow the latter into the community, as they could move freely from the camps where they were held, while people from across the border, many of whom would have had relatives in Hong Kong, were caught and repatriated. In July 1982, the closed camp policy was introduced whereby all Vietnamese were kept as de facto prisoners, under the control of Correctional Services Officers, until they could be resettled. While Hong Kong has been criticized internationally for implementing such a policy, it made its own immigration policy consistent in the eyes of a community that was becoming increasingly critical of the continuous arrival of Vietnamese.

The period 1982-87 was one of relative stability as far as Vietnamese arrivals and departures to and from Hong Kong were concerned (Table 1). As a result, the numbers held in camps dropped to just over 8000 by the end of 1986. This period of relative stability was marked by a blip in

1987, not of increased numbers of arrivals from Vietnam but from a surge of 7406 ex-China Vietnamese illegal immigrants, or ECVIIs in local jargon. These were Vietnamese who had moved into China in the late 1970s and were now moving to Hong Kong. They were not reaching Hong Kong as a place of first asylum and hence were not eligible for resettlement in the West. They were treated by Hong Kong almost as if they were illegal immigrants from China itself, the only difference being that special permission had to be sought from China for their repatriation and that they were held in different detention centers. In 1987, China very quickly agreed to take them all back, but this problem of ECVIIs is returning to haunt Hong Kong in the 1990s.

THE RISE OF THE ECONOMIC MIGRANT

The years 1988 and 1989 saw a renewed upsurge of boat people from Vietnam. From 3395 in 1987, numbers increased to 18,328 in 1988, and 34,112 in 1989, the highest since the influx of the late 1970s. In common with the flows since 1980, the vast majority of this new surge were ethnic Vietnamese, although over the decade there had been a shift in their place of origin. In the early 1980s, most were from the south of Vietnam; in the flows of the late 1980s, the majority were from the north. This introduced the issue of whether ethnic Vietnamese leaving their own system could be thought of as refugees. At the end of 1987, the number in closed camps was just over 9537. This had increased to 25,673 by the end of 1988 and 55,728 by the end of

TABLE 1

STATISTICS ON VIETNAMESE MIGRANTS TO AND FROM HONG KONG, 1975-93

	Arrivals from Vietnam	Ethnic Origin of Arrivals				Resettlement	Repatriation*	Number in Hong Kong at Year's End
		Chinese from		Vietnamese from				
		South Vietnam	North Vietnam	South Vietnam	North Vietnam			
1975								
1976								
1977	1,001							
1978	9,115							
1979	68,748†	17,972	37,536	9,825	3,341	24,377	—	50,609
1980	6,788	62	43	5,599	1,084	37,468	—	21,657
1981	8,470	87	61	6,050	2,272	17,818	—	12,960
1982	7,836	91	27	6,051	1,667	9,247	—	12,627
1983	3,651	47	11	1,904	1,689	4,200	—	12,766
1984	2,230	49	21	1,563	597	3,694	—	11,892
1985	1,112	13	10	687	402	3,953	—	9,443
1986	2,059	50	25	914	1,070	3,816	—	8,011
1987	3,395	13	23	999	2,360	2,212	—	9,537
1988	18,328	82	162	5,012	13,072	2,772	—	25,673
1989	34,112	1,717	486	3,032	28,877	4,754	918	55,728
1990	6,595	4,256	296	1,861	182	7,656	5,452	52,030
1991	20,206	2,319	222	8,586	9,079	6,467	7,747	60,022
1992	12	9	0	1	2	3,439	12,612	45,317
1993‡	24§	—		—	22	1,317	3,841	40,697

SOURCE: Hong Kong Government, *Monthly Statistical Report*, June 1993.

NOTE: Statistics exclude ex-China Vietnamese illegal immigrants.

*From 1989 only.

†The 1979 total of arrivals includes 74 who were of "other" ethnic group, neither Chinese nor Vietnamese.

‡To 7 July.

§No information on the ethnic origin of two arrivals in 1993.

1989. In response to this renewed influx, in June 1988 Hong Kong introduced screening, with repatriation for all those screened out. Arriving Vietnamese were to be considered not as refugees but as migrants or, more commonly, economic migrants.

This was a major change of policy. Hong Kong had unilaterally broken from the 1979 accords, but this decision was taken in the face of a potential flood of Vietnamese to Hong Kong and to other destinations in the region. For example, the numbers going to Malaysia between 1987 and 1989 doubled, from 8287 to 16,718, and those going to Indonesia increased from 1672 in 1987 to 13,833 in 1990. A radical shift in direction was required if this migration was to be tackled; Hong Kong provided the lead.

The years 1987 and 1988 were crisis years for the economy of Vietnam, particularly in the north, where rice production was down by some 700,000 tons in 1987. The following year was the worst since the virtual economic collapse of 1979. There was famine in a dozen northern provinces, and inflation was approaching 1000 percent.[14] It is thus hardly surprising that tens of thousands chose to leave Vietnam. Here again there were dilemmas and contradictions: the Chinese who could buy their way out of the economic difficulties of 1979 were quickly seen as refugees, whereas Vietnamese fleeing famine a decade later were classified as economic migrants to be repatriated. The

intervening decade had seen major changes in local and international attitudes toward people moving across international boundaries. International migration, whether of settlers, laborers, students, the undocumented, or refugees, grew dramatically over this period, as had awareness that these movements had to be monitored and regulated, if possible.

Numbers leaving continued to increase in 1989, when some 34,112 Vietnamese came to Hong Kong by boat from Vietnam. The economy, however, turned around in that year, and there were considerable rice surpluses not only in the Mekong river delta in the south but also in the densely populated northern provinces. In fact, during 1989, Vietnam became the third-largest rice exporter in the world. This improvement in the economy did not initially appear to stem the outflow, although by 1990 the numbers leaving Vietnam dropped dramatically, with only 6595 arriving in Hong Kong that year. Hong Kong government authorities like to think that their strong action in forcibly repatriating 51 screened-out boat people acted as a strong deterrent. The improved conditions in Vietnam certainly should also not be overlooked in explaining the reduced flow, but, as will be suggested, there were most probably other factors involved, too.

SCREENING AND REPATRIATION

Since screening was introduced, the majority of Vietnamese have been screened out. As of June 1993, some 50,048 people had been screened, only 5729 of whom had

---

14. The information on the economy of Vietnam given in this article is taken from the *Asia Yearbooks* published by the *Far Eastern Economic Review*. The data in this section come from the 1989 yearbook.

been allowed in as refugees. Those who are identified as genuine refugees are moved to a holding center in the Philippines at Bataan. Some 4654 refugees have been moved to Bataan so far to await resettlement. Those who have been screened out have the opportunity to appeal, and, of 16,622 cases involving 35,549 people who had gone through this stage by June 1993, a further 2080 persons were deemed to be refugees. In other words, of those screened to date, only 15.6 percent were identified as refugees. If United Nations High Commissioner for Refugees (UNHCR) personnel disagree with any decision to screen a particular person out, they have the right to declare any migrant a refugee.

The screening procedure has been one of the most controversial of the Hong Kong policies. Accusations grew that those who carried out the screening were ill prepared for their task and that, given the work load involved, they could not devote sufficient time to each case. Interpretation services were also seen to be inadequate. Difficulties undoubtedly arose during the early implementation of the scheme, and it has been seen that the "process fails to conform to general principles of natural justice which form part of the territory's own legal system."[15] In 1991,

the whole system was subject to a three-month judicial review that concluded that the screening was "fair and practical" given the constraints of a two-year backlog in some cases.

The fact that the Vietnamese continued to leave for Hong Kong after the introduction of screening on 16 June 1988 showed that, unless the government could show it was serious by repatriating screened-out boat people, screening was not a significant deterrent to those who wanted to leave. Repatriation clearly required the agreement of Vietnam to take migrants back and also, preferably, the agreement of the migrants themselves. In June 1989, the Comprehensive Plan of Action was drawn up for UNHCR to establish a voluntary repatriation scheme throughout the East and Southeast Asian region where Vietnamese were languishing in camps. This ambitious program took some time to set in motion. In the meantime, the Hong Kong government decided to repatriate forcibly a small group of boat people in December 1989 to act as a deterrent. The handling of this incident turned out to be a public relations bungle that brought condemnation of the government from virtually every quarter.[16] Although the drop-off in

---

15. Rhoda Mushkat, "Balancing Western Legal Concepts, Asian Attitudes and Practical Difficulties—A Critical Examination of Hong Kong's Response to the Refugee Problem," in *Asian Yearbook of International Law*, ed. Ko Swan Sik et al. (Norwell, MA: Kluwer Academic, 1993), pp. 62-63. The most exhaustive discussion of the legal aspects of Hong Kong's approach to refugees can be found in ibid., pp. 45-112. Useful summaries of the screening

procedures can be found in John Torgrimson, "Vietnamese Boat People," in *The Other Hong Kong Report 1991*, ed. Sung Yun-wing and Lee Ming-kwan (Hong Kong: Chinese University Press, 1991), pp. 103-15; Stephen H. B. Yau, "Vietnamese Boat People," in *The Other Hong Kong Report 1992*, ed. Joseph Y. S. Cheng and Paul C. K. Kwong (Hong Kong: Chinese University Press, 1992), pp. 111-25.

16. See Bale, "Vietnamese Boat People," for a balanced summary of the events.

numbers during 1990 was seen as a justification of the deterrent value of this forced repatriation, there were almost certainly other factors accounting for the sharp decline in 1990. No other forced repatriations were attempted for almost two years, when they were resurrected as the Orderly Repatriation Program, by which time the principles of return had been well established.

The voluntary repatriation scheme took some time to get under way. During 1990, some 5452 were repatriated voluntarily. In addition, resettlement of refugees also increased in that year to 7656 following the Comprehensive Plan of Action of the previous year. Voluntary repatriation continued to grow over the following two years as the program became more widely accepted by the international community, by Vietnam, and by the migrants themselves. Numbers repatriated grew to 7747 in 1991 and reached 12,612 in 1992 (Table 1). Clearly, there had to be an incentive for the migrants to return, and US$360 for every man, woman, and child was given as "reintegration assistance" by UNHCR, plus US$50 "pocket money" for every adult and US$25 for every child. These were substantial amounts of money in Vietnam, where per capita gross domestic product in 1990 was around US$200. It was hardly surprising that some people turned right around, often with their families, to return to Hong Kong hoping to claim the allowances again. Virtually 80 percent of those volunteering for repatriation in 1991 had arrived in 1991, or 5963 out of a total of 7660. The so-called "double backers" be-

came such an issue that those arriving after 27 September 1991 were not entitled to reintegration assistance, irrespective of whether it was their first or second time of arrival in Hong Kong; only the US$50 and US$25 pocket-money payments were to be made.

The numbers arriving in Hong Kong from Vietnam increased dramatically in 1991, to 20,206, from the 1990 figure of 6595. The reintegration allowance almost certainly had a major part to play in this upsurge as 92 percent of those leaving Vietnam in 1991 headed for Hong Kong. Arrivals continued to drop dramatically for other Association of Southeast Asian Nations countries of first asylum: to zero for Malaysia, to 1260 from 13,833 for Indonesia, and to 229 from 1108 for the Philippines. Certainly, 1991 was a bad year for the Vietnamese economy, with rice exports down 70 percent, the worst floods in 13 years in the Mekong, and, most tellingly, the loss of Soviet assistance from the beginning of the year. However, this was not reflected in increased outmovement to destinations other than Hong Kong.

There is one other factor in this complex chain of causation of out-migration from Vietnam. We have seen how there was official collusion, even control, in the exodus during 1978 and 1979. To what extent has it been in Vietnam's interest to allow its population to leave? In the late 1970s, Vietnam was combining commercial return from the export of people with the benefit of ridding itself of those who were ideologically incompatible with the regime. More important, each person leaving Vietnam was a potential source of remittances. It has been estimated that in 1990 about US$500 million, equal to about one-quarter of Vietnam's export earnings in that year, were remitted by overseas Vietnamese.[17] In such times of stress as in the late 1970s and in 1988 and 1989, it made perfect sense to allow, even encourage, this potential source of earnings to leave Vietnam and try for resettlement elsewhere—even if the possibility was remote. Certainly, rumors of amnesties, or the possibilities of gaining employment in Kuwait, might cause minor fluctuation,[18] but the factors controlling the main directions of the flows are likely to have been macropolitical and economic.

The converse to this argument also holds. When it is in Vietnam's interest to control the outflow, it will do so. This appears particularly to apply to the recent trends in out-migration. With the disintegration of the Soviet Union and the withdrawal of aid, Vietnam needs to integrate itself much more into the West, and, more important, into other Southeast Asian economies. The Vietnamese are only too conscious of the economic growth achieved by Thailand and Indonesia and, indeed, Hong Kong over the last decade. It makes no sense to alienate these economies by allowing its own people to accumulate endlessly in their camps without hope of resettlement. This thinking, although not articulated as explicitly, was surely behind the "breakthrough" in the agreement of October 1991 between Vietnam,

Hong Kong, and the British government, which accepted that all nonrefugees should be returned to Vietnam.[19] As noted, voluntary repatriations were up markedly in 1992 and arrivals were down. Only 12 Vietnamese boat people arrived in Hong Kong in 1992 and by June 1993 only a further 24 had arrived. This decline in numbers also applies to other countries of first asylum, none of which has introduced an Orderly Repatriation Program. Vietnam's wish to accommodate itself more with the international community is evident in another way, too: so far, there have been no cases of persecution of returned migrants. They appear to have been allowed to integrate back into their communities. Screening in Hong Kong is likely to be phased out by the middle of 1994, and government officials can now perhaps see the end of one of the most explosive phases of emigration from Vietnam.

THE FUTURE

There were, in early July 1993, still over 40,000 Vietnamese in Hong Kong: 2191 refugees awaiting resettlement, some 31,600 migrants awaiting repatriation, and almost 7000 awaiting screening. The rate of voluntary repatriation has slowed: only 3581 had applied for repatriation as of early July 1993, compared with the 12,600 repatriated in 1992. Herein again lies a dilemma. One of the difficulties in reducing the number of volunteers is the conditions in the camps themselves. Unquestion-

17. Cited in the *Far Eastern Economic Review*, 23 Jan. 1992, p. 19.

18. These are discussed in Torgrimson, "Vietnamese Boat People."

19. For details of the "breakthrough," although not for the interpretation presented here, see Yau, "Vietnamese Boat People."

ably, pitiful conditions exist in some camps, and rape, murder, and rioting are not infrequent events.[20] However, it is estimated that some 65 percent of the population of working age is gainfully employed in the camps— about 40 percent employed by the Hong Kong government and the balance by various nongovernmental organizations. Each earns about US$23 per month, and, if there are two family members working, they have essentially US$46 per month pocket money, as all their food, accommodation, medical expenses, and so on are paid for. This is much more than the average family could hope to save back in Vietnam. Hong Kong is the only area of first asylum that permits employment to such an extent, and it is significant that only about 10 percent of those employed have volunteered for repatriation.

Given the amount of money circulating in the camps and the potential for graft, extortion, and prostitution, it is clear that many are much better off in the camps than if they returned to Vietnam. Those who have access to more money, and hence influence, are likely to intimidate those who do not, further reducing the numbers volunteering for repatriation. Paradoxically, this situation appears to be the result of welfare and the relative affluence in the camps. To combat this problem, the number of services in the camps is being reduced. Vocational training, adult education, and the number of jobs are being reduced on the justification that such programs and opportunities are available in Vietnam as part of the UNHCR and European Community packages for reintegration. UNHCR intends to cut the reintegration assistance for those who arrived before 27 September 1991 but did not volunteer for repatriation before 30 October 1993. This assistance is being reduced from US$360 to US$240 per capita, and the change is being publicized to encourage more to volunteer.

While the "problem of the boat people" has not entirely disappeared from Hong Kong, the further reintegration of Vietnam into the world economy, given impetus by the recent American decision not to block International Monetary Fund loans to the country, should see the exodus from Vietnam to Hong Kong continue to slow. The black cloud on the horizon from the perspective of mid-1993 is the sudden upsurge of ECVIIs. During July 1993, when this article was being written, some 1500 entered Hong Kong by boat. There are rumors that up to 10,000 may be on their way to the territory. This new influx is, however, a matter between Hong Kong and China and does not involve Vietnam. It does show conclusively that Hong Kong is likely to experience echoes of the past exodus from Vietnam for some time to come.

20. The worst case was a fire at the Sek Kong detention center in Feb. 1992 in which 24 Vietnamese were killed, including 12 children, and 114 were injured. The fire was started during a quarrel over alcohol debts. See Yau, "Vietnamese Boat People," pp. 119-23. Violence in the camps is a major theme in Leonard Davis, *Hong Kong and the Asylum-Seekers from Vietnam* (London: Macmillan, 1991).

CONCLUSION

In the 18 years since people first started coming to Hong Kong from

Vietnam in boats large and small, not one person has been turned away. Almost 200,000 Vietnamese have landed in the territory during those years. Hong Kong, alone among the areas of first asylum, abided strictly by the terms of the 1979 agreement until its introduction of screening. Its policies have been open to international scrutiny. It is wrong to see inherent contradictions and inconsistencies in the government's policy toward the Vietnamese.[21] That policy has been a very pragmatic response to changing pressures from three distinct directions: the numbers of arrivals; the international community in terms of numbers of people being resettled and the perception of who is, or is not, a refugee; and the local community in terms of the increasing economic burden on the economy. The cost of the operation has been significant, and the bulk of this has been borne by the Hong Kong taxpayer. From financial year 1979-80 to 1992-93, the cost to Hong Kong has been about US$635 million. The British government has contributed US$83 million, and UNHCR, US$121 million over the same period. Current annual costs to Hong Kong are over HK$1 billion (approximately US$128 million), and UNHCR and British funding are being reduced markedly. Having borne the greater part of the expenditure for so long, it is little wonder that the Hong Kong government, which has to respond to an increasingly vocal Legislative Coun-

cil, has had to take a strong stance on screening and repatriation. At a cost to Hong Kong of over US$3000 per Vietnamese per year, it seems only a matter of time before a financial deal will be struck with Vietnam. The boat people are—in fact, always were—for all intents and purposes bargaining chips in Vietnam's quest for economic and political development.

Many contradictions remain. Hong Kong was largely the creation of refugee movements. Yet many of these same refugees would, in another era, have been called "economic migrants." Hong Kong has operated a very restrictive migration policy since 1980, and under such circumstances the issue of who is or is not a refugee becomes of critical concern.[22] The contrast between Vietnam and a prosperous, stable Hong Kong made Hong Kong a target for movement, both from the point of view of the migrant, who had little to lose, and from the point of view of Vietnam, which was attempting to export potential revenue earners to prosperous areas and also had little to lose. The final contradiction involves the return of Hong Kong to the sovereignty of the People's Republic of China from 1 July 1997. Those who fled from a Communist system are now being handed back to a state controlled by the Communist Party. Is there likely to be a wave of refugee migration from Hong Kong itself so that the receiver becomes the sender? This is another complex issue which I have examined in depth else-

21. See Chan Kwok Bun, "Hong Kong's Response to the Vietnamese Refugees: A Study in Humanitarianism, Ambivalence and Hostility," *Southeast Asian Journal of Social Science*, 18(1):94-110 (1990).

22. See Zolberg, Suhrke, and Aguayo, *Escape from Violence*, chap. 1.

where.[23] As far as the Vietnamese in Hong Kong are concerned, China has made it clear that all must be resettled or repatriated in accordance with existing international agreements before July 1997.

23. See Ronald Skeldon, ed., *Reluctant Exiles? Migration from Hong Kong and the New Overseas Chinese* (New York: M.E. Sharpe; Hong Kong: Hong Kong University Press, 1994).

ANNALS, *AAPSS*, **534**, July 1994

Immigration Control in Australia

By ROBERT BIRRELL

ABSTRACT: Like Canada and the United States, Australia has encountered increasing difficulties in regulating international migration movements. Australia's physical isolation and rigorous entry procedures have limited the arrival of undocumented migrants to a trickle. But the number coming as students, visitors, and under other short-term visas who subsequently overstay these visas and apply to change their status to permanent residence while in Australia has increased sharply since the early 1980s. The management of these claims has proved difficult because of judicial leniency and the advocacy of humanitarian and ethnic lobby groups. However, since the late 1980s, the Australian government has introduced a series of tough legislative and administrative measures that appear to have significantly diminished the problem. These measures have been much tougher than those enforced in North America. It is argued that this Australian response can be traced to the heritage of control that has shaped Australia's immigration policies and Australians' conceptions of themselves as a nation.

Robert Birrell received his Ph.D. in sociology at Princeton University. He is reader in the Department of Sociology and director of the Centre for Population and Urban Research at Monash University in Melbourne, Australia. He is the joint editor of People & Place, *an Australian journal specializing in immigration issues, and a member of the Australian government's National Population Council. He contributed to the 1992 National Population Council's report* Population and Australia's Future.

IT is an open question whether liberal democracies like Australia, Canada, and the United States can unilaterally determine the numbers and types of migrants they receive. Australia's recent experience, however, suggests that, relative to the recent experience of the United States and Canada, a high degree of control is possible.

The Australian government has succeeded in preventing all but a handful of undocumented migrants from entering Australia through its main international entry points. But it has faced an increasing problem of documented entrants who subsequently remain illegally and, since 1989, the arrival of 650 boat people who, without authorization, simply sailed to Australia's unprotected northern shores. Nevertheless, those who have sought to change their status to that of permanent resident face much tougher rules than their equivalents in Canada or the United States. This particularly applies to asylum seekers.

Australia's physical isolation as an island continent has contributed to this outcome, but this is only a part of the story. There has been a dramatic increase in the numbers of students, tourists, and visitors coming to Australia, including from Third World countries where migration push pressures are intense. Some of these have sought to change their status once they have arrived here. As in North America, humanitarian and ethnic community groups in Australia tend to support such claims. Also the Australian courts have sharply increased their involvement in the onshore immigration decision-making process since the early 1980s. The courts have taken a liberal, permissive approach, cutting across the strict control agenda pursued by the immigration bureaucracy. But this liberalizing trend has been resisted by the Australian government in what has become a contest between the parliamentary and executive arms of government, on the one hand, and the judiciary and those representing asylum and other claimants, on the other.

This resistance reflects Australia's distinctive traditions of immigration management, the immigration bureaucracy's firm commitment to control, and, above all, majority domestic political opinion favoring such policies. This opinion has translated into a political will, shared by both major political parties, to implement effective immigration control measures.

PAST POLICIES OF IMMIGRATION MANAGEMENT

Concern about immigration management has long been linked to Australians' views of themselves as a nation. The infamous "White Australia" policy is the best known expression of this. The last remnants of racist criteria in Australia's immigration policies were abolished only in 1973, well after similar rules were dispensed with in the United States or Canada. But this policy was also an expression of the social aspirations of both the liberal and labor leaders who dominated Australian politics during the foundation years of the federation, which extended from the 1890s to World War I. Their central ideal was the creation of a nation free of Old World social and religious cleav-

ages, in which all could live a digni-
fied lifestyle. It was believed that the
importation of migrants who were
Asians or Pacific Islanders would undermine these ideals by degrading
the dignity of manual labor. For example, in 1903, the liberal leader and
Prime Minister Alfred Deakin declared that "White Australia"

means equal laws and opportunities for
all, it means protection against the underpaid labor of other lands; it means
social justice as far as we can establish it,
including just trading and payment of
fair wages. A White Australia means a
civilisation whose foundations are built
upon healthy lives, lived in honest toil,
under circumstances which imply no degradation. . . . A White Australia is not a
surface, but it is a reasoned policy which
goes to the roots of national life, and by
which the whole of our social, industrial
and political organisation is governed.[1]

Immigration control was thus
linked to the more progressive elements of Australian politics. For many
years "White Australia" was regarded as a key component of Australian social aspirations. The United
States was seen as flawed by comparison, because of its early reliance
on slave labor and the legacy of deep
social divisions that this left behind.

At times, would-be migrants from
continental Europe were also excluded. Before World War II, there
was no parallel in Australia to the
flow of Eastern and Southern European migrants who moved to North
America, or any accompanying
myths about welcoming the poor and
disadvantaged. Organized labor even
opposed the arrival of their kith and

kin from Britain when such movements threatened the labor market
situation of union members. This opposition can be linked to a distinctive
feature of working-class accommodation with capital at the beginning of
this century. Capital would retain its
ownership of the productive process,
but, in return, workers would be
guaranteed work under fair wages
and conditions. This outcome was to
be achieved by building a protected
economy, dependent on tariffs
against goods embodying low-cost labor (or more efficient practices), and
immigration restrictions defending
Australian workers against direct
workplace competition.[2]

IMMIGRATION POLICY
AFTER WORLD WAR II

This restrictive approach to immigration also characterized the migration selection policies pursued by
both Labor and Conservative governments after 1945. The consensus was
that Australia needed to boost its
population through immigration, for
both defense and nation-building
purposes. But successive governments went to great lengths to reassure the electorate that this would
not be at the expense of Australian
workers' privileges. The strategies
included requiring those who arrived
during the 1940s and 1950s as refugees and other government-assisted
continental European migrants to
sign two-year contracts permitting
the Australian government to specify
their initial employment. One purpose was to ensure that these mi-

1. Alfred Deakin, "Policy Speech of the
Deakin Government," Ballarat, 1903, p. 12.

2. Francis Castles, *Australian Public Policy and Economic Vulnerability* (Sydney: Allen
& Unwin, 1988), pp. 101-2.

grants did not compete with the unionized workforce.

An important legacy of these measures was the growth of a powerful immigration bureaucracy. Unlike the United States and Canada, a separate immigration ministry and accompanying bureaucracy has been maintained through most of the postwar era. Its task has been both to recruit migrants and to persuade the Australian public of the merits of high migration. The latter was not easy given the role of immigration control in the labor movement's accommodation with capital. The government has sought to allay these concerns by insisting that the Immigration Department (currently entitled the Department of Immigration and Ethnic Affairs) would control the flow of migrants such that there would be no conflict with the welfare of Australian workers and there would be no flow that would challenge Australians' national identity—thus the insistence until the 1970s that migrants become "New Australians."

Nevertheless, in the pursuit of a vigorous immigration policy after World War II, about a third of the Australian intake during the 1950s and 1960s came from Southern and Eastern Europe. Most of these came via sponsorships of family members in Australia. They were people from rural backgrounds who had no choice but to take up low-skilled positions in the workforce, seemingly in contradiction to the traditions outlined earlier. This outcome was an unintended outcome of the pursuit of high migrant intakes. It reflected the inability of the Australian government to recruit as many British and other Western European migrants as it wanted, following the postwar economic recovery in Europe.[3] Basically the Immigration Department rationed the number of family sponsorships it accepted in order to achieve its annual program targets.

Successive Australian governments have been aware that if immigration appeared to threaten Australian living standards or social ideals, then this could undermine public acceptance of the entire program. If the immigration program was to be successful, it had to be seen as under control. Any downturn in the Australian economy has usually been followed by a quick contraction in the immigration intake. It was no surprise that when the conservative Fraser government enumerated a set of nine principles guiding immigration policy in 1978, the first was the following: "It is fundamental to national sovereignty that the Australian Government should determine who will be admitted to Australia. No person other than an Australian citizen, or a constituent member of the community, has a basic right to enter Australia."[4]

The government's resolve was to be sorely tested in the years immediately following this statement, when some 2000 Indochinese boat people arrived uninvited on Australia's northern shores. They were not wel-

3. Robert Birrell and Tanya Birrell, *An Issue of People: Population and Australian Society* (Melbourne: Longman/Cheshire, 1987), pp. 54-55.

4. Michael Mackellar, "Ministerial Statement" (Department of Immigration and Ethnic Affairs, Australia, 7 June 1978).

comed. There were expressions of sympathy from humanitarians, but they were swamped in a tide of public opposition to what many saw as an invasion. The government responded by pursuing an "orderly departure program." This required major concessions to the nations of first asylum that belonged to the Association of Southeast Asian Nations. Australia had to promise to take a substantial number of the Indochinese refugees through formal channels in return for Malayan and Indonesian cooperation in not facilitating the unauthorized movement of boat people to Australia. This was to be the first of a series of challenges to the Australian government's ability to "determine who will be admitted to Australia."

CHALLENGES TO
THE CONTROL REGIME

By the late 1980s, the Australian government was struggling to manage a sharp increase in the number of change-of-status claims made by persons who had entered Australia without permanent residence visas. One source of the problem was expansion in the family reunion program during the 1980s. In 1981, in response to pressure from Southern and Eastern European ethnic communities, the Fraser government extended family reunion rights to include a sibling category. The Hawke Labor government extended this concession when it took office in 1983. The result was much like that which occurred after the 1965 U.S. immigration reforms. The concession was largely taken up by the then small non-European communities resident in Australia. By the end of the 1980s, the family re-

union intake had doubled, with most entrants coming from the Third World, particularly the Philippines, Hong Kong, Vietnam, and Lebanon. The rapid increase in the size of these communities opened up social links to areas of intense migration push pressures.

Additional pressures resulted from the government's attempts to sell educational services to overseas students. Colleges providing English courses for non-English speakers boomed between 1987 and 1989. By July 1989, when the Tiananmen massacre occurred in Beijing, there were in Australia 13,500 nationals from the People's Republic of China (PRC) who originally arrived as English students and thousands more in the pipeline. Subsequently, about 20,000 of these came to Australia. Their recruitment had been organized by the Department of Education. It did not check the bone fides of these students. All an applicant had to do to obtain a student visa was to prepay English language fees and accommodation expenses for six months—around A$6000. The PRC nationals in Australia at the time of Tiananmen have since been granted four-year temporary permits, which expire in 1994. Most of the 20,000 post-Tiananmen students have since sought refugee status in Australia. As of mid-1993, they dominate the onshore asylum backlog of around 21,000 claimants.

It is significant that throughout the internal government debate over what to do about the PRC students, the Immigration Department led the effort to restrict their entry. Well before July 1989, it had sought to take over the recruitment process from the Department of Education. This battle was won by 1990, and since that time a strict bone fides test has been implemented that effectively debars PRC nationals from enrolling in vocational courses.

A further major challenge to the government's control agenda has been the increased involvement of the courts in immigration decisions. Until the 1980s, there were few restraints on the Immigration Department's decision-making authority. This is no longer the case, largely because of the extension of administrative law to immigration decisions covering onshore change-of-status applications. All such decisions are now subject to client accountability, with those aggrieved able to appeal their case in the courts if they believe that the decision was not made properly. The grounds for such appeals include the provisions of natural justice, such as whether the decision maker took into account all the relevant facts, or whether the applicant had been advised of the decision maker's case against him or her. The government did not intend to open up the immigration decision-making process in this way and especially not to those illegally in Australia. It has proved difficult, however, to quarantine immigration decisions on illegal migrants from the larger movement for administrative accountability that has marked the Australian legal system in recent years.

As in Canada and the United States, the Australian judiciary has been influenced by the greater currency of human rights ideals among liberal elites and by the growing body of international case law influenced by such ideals. This situation has given those opposed to Australia's tough control regime an avenue to attack it. The challengers include religious leaders, academics, sections of the ethnic movement, refugee advocates, and, most recently, specialist immigration lawyers.

An important outcome is that the courts have adopted broader definitions of the criteria used to assess onshore change-of-status applications than was originally intended by the Immigration Department. This has applied particularly to claims based on humanitarian or compassionate grounds. Also, much tougher standards of administrative justice have been applied. In the case of claims made on the basis of marriage, by the end of the 1980s, the Federal Court's standards for proving that marriages were not bone fide were so tough that almost all such claims were being accepted. Partly as a consequence, the number of spouse applications grew sharply, to around 10,000 per annum. To rub salt into the Immigration Department's wounds, a survey of the applicants revealed that 40 percent were in Australia illegally at the time of their change-of-status application.[5]

By the end of the 1980s, the situation was delicately poised. Apart from the problems just discussed, the Australian government was also facing an upsurge in asylum claims deriving from the PRC students. Then, beginning in November 1989, there

5. "Grant of Resident Status on Spouse/De Facto Spouse Grounds to Visitors" (Report by a working party, National Population Council, Canberra, June 1990), p. 13.

was a renewed flow of boat people, which, by October 1992, had delivered 650 Indochinese in 14 separate boats to our shores, almost all of whom claimed asylum. Their cases, too, had to be dealt with in a context of judicial activism.

THE REASSERTION OF CONTROL

Though these events prompted a renewed government effort to regain control of the migration process, North American readers might wonder what all the fuss was about. Relative to Canada and the United States, Australia has received far fewer undocumented migrants and, partly because of this, has been subject to a smaller number of onshore asylum claims.

This limited undocumented entry reflects a combination of Australia's zealousness in controlling entry and its physical isolation. Unlike the Canadian government, the Australian government has long required all those wishing to travel to Australia to possess an authorized visa before embarking. Recent innovations in the processing of these visas has made fraudulent entry unlikely. The new Travel and Immigration Processing System, installed in 1991, enables entry officers to refer to a computerized data bank in order to check the traveler's documents against the details of visas issued at the overseas posts and against alert lists assembled to track those suspected of fraudulent entry. This system also enables the government to match exits against entries and thus accurately assess the number and identities of those overstaying their visas.

Physical isolation has also facilitated entry control because there are only a small number of final embarkation points from which to enter Australia. The Immigration Department has been able to insist on close monitoring of entry documents at these points—like Singapore Airport—and thus screen out most of those who might wish to enter Australia illegally.

As a result, very few persons without a valid visa make it to an Australian airport. In the case of Sydney, Australia's busiest international airport, only around 150 a month arrive without valid documents.[6] Of these, only a handful make asylum claims. Strict criteria are followed in issuing temporary entry or tourist visas when the record indicates that people from particular places show a high risk of visa overstaying. The PRC intake was a brief but significant exception. As of May 1992, the Immigration Department estimated that there were 81,000 illegal migrants in Australia, with the great majority of these having overstayed their original entry permits.

The main focus of recent government efforts to regain control over the migration process has therefore been on those entering Australia on temporary visas who then seek to change their status to permanent residence. The objective has been to limit the opportunities for political lobbying on behalf of particular cases and to minimize judicial interpretation of the change-of-status rules. To

6. Australia, Department of Immigration and Ethnic Affairs, *Review '92* (Canberra: Australian Government Publishing Service, 1992), p. 109.

this end, a new Migration Act was introduced in 1989, which, with its accompanying regulations, specified in precise detail the entry criteria for each migrant category. The purpose was to leave few openings for subsequent challenge of Immigration Department officers' decisions and thus limit the scope for judicial review. The act also removed the Minister for Immigration from any role in the decision-making process, thus limiting the exercise of political influence in the outcome of individual claims.

After wide public debate through 1990 and 1991, the government also narrowed the definitions of some key grounds for change-of-status claims. Because of judicial intervention, by 1988 the humanitarian category was being defined very broadly to include individuals "who because of membership of a particular group/class or because of beliefs held, [have] been or would be singled out for severely disadvantageous treatment by the state in the applicant's country of origin or last permanent residence." "Disadvantagous treatment" included circumstances of "war, revolution and inter-communal violence" in the country of origin.[7] This definition was narrowed in 1991 to those who could show that their "particular circumstances and personal characteristics provide them with a sound basis for expecting a significant threat to personal security on return as a result of targeted action by persons in the country of return."[8] In the case of compassionate claims, the definition was narrowed to exclude all cases except those where the applicant had a close family relationship to an Australian resident.

There was less change in the regulation of onshore marriage claims. The government's initial proposal included requiring all such applicants to leave Australia and apply overseas. But after much debate, this proposal was withdrawn. The main change has been that, since 1991, claims based on marriage are only granted on a two-year temporary basis, with the parties required to prove the bone fides of the relationship at the end of this period. Only then can the immigrant partner be granted permanent residence.

Finally, those overstaying their visas now have less access to change-of-status claims or to the courts should their claims fail. They can still claim to stay permanently on marriage grounds, but only if they apply within 28 days of becoming illegal. More resources have been put into locating illegals, with compliance staff trebled—from an admittedly low base—to 150 in 1990. The weak point in this response is that when persons who have overstayed their visas are located, they can make a claim on asylum grounds. This frequently occurs because it is the last option available for most illegals.

THE ASYLUM ISSUE

Australia's capacity to control migration has been most sorely tested

7. Australia, Department of Immigration and Ethnic Affairs, *Department of Immigration, Local Government and Ethnic Affairs Instruction Manual*, Grant of Residence Status, no. 10, 1988.

8. Australia, Minister of Immigration, Local Government and Ethnic Affairs, Media release, no. 15, 1991.

by the availability of asylum claims. Once such a claim is made, it provides access to a long process of administrative and perhaps judicial review. Welfare assistance is also available, though via a semi-charitable system separate from the government's social security system. Employment is permitted if, after a preliminary official review, the case is determined not to be frivolous.

The Australian government has been well aware that exploitation of the asylum system can undermine its control objectives, especially if the time taken to complete the process is prolonged. But as a signatory of the United Nations Convention and the 1967 Protocol Relating to the State of Refugees, the government cannot unilaterally redefine the meaning of asylum, as it has with humanitarian claims. It has had to use the convention criteria, that is, a well-founded fear of being persecuted for reasons of race, religion, nationality, membership in a social group, or political opinion. This definition leaves open how a nation should determine such uncertain questions as whether a claimant's fear of persecution is well founded or not. Is it to be based on the subjective view of the claimant or the objective view of an independent expert after an examination of the case? What types of acts should be defined as persecution; should they involve physical punishment or is verbal abuse enough?

Since different answers can be given to these questions, the field has been wide open to judicial interpretation. The Australian courts have drawn selectively on international legal precedent. Given the judicial

leaning toward a humanitarian perspective, the tendency has been to choose the more liberal case law in judgments on the substance of asylum claims.[9]

THE PROCESSING OF ASYLUM CLAIMS

As noted earlier, by mid-1993 there was a backlog of around 21,000 claims, not including the pre-Tiananmen PRC students. In November 1993, the government decided that the latter would be granted permanent residence, subject to health and character checks. Most of the 21,000 backlog derives from post-Tiananmen PRC students. In their absence, Australia's asylum problem would be relatively insignificant by North American standards.

Asylum claims are processed at a primary stage by Immigration Department officers, then through a review stage should those rejected wish to appeal. Very few of such claims have succeeded. For the first nine months of 1992-93, of 9004 cases finalized at the primary state, only 4.4 percent, or 400, were granted asylum, while at the review stage, 1430 were finalized, with only 93, or 6.5 percent, approved. By contrast, 21,202 onshore asylum cases were approved in Canada during 1992 as well as 32,029 cases under the Canadian government's backlog clearance program. The great majority of those making asylum claims in Canada

9. Robert Birrell, "Problems of Immigration Control in Liberal Democracies: The Australian Experience," in *Nations of Immigrants,* ed. G. Freeman and J. Jupp (Melbourne: Oxford University Press, 1992), pp. 29-30.

have succeeded, though recently the success rate has declined to near 50 percent.

The asylum issue has generated intense debate in Australia, mostly in relation to the processing of the asylum claims of the 650 boat people. They were all detained in custody pending the outcome of their cases. Some have been in detention for over three years. As of September 1993, 300 remained in custody, though all had been rejected as asylum claimants at both the primary and review stages. But refugee advocates and lawyers supporting their claims have been able to delay their return to Indochina through a series of appeals to the judiciary on administrative law grounds. The boat people have received passionate support from their advocates as well as emotion-laden publicity when some of the claimants demonstrated their desperation through hunger strikes, attempted suicides, and other dramatic acts. It is a measure of the government's resolve that, despite the small numbers involved, it has resisted all appeals to release them from custody. The conservative party opposition has urged an even tougher stance, accusing the government of a "failure to act with courage" in bringing the boat people's claims to completion. According to the opposition's spokesperson, this inaction "sends a clear message to the international community that we cannot control our borders."[10]

The government has responded, with the support of the opposition, by legislating new measures designed to prevent the appeal courts from releasing asylum claimants while their cases are being heard and to limit the jurisdiction of the courts when asylum decisions are appealed.

In foreshadowing new legislation to these ends in May 1992, the Immigration Department Minister, Mr. Hand, declared,

I believe it is crucial that all persons who come to Australia without prior authorisation not be released into the community. . . . The Government is determined that a clear signal be sent that migration to Australia may not be achieved by simply arriving in this country and expecting to be allowed into the community.[11]

Legislation was passed in May 1992 prohibiting "designated people," including the boat people, from being released into the community before their cases have been finalized. One clear purpose has been to deter others from considering an unauthorized trip to Australia.

Another broader piece of legislation, the 1992 Migration Reform Bill, passed late in 1992, allows the government to detain all persons who are in Australia illegally. Those who can establish a valid basis for continued residence will be released on bridging visas, pending a decision on their claim. But no release will be allowed for those who arrive in Australia without authority, such as boat people or undocumented airline arrivals. The purpose of the legislation is to limit the courts' authority to release the latter from custody.[12] The

---

10. Australia, *Commonwealth Parliamentary Debates* (House of Representatives), 7 Nov. 1991, p. 2676.

11. Ibid., 5 May 1992, p. 2372.

12. Kathryn Cronin, "A Culture of Control: An Overview of Immigration Policy-Making,"

message from the legislators to the judiciary has been openly stated. When Mr. Hand introduced the bill in the Parliament, he declared that

a primary objective of the migration Act is to regulate, in the national interest, the entry and presence in Australia of persons who are not Australian citizens. . . . An objects provision will be inserted in the Act to remind the community, the administrators and the courts of this intention.[13]

Additional provisions of the Migration Reform Bill stipulate that the grounds on which rejected asylum claimants can appeal to the courts will be curtailed. Onshore asylum claimants are to have access to a merits review of their cases before an immigration review tribunal. But further appeal can no longer be based on alleged failure to follow the rules of natural justice or on the alleged lack of the reasonableness of the decision, two of the most important grounds previously cited by those appealing asylum decisions.

In November 1993, the Australian government took action to resolve the situation of the Cambodian boat people and also the backlog of asylum applications from post-Tiananmen PRC students. The several hundred of the former remaining in detention were offered permanent residence if they first returned to their home country for a year. All existing onshore asylum seekers, including those from the PRC, were offered permanent resi-

dence if they met certain English-language and educational criteria. These decisions represented a significant breach of the government's past stance. They reflected a judgment that these cases might be tied up in the courts for years, implying high legal, financial, and perhaps political costs, given the public controversy they generate. The decisions do not mean an end to the will to control entry. On the contrary, both major political parties are especially anxious to ensure that there will be no repetition of the unregulated entry that produced the original problems.

CONCLUSION

Australia, like other Western societies, has found it difficult to manage migration movements and to deal with the contentious issues raised by a tough control regime. There were times during the 1980s when other goals, like selling educational services, led to an upsurge in change-of-status claims that temporarily overwhelmed the government's capacity to manage the demand. But these difficulties have prompted a vigorous political response leading to solutions that promise to diminish the earlier problems.

Though this response has been facilitated by Australia's physical isolation, at root it reflects a political will to act resolutely. This is not nearly so evident in either Canada or the United States. At first glance, this is puzzling, given Australia's record as a country of high migration. By 1991, 23 percent of Australia's population was born overseas, a far higher proportion than in North America. But

in *The Politics of Migration*, ed. J. Jupp and M. Kabalda (Canberra: AGPS, 1993), pp. 101-2.

13. Australia, *Commonwealth Parliamentary Debates* (House of Representatives), 4 Nov. 1992, p. 2621.

as indicated, Australia's postwar migration program has been accompanied by a parallel effort to ensure that the immigrants were selected on Australian terms.

The tough control line pursued after the excesses of the 1980s depended on the larger political situation. If the Labor government had been faced by an opposition responsive to ethnic and humanitarian appeals, then the immigration reforms pursued since 1989 could not have occurred. The fact that the conservative opposition supported these reforms, despite its long record of support for migration, can be traced to the politics of immigration during the 1980s.

Immigration became a highly contentious issue during the 1980s because its scale and diversity—reflecting family and refugee movements —generated a sharp public reaction. Those opposing these trends appear to have tapped into a strong ethnocentric reaction. This suggests that many Australians felt their identity as a people was being challenged by both the fact of diversity and the accompanying rhetoric of multiculturalism. By the end of the 1980s, opinion polls consistently showed around 60 to 70 percent of Australians to be in favor of reducing immigration and opposed to multiculturalism. The issue was at such a high threshold in the public consciousness that it was often on or near the front pages. It was only a matter of time before some politicians sought to mobilize voters around the issue.

Sections of the conservative party were the first to take up a critical stance in the late 1980s. Since the beginning of Australia's current recession in 1990, new concerns about the welfare costs of migration and job competition with Australians have added additional fuel to the debate. The conservatives have responded by featuring an anti-immigration position in their electoral platform and by stressing a firm line on immigration control, particularly in relation to asylum seekers. The Labor government has moved in the same direction, though not so outspokenly. It has cut back the formal immigration program from 140,000 in 1988-89 to 76,000 in 1993-94. The decision to accompany this with a renewed emphasis on control can be understood in part as a desire to reassure a critical public that the government has not lost control over migration entry.

Though those favoring a less rigorous and more open response to asylum claims have sought public support on the grounds of compassion and humanitarianism and by appealing to newer ideals about Australia as a "nation of migrants," these appeals do not generate the support found in North America. I believe this can be traced to the absence of such traditions in Australia's migration experience. Most Australians do not think of themselves as a multicultural society (in the sense of an ideal to be pursued, rather than as a reality to be tolerated) or as cultural mosaic as the Canadians do, let alone a land welcoming the downtrodden as do so many Americans.

From the Campaign against Illegal Migration to the Campaign against Illegal Work

By CLAUDE-VALENTIN MARIE

(Translated by Mark J. Miller)

ABSTRACT: The French effort to curb illegal immigration, which began in earnest in the mid-1970s, had become increasingly subsumed under a broader campaign to prevent and punish illegal employment by the early 1990s. Illegal alien employment remains a significant concern, but most illegal work involves French citizens. Over the past two decades, France has fine-tuned and reinforced a panoply of laws punishing illegal employment, but socioeconomic trends have tended to exacerbate it. Nonetheless, the government's ability to punish and deter illegal work, including illegal alien employment, is more considerable and credible today than it was two decades ago.

Claude-Valentin Marie is one of the French government's most prolific immigration specialists. In recent years, he has been in charge of research at the interagency group monitoring and facilitating coordination of the French governmental effort to curb illegal work. His most recent publications include Travail clandestin, trafics de main d'oeuvre et formes illégales d'emploi *(1992);* Travail illégal et suites judiciaires *(1993);* Les politiques d'immigration dans les états membres de la Communauté Européenne: Entre l'exigence de contrôle et l'impératif de l'intégration *(1993).*

DESPITE the official decision in 1974 to curb most legal recruitment of foreign labor and despite the increased unemployment of aliens already resident in France, new migrants have continued to enter the country and to seek employment without legal authorization. Until the early 1980s, this new irregular immigration remained little known. It was the legalization of August 1981 that opened the way to renewed and more exact understanding of illegal employment of aliens and, beyond that, of illegal employment as a whole. Two studies undertaken at that point facilitated better understanding of the new inflows, the characteristics of the aliens involved, and the specifics of their utilization by certain economic sectors and in certain jobs.[1]

The first important lesson drawn from these studies pertained to the close connection disclosed between the changes affecting production systems, the employment of aliens without authorization, and the evolution of employment of aliens legally resident in France. In 1982, 150,000 foreign workers applied for legalization and 140,000 received a favorable reply. Two-thirds of them had beforehand been illegally employed in the building industry (30 percent) and in services (36 percent). In contrast, unauthorized alien workers were virtually absent from the major industrial sectors, such as automobile construc-

1. For an English-language translation and summary of these reports, see French Ministry of Social Affairs, "The Employment Market and Immigrants in an Irregular Situation: Lessons from the Recent Legalization Exercise in France," *International Migration Review*, 18(3): 558-78 (Fall 1984).

tion and steel, which were then laying off large numbers of foreign employees who had been recruited massively over the two preceding decades. Unlike those foreign workers who had arrived during the period of rapid economic growth and who had been recruited above all by large firms for relatively stable jobs, illegal hiring of foreign workers in the 1980s and early 1990s was done essentially by small firms with fewer than 10 employees. In these small enterprises, the new foreign workers typically performed jobs that required scant training or few qualifications, involved difficult working conditions, and often paid at levels beneath legal minimums.

Incontestably, the official suspension of most legal immigration for employment purposes, the progression of layoffs in industry, and mounting unemployment did not stop the arrival of new foreign workers and their illegal employment in certain economic sectors. But, contrary to the common portrayal, the reinvigoration of illegal economic practices linked to economic crisis and restructuring of production systems was not limited solely to illegal unemployment of aliens. Worse, this long-exclusive stigmatization contributed to obfuscation of other illegal economic activities and, above all, the socioeconomic mechanisms that engendered them. The ambiguities of the term "clandestine," which was commonly thought to refer to illegal alien employment, played an important role in the obfuscation. Reduced to a designation for foreigners residing and/or working without authorization, usage of this term led to an abusive confusion between the irregularity of the administrative status of aliens and the entirety of illegal practices of which employers are guilty.

If, because of the ambiguities evoked, unauthorized employment of aliens remains the illegal employment practice most commonly denounced, factual examination reveals that it rarely constitutes an isolated infraction. The results of recent enforcement in the garment and leather-making, transportation, and building sectors reveal that the infraction typically occurs along with other violations of socioeconomic public order: employment that is undeclared to social security and other organs of social protection, illegal employment, fiscal fraud, and false bookkeeping. This recent enforcement also reveals that the majority of illegally employed workers are not aliens legally resident in France. Above and beyond a particular category—that of foreigners in an irregular situation—what is most striking is the growing importance of the numbers of at-risk, vulnerable workers. There are ever growing numbers of French and legally resident foreign workers whose employment is not in conformity with the law.

THE SCOPE OF ILLEGAL WORK

To facilitate a more rational and complete understanding of these new realities, we propose to utilize a new notion of illegal work. The notion designates here an ensemble of legal offenses against socioeconomic order that can be grouped into two major categories. The first involves irregular work and employment associated with black market or underground work in general, undeclared employment, and illegal multiple employment, such as violation of the ban on public employees from having private sector, paid employment. The second involves labor trafficking with, on the one hand, the infractions specific to utilization of foreign manpower, direct or indirect employment of an alien without employment authorization, abetting illegal entry and stay, and so on and, on the other hand, the offenses not specifically related to alienage such as contravention of rules pertaining to temporary work, illicit leasing of workers, and the like.

First among those infractions pertaining to illegal work is clandestine work. This is legally defined as the exercise of an independent activity by a person, moral or physical, with the intention of circumventing a series of obligations whether (1) professional, such as mandatory registration with various regulatory bodies like the Repertory of Occupations and the Registry of Commerce and Firms; (2) financial, such as fiscal and social declarations; or (3) social, such as, in the case of employment of salaried workers, presentation of attestations of payment of salary, entry of employee names upon the personnel registry, or their inclusion in a mandatory book noting salary payments by employers. All contraventions against one of these obligations renders one guilty of an offense that harms either (1) the economic equilibrium of one's profession (disloyal competition); (2) the interests of salaried workers, for instance, the absence of social protection; or (3) the interests of collective society (fiscal fraud). Equally subject to punishment are physical or moral persons who have knowing recourse to clandestine enterprises or firms.

This definition of clandestine work clearly shows that three dimensions of economic activity by firms are targeted: the legal conformity of a firm as a firm, the legality of its activities and products, and the conformity of the conditions under which it employs people. This definition thus has the merit of being applicable to very diverse situations—that of an artisan who does not enroll on the registry of occupations and thereby is unknown to fiscal authorities and to social security, as well as that of another artisan who is enrolled and who does list all of his or her personnel on the personnel registry. Moreover, it applies equally to those firms that merit the most condemnation, the totally clandestine enterprises that are not registered at all. All of these clarifications indicate that, contrary to what, unfortunately, is connoted by the term "clandestine worker," this offense cannot be committed by salaried workers. In no way can a dissimulated employee be equated with a clandestine worker. As a victim of clandestine work organized by his or her employer, such a worker cannot be held responsible or co-responsible. Moreover, and this is essential, in defining clandestine work, lawmakers made no reference to aliens as such.

Totally different, in fact, is the prohibition likewise found in the Labor Code (article L 341-6) against employment of an alien who has not received prior authorization to take up salaried employment in France. This indicates that, contrary to the commonplace confusion on this theme, French law establishes no unequivocal causal relationship between the irregularity of the administrative status of aliens and clandestine work. The scope of the former infraction often overlaps with the scope of the latter offense, but the latter's scope also exceeds that of the former by far.

In sum, the notion of illegal work designates all those practices that, above and beyond their juridical diversity and their economic specificity, aim at dissimulation of all or part of professional life in order to escape obligations established by fiscal, economic, and social regulations. This approach is, in any case, more in conformity with the lessons drawn from legal proceedings begun by enforcement services from 1989 to 1991. To the notion of illegal work has been attached that of troubling economic public order. Utilized under criminal law, this latter notion designates the damage caused to the collectivity, such as financial losses to governmental (state) organisms, disloyal competition undercutting firms that comply with the law, and the damage caused to employees, such as absence of social protection and loss of mandatory guarantees. In the nomenclature used in the publications of the Ministry of Justice, illegal work encompasses part of the offenses against policing of aliens and part of the damages to social order. All of the contentious matters studied here have been the object of an important lawmaking effort. Since the begin-

TABLE 1

TOTAL INFRACTIONS BY SECTOR AND
BY PRINCIPAL OFFENSES, 1989-91 (Percentage)

	Total	Unauthorized Alien Employment	Clandestine Work	Illicit Lending of Workers or Labor Trafficking
Agriculture	11.16	11.9	10.9	1.4
Building	36.2	42.8	29.1	78.5
Garment	7.9	10.8	7.2	5.4
Commerce	9.5	4.0	15.3	1.7
Hotels, cafés, restaurants	9.1	10.6	10.1	0.1
Automobile	3.0	0.7	5.4	—

SOURCE: Claude-Valentin Marie, *La verbalisation du travail illégal et sa condemnation par les tribunaux* (Paris: Interministerial Liaison Mission to Combat Illegal Work, Undeclared Employment, and Manpower Trafficking, 1993).

ning of the 1980s, Parliament has voted on nearly a dozen laws concerning them, and the government has published an even larger number of regulations of various kinds, such as decrees.

TWO OF THE MOST AFFECTED SECTORS: THE BUILDING AND AGRICULTURAL INDUSTRIES

The building sector is incontestably one of the economic sectors where regulations affecting the activities of firms and employment of workers are the least respected. As seen in Table 1, whatever the offense, it is committed most frequently in this sector.

Equally remarkable is the close connection between the number of infractions written up and the evolution of the economy. This was particularly evident from 1986 to 1989, a boom period for the building industry. After ten years of economic crisis, this period witnessed the creation of nearly 60,000 jobs in the industry. However, infractions for unauthor-

ized employment of aliens also more than quadrupled. In 1987, this sector alone witnessed more than half of all infractions reported to the Interministry Liaison Mission to Combat Manpower Trafficking.

It is with this same logic that there evolved in a parallel fashion in the 1980s other forms of precarious, but authorized, employment, particularly part-time and limited contract employment, and frequent abuse of public assistance measures designed to facilitate integration of at-risk youths. In the 1989 annual report of the Cour des Comptes, an important administrative tribunal with the mission of overseeing public bookkeeping and the finances of various administrations, this parallel abuse of public assistance measures was strongly denounced. "While [these measures] are intended to enable youths between 16 and 25 who either need a job or who otherwise are in difficulty to build a professional future, [they] often were used by firms to provide seasonal or temporary employment." "It was noted in numerous cases that the work days imposed upon the trainees were unusually long." Unquestionably, in a context marked by twin dynamics of economic boom and evolution of labor management, illegal work constituted a complementary factor of flexibility. The hypothesis is confirmed inversely by developments in 1991, when there was a slowdown of economic activity in the building sector and a concomitant dip in the number of infractions reported to the liaison mission.

Unlike the pattern in the building industry, infractions for unauthorized employment of aliens in agriculture have declined in recent years while those for clandestine work have increased. This relative substitution has been encouraged by heightened recession in rural areas, the absence of alternative employment in nearby industrial areas, and, as a consequence, continuous growth in underemployment and unemployment. This degradation of the socioeconomic milieu has had the direct consequence of lowering the level of expectations concerning wages, working conditions, and employment of local populations.

Under the pretext that the payroll taxes involved with normal hiring excessively raise production costs, many growers have taken advantage of this increasing precariousness to develop further illegal practices. This has meant more frequent recourse to clandestine work, by nondeclaration of French and alien employees, abusive lengthening of work days, and nondeclaration of overtime. Some have proceeded to fictitiously fire employees, who consequently qualify for unemployment relief, and then rehire these same employees at lower and undeclared wages. By such means, these growers seek to maximize ratios of harvest size to labor cost. Through a form of hiring blackmail, they exert permanent pressure to lower or, if not that, to maintain wages below legal minimums. In this system of generalized precariousness, unauthorized alien employment constitutes only one offense among many others, because, in reality, social legislation no longer applies. Certainly, overall, resident aliens and foreign seasonal workers, whether legally resident and employed or not, figure prominently among those exploited for their labor, but, and one cannot overemphasize this point, they are far from being the only ones.

TRANSPORTATION: BOOMING
ILLEGAL PRACTICES
AND WORSENING
WORKING CONDITIONS

Transportation was one of the sectors most affected by changes in production systems and by the "just in time" pattern. These can be found in, for example, shopping malls that impose short delivery terms or manufacturing industries, such as the automobile industry, that require from carriers regular and punctual delivery of spare parts needed for the assembly line. In this context, in 1987, transportation demand soared whereas competition increased and prices dropped. To minimize costs and risks, major transportation companies increasingly have recourse to subcontractors, that is, to independent carriers. This has both developed subcontracting practices and jeopardized small companies' finances. But constant pressure pushes the former to deviate from Labor Code norms and, more generally, from security rules, such as those concerning overtime work and speed limits. According to the president of the French carriers union, the Union Nationale des Organisations Syndicales des Transporteurs Routiers, "When price controls were removed in 1986, prices dropped and misuses of subcontracting practices soared. Some companies misuse subcontractors and thus take part in worsening social conditions." Thus, modernization of productive systems has brought about precarious working conditions and has encouraged illegal work: nonregistered artisans, clandestine work, undeclared employees, and misuse of subcontracting. The transportation industry resorts to the same practices as the building industry except, significantly, for the hiring of unauthorized aliens.

THE STATE CONFRONTS THE EVOLUTION AND GROWING SOPHISTICATION OF ILLEGAL WORK

It is this diversity and sophistication of forms of delinquent economic activity and employment—no longer the mere unauthorized employment of aliens—that enforcement services encounter today. It is precisely this diversity and sophistication that the important lawmaking and regulation effort undertaken over the past decade has sought to understand to enable enforcement services to better respond. But the determination of public authorities has also been manifested through reinforcement of resources made available to enforcement services.

Since adoption of a 1987 law redefining clandestine work, a series of legislative and regulatory modifications has sought to give enforcement agents means of intervention better suited to the evolution of realities encountered in the field. The most significant of these measures include clarification of the definition of illegal work (the law of 13 January 1989); strengthening sanctions against illegal work, against unauthorized employment of aliens, and against illegal recruitment of foreign workers; as well as a new measure punishing the employment through an intermediary, for instance, a subcontractor, of an unauthorized alien (the law of 10 July 1989). Additionally, there has been modification of Labor Code provisions relative to subcontracting and labor leasing complemented by strengthening of penalties in the event of infractions (the law of 12 July 1990); reform of the organization of interministerial coordination of the campaign against illegal work (decree of 25 July 1990); extension of the power to bring charges for transgressions against the ban on illegal work to enforcement agents specializing in social security compliance (the law of 3 January 1991); and reinforcement of the powers of judicial authorities within the departmental commissions established in the framework of interministerial coordination of the campaign against illegal work (decree of 30 October 1991).

All of these initiatives aim to accomplish three goals: reinforcement of the means of deterrence, expansion of the scope of intervention, and, above all, better operationalization. This has meant, in the first instance, recruitment of additional labor inspectors, extension of enforcement powers to social security compliance agents and maritime affairs agents, and, subsequently, an amelioration in the functioning of the departmental commissions along with development of joint enforcement operations involving various agencies. The latter have been facilitated by the suppression of the ban against sharing information between enforcement agents from different agencies. One must underscore how essential institutionalized dialogue between agencies has been to the progress made in recent years in understanding the phenomenon of illegal work. The law adopted on 31 December 1991, which capped the development of this capacity to deter illegal work, also bears the imprint of this institutionalized dialogue.

As the culmination of this long legislative and regulatory effort undertaken since the mid-1980s, the law of 31 December 1991 can be considered as the first major law pertaining to illegal work, even though its title refers only to clandestine work. This law represents, in effect, a radical change in perspective over that of the past in at least three ways. First, the law of 31 December 1991 brings together into one coherent legal text what heretofore had been scattered throughout a multitude of laws and regulations. Moreover, for the first time, this law takes into account the diverse forms of illegal work: clandes-

tine work, unauthorized employment of aliens, undeclared employment. It endeavors in particular to adapt itself to the most sophisticated forms of illegal work: irregular subcontracting and illicit leasing of workers. Finally, it attempts to reconcile the two end goals of governmental action: deterrence and punishment. In this respect, it strengthened penalties and sought to render enforcement more efficacious while encouraging employers to voluntarily respect laws and regulations pertaining to them.

With regard to these objectives, several fundamental points can be made that suggest the new directions of the action undertaken. One of the first concerns of the law of 31 December 1991 was to remove the oft remarked-upon ambiguity between the individual responsible for clandestine work, an independent worker or an enterprise, and the salaried worker(s) employed without being declared. This concern with clarity and greater rigor is found in the innovation that enables punishment of the veritable beneficiaries of clandestine work. This is what was accomplished by the insertion into the Labor Code of the new notions of recourse to intermediaries or indirect recourse to clandestine work that one frequently sees in subcontracting operations. The same objective motivated the introduction into the Labor Code of the notion of financial solidarity between the person responsible for clandestine work and the person who knowingly had recourse to his or her services. Hence, for the first time, it is possible to penalize a general contractor or the individual who knowingly orders a job done, notably in complex subcontracting schemes where it is the most difficult to establish responsibility. The principle that informed this initiative was to furnish enforcement agents with the means to penetrate the appearances of legality offered by juridical forms of supplying services.

This new approach is supported by the strengthening of sanctions for all illegal work infractions and the creation of complementary punishments. In cases of clandestine work, judges can from now on confiscate the direct or indirect products of clandestine work in addition to inflicting previously mandated punishments. Moreover, a judge can now ban transgressors from the exercise of a profession and/or exclude the individual from public markets for a period up to five years. Alien transgressors can now be excluded from French territory for five or more years. These same sanctions are applicable in cases of violations of regulations concerning aliens. Concomitantly, the principal penalties applied, imprisonment and fines, have been strengthened. Finally, sanctions for labor trafficking and illicit lending of workers have been aligned with the principal penalties for clandestine work, namely, two months to two years of imprisonment or a fine of 2000 to 200,000 French francs (approximately $400 to $40,000) or both.

Not only is the number of enforcement services engaged in the campaign against this delinquency larger, but the object of their enforcement has simultaneously been clarified and expanded. Most recently, to facilitate the efforts of these services

and to further deter illegal work, a new legal provision has complemented the law of 13 December 1991. On 31 December 1992, Parliament approved a measure requiring all employers to declare all employees to social security agencies prior to their hiring. These declarations are computer accessible to all authorized enforcement services, which receive a confidential code, itself changed on a regular basis. From now on, ignoring the mandatory requirement for employers to declare all employees to social security agencies prior to their hiring can be considered material proof of dissimulation of an employee, a clandestine work offense.

The corollary law of 31 December 1992 also equipped the Ministry of Labor with a credible instrument to analyze all evidence and information available concerning illegal work. This information-gathering system seeks to elucidate the social and economic determinants of illegal work and to create statistics necessary for a rational approach to preventing it. This system will enable authorities to ascertain the relative frequency of clandestine work or of undeclared employment according to region and economic sector. It thereby will facilitate the understanding of patterns of multiple offenses, relationships between related forms of delinquency, the significance, for instance, of the utilization of independent status as a means of disguising employee status, or the effects of free circulation and provision of services within the European Union on the sophistication of ongoing processes of international labor trafficking and social dumping.

TABLE 2
LEGAL COMPLAINTS BY TYPE OF INFRACTION, 1989-91

Type of Infraction	1989	1990	1991	1989-91
Clandestine work	4,426	4,983	5,283	14,692
Unauthorized alien employment	3,107	3,858	3,808	10,773
Labor trafficking and illicit lending of workers	292	763	768	1,823
Other infractions	1,412	2,083	2,699	6,194
Total	9,237	11,687	12,558	33,482

SOURCE: Marie, *Verbalisation du travail illégal.*

THE BALANCE SHEET OF LEGAL COMPLAINTS, 1989-91

Important in qualitative terms as witnessed by the intense legislative and regulatory efforts described previously, the balance sheet of the campaign against illegal work also has had nonnegligible net results in quantitative terms. As seen in Table 2, over the three years between 1989 and 1991, enforcement services transmitted to legal authorities more than 14,600 cases, with a total of 33,480 infractions against the Labor Code and the legislation pertaining to employment of aliens.

Detailed analysis of these results shows a preponderance of infractions for clandestine work over infractions for unauthorized employment of aliens. If these results were not interpreted with greater precaution than was the case with those published previously, the progression would appear considerable. In reality, such a comparison would lack rigor as the scope of the infractions enumerated and the cases considered has been widened and therefore differs considerably from previous periods. This noted, such a comparison is not totally devoid of interest. This difference and the evolution that it brings

to light signify the will of public authorities to intensify a campaign against what is today considered a social plague.

Examination of the classification of infractions detected by type of activity reveals, on the other hand, remarkable continuity in the economic sectors with the greatest propensity for this type of delinquency. As seen in Table 3, the building industry, agriculture, commerce, and hotels, cafés, and restaurants remain the most affected. In 1991, 7 out of every 10 cases counted targeted one of them. The building industry alone was the subject of a third of the cases established. Nearly 40 percent of the infractions cited concerned it, making it responsible for 70 percent of the progression in total infractions from year to year. If unauthorized employment of aliens and clandestine work are the most frequent offenses, this industry also is the center for the bulk—7 of 10 cases in 1990—of infractions for illicit lending of workers and labor trafficking. This observation is confirmed by the reports of the departmental commissions. Over the same period, they indicate that the building sector is the origin of 40-70 percent of the infractions cited and

TABLE 3

**EVOLUTION OF LEGAL COMPLAINTS AND INFRACTIONS
FOR ILLEGAL WORK BY ECONOMIC SECTOR, 1989-91**
(Percentage of annual total)

Sector	Legal Complaints			Infractions		
	1989	1990	1991	1989	1990	1991
Agriculture	9.0	9.0	9.5	10.7	11.5	12.5
Building	31.8	34.5	31.7	31.6	39.8	38.5
Commerce	11.2	13.3	14.4	8.6	10.2	10.3
Hotels, cafés, restaurants	11.2	11.9	11.7	9.1	9.2	9.7
Automobile	4.8	4.4	4.9	3.2	2.8	3.0

SOURCE: Marie, *Verbalisation du travail illégal.*

that it experiences all forms of illegal work. The departmental reports also confirm the growing number of infractions concerning labor trafficking and illicit lending of workers, which, as a general rule, are detected along with other offenses in the more or less complex cases called false subcontracting.

MORE MOTIVATED SERVICES

These results confirm, in the first instance, an important mobilization of enforcement services that is reflected in the augmentation of cases established and infractions cited between 1989 and 1991, respectively 12 and 30 percent more. A firmer engagement of different agencies above and beyond the enforcement of agents from the external services of the Ministry of Labor and Employment was manifest in their presence on the ground in larger numbers than previously. In addition to the multiplication of their investigations and field operations, one also observes a clear-cut evolution in their approaches. The more rapid growth of

infractions cited relative to cases written up shows real progress in this domain. It demonstrates a greater capacity for agents to deal with the most complex matters, in which there are several infractions often masked by fictitious legality. This evolution bodes well for the future, especially if a related program of training for enforcement agents continues.

Steady improvement in the competencies of enforcement agents appears all the more imperative because the types of offenses to which they must be attentive and their fields of investigation are steadily growing. In comparison with evaluations made of enforcement in this area that were proffered in the mid-1980s and that reflected the results of action almost exclusively centered on detection of illegal employment of aliens and a campaign against irregular immigration, this evolution also appears significant.[2] In the field,

2. See *La lutte contre les trafics de main-d'oeuvre en 1986-1987: Rapport au Ministre du travail, de l'emploi et de la formation professionelle* (Paris: La Documentation Française, 1988).

TABLE 4
**TOTALITY OF SINGLE AND MULTIPLE INFRACTIONS
SANCTIONED BY TRIBUNALS, BY TYPE OF INFRACTION, 1988-89**
(Absolute number and percentage)

	Number of Infractions	Percentage
Illegal work		
Clandestine work	4,131	57.0
Employment of aliens		
(of which unauthorized alien employment)	1,814 (1,754)	25.0
Labor trafficking and illicit worker lending	471	6.5
Absence of required professional papers for aliens	52	0.7
Infraction of employment regulations	10	0.1
Subtotal	6,478	89.3
Associated infractions		
Aliens police related to immigration	293	4.0
Other endangerment of socioeconomic order	230	3.2
False documents	55 ⎱	
Fraud	58 ⎰	3.4
Other infractions	130 �	
Subtotal	766	10.6
Total	7,244	100.0

SOURCE: A. Brizard and Claude-Valentin Marie, *Travail illégal et suites judiciaires* (Paris: Ministry of Labor and Ministry of Justice, 1993).

most agents now watch as much for the legality of alien employment in an enterprise or on a site as they do for respect for rules forbidding all other illegal forms of employment and other economic activities.

MORE CONVICTIONS
FOR ILLEGAL WORK
THAN FOR ILLEGAL
EMPLOYMENT OF ALIENS

In 1992, for the first time, conviction records pertaining to illegal work were analyzed in collaboration with the statistical service of the Ministry of Justice. This analysis covered the years 1988 and 1989. The results obtained confirm and complement those elaborated earlier in this article. During these two years, more than 6131 persons were convicted by tribunals, for a total of 7244 punished infractions. Growing sharply since 1987, convictions for clandestine work arrive in first place. As seen in Table 4, this offense was the cause of almost two-thirds of the convictions over the 1988-89 period.

In second place, one found infractions against regulations concerning alien employees. They were two times less numerous than convictions for clandestine work and progressed more moderately than the former. Nonetheless, they constituted a quarter of the cases examined.

Classification of the persons convicted for these offenses reveals that French citizens—69 percent—and, more broadly, citizens of the European Community (EC)—75 percent —constitute a very large majority of the persons involved. The presence of aliens from non-EC countries is not less remarkable. Among the convicted, they are found in a much higher proportion—21.5 percent—than their share of the workforce—6.6 percent. North Africans predominate among convicted non-EC aliens. One also observes a clear difference in behavior between French citizens and aliens from non-EC countries relative to the type of offense most frequently committed. Citizens have a higher propensity to be a party to clandestine work, whereas non-EC aliens appear more tempted to employ aliens without authorization. Three-quarters of convictions for clandestine work were leveled against French citizens and only 15 percent against aliens from non-EC countries. Conversely, of those convicted for unauthorized employment of an alien, 52 percent are citizens, while 37 percent are non-EC aliens, the latter being clearly overrepresented.

SEVERITY OF PUNISHMENT

With a level of incarcerations exceeding 25 percent of convictions made, clandestine work and unauthorized alien employment undoubtedly are the object of more severe punishment than other related offenses. Three major traits characterize the punishment of unauthorized alien employment as compared to that meted out for clandestine work: it is more severe; it is the object of more extreme views by judges; and fines for it are heavier. Incarcerations are slightly more prevalent in cases

of unauthorized alien employment and sentences rarely are partially suspended as judges opt for either incarceration or total suspension of sentence. The level of fines levied for unauthorized alien employment is superior to that levied in cases of recourse to clandestine workers. Regardless of the type of infraction, aliens from non-EC countries are punished more severely than are French citizens.

The first means of appreciating the importance of cases pertaining to illegal work follows from their rapid progression since 1987, which essentially is due to the growing attention given to clandestine work by special prosecutors. This evolution reflects the effects of the law of 27 January 1987, which clarified and extended the grounds for incrimination for this offense. Despite the criticisms that have been leveled, this law also facilitated, as witnessed by the results considered here, genuine progress in the adjudication of the new offense. This upward trend apparently held steady in 1990 and 1991. The information currently available strongly suggests this as there appears to have been a sharp upsurge in legal complaints for illegal work.

From now on, against this backdrop of mobilization of enforcement agents with its consequences for caseloads, the question obviously becomes one of the capacity of the tribunals most affected to handle the exponential growth in illegal work cases. Already voices have been raised warning against a flood of such cases. Some fear that this will necessitate either granting a priority to illegal work to the detriment of other legal matters concerning socioeconomic order or expediting legal procedures in cases involving illegal work. Neither of these alternatives are satisfactory to enforcement services.

The final observation that can be made from analysis of convictions for illegal work pertains to the unimportant number of convictions for labor trafficking and illicit lending of workers as well as their relatively modest progression since 1985. These results underscore, if underscoring is still needed, the difficulties encountered by enforcement services and tribunals in dealing with this type of infraction. The cases involved are, in effect, the most complex ones in the realm of illegal work. But they also are those that enforcement agents are and will be confronting more and more. The task of enforcement agents becomes more difficult due to the multiplication of cases in which the protagonists are foreign enterprises that operate temporarily on French soil under the cover of a contract for provision of services.

FROM NOW ON,
A EUROPEAN CONCERN

This double characteristic of contractual relations, involving complex subcontracting associated with transnational delivery of services, constitutes an important dimension of the contemporary organization of productive activities. One can only acknowledge that it adds to the complexity of facts that enforcement agents must master and adds to the difficulty of describing them and, for the courts, of judging them. The contradiction between the growing interdependence of labor markets within the EC and the heterogeneity of laws governing them in various member states contributes to this evolution. Each passing day, it favors growing sophistication of lawbreaking. This point is one that must retain the attention of institutions concerned with illegal work. It concerns not only France but the whole EC. This is what the Federal Labor Ministry in Germany is concerned about. German authorities appear increasingly preoccupied by circumvention of their laws pertaining to temporary workers and subcontracting by Community firms, most notably from Belgium.

As much as in France, the questions debated here have taken on a high-profile saliency throughout the highly developed European states that, during the two preceding decades, largely encouraged foreign labor migration. For a long time, European institutions ignored these questions before radically changing their attitude in the early 1980s. In this respect, 1983 marked a turning point. For the first time, on the basis of a French initiative, a European institution—in this instance, the Council of Europe—received a proposal aiming at harmonization not so much of immigration policies as of control of migratory flows. In a domain where every state was, until then, very watchful of its independence, the idea of a harmonization of norms regulating conditions for the entry, sojourn, and circulation of persons marked the start of a dramatic departure. In effect, once accepted, the hypothesis of harmonization would require that all member states surrender at least some sovereignty on the particularly sensitive subject of control over circulation and installation in their respective territories. This is where the essential change began. Even if the desired harmonization still encounters numerous obstacles, this breakthrough in conceptualizing the phenomenon had a considerable impact on approaches to migration questions and their treatment. Most notably, it brought about a very pronounced modification of the internal dispositions in each state.

Most of the European states still concentrate on curbing irregular immigration and employment of unauthorized aliens while overlooking other illegal employment practices. French experience, however, shows that unauthorized aliens cannot be held responsible for illegal employment; conversely, irregular jobs determine when, how, and in which sector unauthorized alien workers will be hired. These jobs can even be offered to authorized aliens or French people. That proves that such jobs depend mostly on the socioeconomic situation of the country and not on the administrative status of the workers.

ANNALS, *AAPSS*, **534**, July 1994

Regulating Migration in Europe: The Dutch Experience, 1960-92

By HANS VAN AMERSFOORT and RINUS PENNINX

ABSTRACT: Like other West European countries, the Netherlands has become an immigration country against its will. Since 1960, three migration flows in particular have contributed to the migration surplus: labor migration from the Mediterranean area, migration from former Dutch colonies, and migration of international refugees. In each case, the measures taken by the Dutch government to regulate the migration have not been successful. This article analyzes why it is so difficult, if not impossible, to effectively implement migration regulations. A very important reason seems to be the contradictory aims of the welfare state that, on the one hand, tries to keep immigrants out but, on the other hand, seeks to ensure full civil rights for the immigrant population settled in the country.

Hans van Amersfoort has a chair in population geography at the University of Amsterdam. His main research interest is in immigration, and he has written a number of books on West Indians, Moluccans, and Moroccans in the Netherlands. He is a staff member of the Institute for Migration and Ethnic Studies.

Rinus Penninx has a chair in ethnic studies and is director of the Institute for Migration and Ethnic Studies of the University of Amsterdam. He has published on Turkish migration, ethnic minorities policies, and immigration in the Netherlands.

L IKE other West European coun-
    tries, the Netherlands has be-
come an immigration country. To
date, 14.9 percent of the population
was born outside the country or is a
child of an immigrant. In the big cities, the share of the immigrant population is much higher.[1]

The Netherlands has never
wanted to become an immigration
country; on the contrary, the country
has for a long time stubbornly denied
that immigration took place.[2] Immigration was—and is—considered to
be undesirable and has at best been
accepted as an unavoidable consequence of the colonial past, the recruitment of labor in the 1960s, or
international treaties with regard to
refugees. The Dutch government has
taken a variety of measures to prevent immigration into the Netherlands and to induce already settled
immigrants to return home. It is obvious that these measures have not
been successful. The history of migration varies somewhat from coun-

try to country in Western Europe but
is basically similar to the Netherlands'. They all have become immigration countries against their will
and the measures taken to regulate
migration have met with very limited
success at best.[3]

Why has the regulation of immigration been so difficult and unsatis-
factory in Western Europe? That is
the question we will address in this
article. We concentrate on the case of
the Netherlands, but we believe that
our analysis is, mutatis mutandis,
also valid for the other member
states of the European Community
(EC).

A preliminary point to be made is
that migration is a general concept
applied to various flows of people that
comprise both aliens and nationals.
We first describe the migration flows
to the Netherlands and the measures
taken to regulate them. Three main
flows deserve attention in this context: labor migration from the Mediterranean area, migration from former Dutch colonies, and migration of
international refugees.

LABOR MIGRATION
FROM BOON TO BURDEN

The Netherlands developed a
great demand for manual labor in the
1960s. In response to this demand, a
more or less spontaneous flow of migrants from Mediterranean countries like Italy and Spain came into
being. Officially, these immigrants
needed a work permit and a residence permit, but in fact many entered the country as tourists and ac-

1. Hans van Amersfoort, "International
Migration and Population in the Netherlands,"
*Tijdschrift voor economische en sociale geo-
grafie*, 84(1):65-74 (1993); Rinus Penninx,
Jeanette Schoorl, and Carlo van Praag, *The
Impact of International Migration: The Case of
the Netherlands* (Amsterdam: Swets & Zeitlin-
ger, 1993). In the present article, we have limited citations mainly to publications available
in English. Full bibliographic documentation
is given in Hans van Amersfoort and Rinus
Penninx, "Migratieontwikkeling en migratie-
beheersing," in *Migratie, bevolking en politiek:
Nederland als immigratieland in een Westeu-
ropese context*, ed. Hans van Amersfoort (Amsterdam: Amsterdam Sociaal-Geografische
Studies, 1993), nr. 46, pp. 57-84.

2. Hans van Amersfoort and Boudewijn
Surie, "Reluctant Hosts: Immigration into
Dutch Society 1970-1985," *Ethnic and Racial
Studies*, 10:169-85 (1987).

3. Tomas Hammar, ed., *European Immigration Policy: A Comparative Study* (New
York: Cambridge University Press, 1985).

quired the necessary documents afterward, when they had found a job. In this way a practice developed in the 1960s in which economic interests were dominant and that led to a de facto legalization policy.

When the flow of migrants increased, the need for government intervention became more urgent. The Dutch government tried to control the migration flows by signing recruitment agreements with a number of countries. These agreements gave both the governments of the sending societies and the Dutch government some say about where and under what conditions labor could be recruited. At the time, all parties concerned—the respective governments and the migrants themselves—considered the labor migration to be a temporary phenomenon.

During the short recession of 1966-67, the labor import stagnated and the days of labor immigration seemed to be over. But the economy recovered quickly, and labor had to be recruited from more distant countries and areas. During the period 1967-73, the Netherlands recruited especially in Turkey and Morocco.[4] Government control of labor migration was extended: it was not possible any longer for migrants to apply for a work and residence permit once they had arrived in the Netherlands. Prospective migrants had to apply for permits before entering the country. In this way the government hoped to

stop the flow of "tourists," who entered the labor market as illegals, creating an entire circuit of so-called black work, especially seasonal labor in horticulture.

After the oil crisis of 1973-74, the idea of a controllable flow of temporary workers proved to be an illusion. The first paradox was that many of these workers, so much in demand a few years earlier, became unemployed. The second was that they did not return home but brought over their families instead. The immigration of dependents not only increased alien numbers, especially Turks and Moroccans in the Netherlands, but it also changed the character of the immigrant communities completely. This flow of immigrants for family reunification was especially strong in the period 1975-85.

After 1985, the process of family reunification was more or less completed, but yet another type of migration developed. The children in the immigrant communities grew up and reached marriageable age. As the ties with the homeland were still strong and the cultural distance to Dutch society was still great, the immigrants tended to look for partners in the homelands. Dutch law gives foreigners legally residing in the country the right to bring over their dependents and marriage partners. This resulted once more in substantial immigration that could not be regulated.

It seems, however, that the flows of dependents and marriage partners have passed their peaks since 1991, at least as far as the Turkish and Moroccan migration is concerned. The number of eligible dependents

4. Rinus Penninx, "Towards an Overall Ethnic Minorities Policy," in *Ethnic Minorities*, ed. Netherlands Scientific Council for Government Policy (The Hague: Netherlands Scientific Council for Government Policy, 1979), pp. 92-105.

has become very small and, in recent years, the number of marriages within the already settled immigrant community and the number of mixed marriages are rising, whereas the number of marriages with a partner from Turkey is decreasing.[5]

The Dutch government not only tried to prevent migration to the Netherlands; it also took measures to induce settled immigrants to return. Returning migrants could profit from a premium, facilities for transport, and rights to unemployment benefits and pensions. Even more ambitious was the idea of stimulating return migration by development programs for regions in the sending societies that were heavily dependent on migrant labor. As elsewhere in Western Europe, these measures met with only very partial success.[6] The only country that attracted a high number of returning migrants was Spain. This points to a set of factors limiting the effect of regulation measures by the host societies: the factors stimulating migration in the sending societies.

Because the Netherlands had recruited labor mainly in Turkey and Morocco, the case of these two countries is particularly relevant. The

contrast with Spain, where the economic, social, and political situation developed favorably after Franco's death, is telling. Demographic developments in Turkey and Morocco continue to create population pressure, especially in the rural areas. The economies suffer from high inflation and severe unemployment. Turkey is characterized by political instability and violence. Morocco has been politically stable but under an autocratic monarchical regime. These factors greatly influence the decisions of people to leave their country or to return to it and lie beyond control of any West European government. Thus did supposedly temporary recruitment of labor lead to the formation of settled immigrant communities. In 1992 there were 215,000 people of Turkish nationality and 164,000 of Moroccan nationality legally residing in the Netherlands. The origins of a state's incapacity to regulate international migration lie in flawed foreign labor recruitment policies.

MIGRATION AS COLONIAL INHERITANCE

Like other European countries, the Netherlands received specific migration flows from countries that were once Dutch colonies.[7] After World War II, the transfer of sovereignty to Indonesia caused a large influx of Dutchmen from the new republic. The political debate around this repatriation focused on the definition of citizenship. A substantial

5. Philip J. Muus and Rinus Penninx, *Immigratie van Turken en Marokkanen in Nederland: Een analyse van de ontwikkeling tussen 1970-1990, een vooruitblik op te verwachten immigratie en de consequenties voor beleid* (The Hague: Ministry of the Interior, 1991).

6. Hans van Amersfoort, Philip Muus, and Rinus Penninx, "International Migration, the Economic Crisis and the State: An Analysis of Mediterranean Migration to Western Europe," *Ethnic and Racial Studies*, 7:238-68 (1984); Rinus Penninx, *Immigrant Populations in Member States of the Council of Europe* (Strasbourg: Council of Europe, 1984).

7. Hans van Amersfoort, *Immigration and the Formation of Minority Groups: The Dutch Experience 1945-1975* (New York: Cambridge University Press, 1982).

number of Eurasians (Indische Nederlanders) successfully claimed the constitutional right of Dutch citizens to settle in the Netherlands.

Dutch citizenship has played an important role in facilitating migration. In 1954, a new Charter for the Kingdom of the Netherlands came into being. It gave Dutch citizenship to the inhabitants of Surinam and the Dutch Antilles. Scarcely anyone grasped the consequences this would have for migration between the Dutch Caribbean and the Netherlands. It has resulted in a continuous immigration of Dutch nationals from Surinam and the Antilles. In 1992, there were 80,000 Dutch citizens of Antillean descent residing in the Netherlands, but the most spectacular flow has come from Surinam.

The relatively small but steadily increasing stream of Surinamese immigrants caused the Dutch government at the end of the 1960s to search for means to halt the migration. This migration so obsessed Dutch politicians in the 1970s that it became the principal reason for trying to end the relationship as defined in the Charter between the two countries. In 1975, partly because of internal political circumstances in Surinam, this attempt succeeded. During the negotiations on Surinam's independence, the Dutch endeavored to prevent Surinamese citizens from coming to the Netherlands and even to deprive all those already settled in the Netherlands of their Dutch citizenship. This proposal, however, proved quite unachievable. In the end, the Dutch delegation agreed to permit a free exchange of persons between Surinam and the Netherlands until 1980, constituting a transitional period of five years.

These policies created the impression, both at the time of independence in 1975 and again when the transitional regulation came to an end in 1980, that there would be virtually no further possibility for Surinamese citizens to enter the Netherlands. This gave rise to a great number of last-minute migrants, first in 1974-75 and then again in 1979-80. It is a remarkable example of counterproductive policy: the measures resulted in precisely what they were intended to avoid.

After 1980, when Surinam was sliding closer and closer to a military dictatorship, the character of the Surinamese migration to the Netherlands changed. In the first place, a number of Surinamese invoked the right of asylum. In addition, the fact that there was already an established Surinamese population in the Netherlands led to requests for residence on other grounds, like family reunification and marriage. It is also evident that a quite substantial number of Surinamese have not returned home after tourist visits to the Netherlands and have become more or less illegal immigrants. Official migration statistics show that legal migration in the early 1990s is not lower than it was in the early 1970s, and the total number of people in the Netherlands of Surinamese origin has increased from 120,000 in 1976 to more than 228,000 in 1990. From the point of view of migration control, therefore, this represents a completely failed policy.

POLICY ON REFUGEES
AND ASYLUM: A COMPROMISE
BETWEEN IRRECONCILABLES

In the post-World War II period, influxes of refugees consisted initially of people displaced by the war and of people fleeing the Communist regimes in Eastern Europe. This picture has changed completely. Now refugees come from all over the world, as oppressive regimes, civil wars, and ecological disasters make people flee to more promising surroundings.

A second important change lies in the legal status of the immigrant-refugees. Until 1980, these people came to the Netherlands mainly as invited refugees. This means that they had already acquired the legal status of refugee—usually in a United Nations refugee camp—before entering the Netherlands. After 1980, there is a sharp increase in the number of people who arrive in the Netherlands without any legal status—and often without documents—and ask for asylum. This starts a procedure in which their refugee status has to be established. When they are not successful in becoming recognized as refugees, such asylum seekers can be expelled. In 1980, less than 1000 persons entered the country as asylum seekers. In 1991, their number had already risen to 21,000, and in 1993, 38,000 were expected to apply for refugee status in the Netherlands.

The burgeoning flow of people seeking asylum has given rise to a number of categorical measures for fending them off. Reception facilities for asylum seekers became more sober, offering only bed, bread, and bath; measures were taken to prevent asylum seekers from entering the country, for example, through visa regulations and holding transport companies responsible for bringing people into the country with valid papers; and the criteria for granting asylum were narrowed and more applications were rejected. On the international level, the Netherlands, along with other West European countries, has taken additional measures such as harmonizing visa requirements, providing for extra protection of the European Union's external border, and exchanging information on asylum seekers.

In the process of handling the growing number of applications for asylum, a number of problems have been encountered. In the first place, the procedures often drag on, partly because of the overload carried by the organizations involved, and partly because of legal protections that have grown up in the welfare states. Legal rights and appeals procedures are fully utilized. Following a negative decision on an application, if the stay has been an extended one, expulsion frequently is no longer thought to be opportune or permissible.

Because the official regulations are so difficult to implement, asylum policy has become deeply ambivalent. A status of "tolerated" has evolved, lodged in a limbo between acceptance and the increasingly common rejection of the request for asylum: a refugee is designated tolerated when the application for asylum has been rejected but the risk involved in expelling the person concerned is deemed too great, at least for the present. There has recently

FIGURE 1
DETERMINANTS OF MIGRATION: A HEURISTIC MODEL

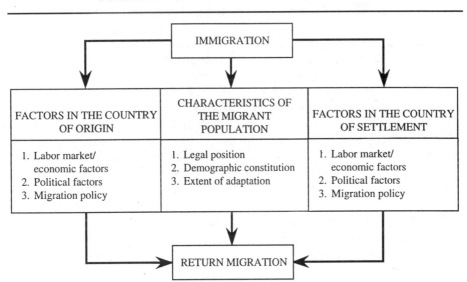

SOURCE: This is a slightly expanded version of a model originally developed by the authors to analyze Mediterranean migration to Western Europe. See Hans van Amersfoort, Philip Muus, and Rinus Penninx, "International Migration, the Economic Crisis and the State: An Analysis of Mediterranean Migration to Western Europe," *Ethnic and Racial Studies*, 7:239 (1984).

been added yet another temporary status, displaced persons, for ex-Yugoslavians: they are offered temporary sanctuary in the Netherlands while awaiting their expected return.

DETERMINANTS OF MIGRATION MOVEMENTS AND POLICY EFFECTIVENESS

In the cases that have been outlined, a number of factors recur; we draw them together now into a heuristic model (see Figure 1). This enables us to draw conclusions concerning the circumstances in the countries of the migrants' origin, the characteristics of the migrant population already established in the country of settlement, and, finally, the factors operating in that target country, including immigration policy.

Factors in the countries of origin

A necessary condition for the commencement and continued existence of economic migration is a lower standard of living for the bulk of the population in the country of origin than in the target country. However, this is not a sufficient condition to generate actual migration. Potential migrants also need to be aware of the possibilities of obtaining a higher income by means of migration, and there must be affordable means of migration as well.

Political migration movements arise as a result of political persecution or repression, but, once again, these factors do not necessarily lead to actual migration. A primary concern is whether departure is even permitted or in any way possible—the situation in the former Soviet bloc comes to mind—and another is that people also need to be aware of the possibility and feasibility of migration.

The economic differences between the countries of northwestern Europe and a large number of others, especially in Eastern Europe and the Third World, have done anything but decline in recent decades. Neither has political persecution outside northwestern Europe diminished. Therefore the prospects for a decrease in migration flows are hardly favorable as far as the necessary conditions for the launch of such movements are concerned.

More important for the migration that we can realistically expect to occur are the changes in what we have termed the facilitating conditions for migration: in the last decades, worldwide communication by means of radio and especially television has penetrated the entire globe, including Third World countries. At the same time, the number of passenger-miles traveled has increased significantly and transport has become cheaper per mile. It can be safely assumed that the powerful growth in the distribution of information and transport facilities is making an important contribution to the increase in migration pressure on northwestern Europe. Distance, which played a significant role as a factor in earlier

migration theory, has now lost much of its importance, as is witnessed by the global distribution of the origins of those seeking asylum. These new migrations are capable, partly depending on immigration policy in the countries of settlement, of evolving into migration movements with their own momentum.

From the point of view of a potential migrant—whether political or economic—the issue of the method of achieving an intended migration is in itself of little relevance. Naturally, there will always be a preference for the method that delivers the most security or profit (in the migrant's terms), so legal residence with all the associated rights is desirable, irrespective of the means employed to achieve that status. If this proves impossible or appears improbable, then the option of an illegal stay, with all the attendant risks, can still be preferable to no migration at all.

Once under way, migration movements achieve their own momentum. In regions with a tradition of emigration, migration becomes such an accustomed, self-evident, and widely used alternative that other ways of obtaining an income begin to be seen as inferior. The social momentum is nurtured by the continuing stream of information, from the impressions of the prosperity of migrants (whether true or not), by means of money transfers and luxury, but also by means of the help provided by those who have migrated to those who have remained behind: nominative recruitment, assistance for relatives and acquaintances who arrive as tourists, marriages between migrants and those remaining behind that can lead to migration, and the like. An environment that encourages emigration can certainly be said to exist in Surinam and in parts of Turkey and Morocco.

In terms of the determinants found in the land of origin, return migration is the mirror image of what has just been described: economic migrants return to sending countries in significant numbers only when the standard of living in the country of origin has risen to the extent that emigration declines, in addition to a number of the earlier emigrants returning, as happened with countries like Spain and Italy after 1975. Only in these circumstances will a country of origin begin to think in terms of a policy on return migration, but until that stage is reached, return migration is likely to be limited and highly selective, involving, for instance, those prone to homesickness, those who see opportunities back in the old country on account of their particular skills or qualities, or pensioners with an income from abroad. Return migration is only likely to take place among political migrants if the political situation in the country of origin has changed, but if this occurs after a long interval has elapsed since emigration, then return migration can be severely hindered by the ties formed by the migrants and their offspring and the position they have attained in the society in which they have settled.

The role of the immigrant populations

The welfare states of northwestern Europe find themselves on the horns of a dilemma: on the one hand, migrants and potential migrants are, on the basis of the ideology of the nation-state, primarily classified as outsiders and may not remain in the country of settlement without permission; this is the principle that governs immigration policy in such countries. However, if migrants actually achieve legal entry and their stay extends in time, another ideology of the welfare state begins to exert mounting influence, namely, that all inhabitants are in principle equal and should have equal opportunities. During the last two decades, the welfare states of Western Europe, and in particular the Netherlands, have attempted to resolve the growing contradiction between the foreigner as outsider and the foreign inhabitant as a person with equal rights by formally evolving a supervised immigration policy, on the one hand, in which decisions on admission are taken prior to the actual arrival, and, on the other hand, by extending the rights of legal residents and operating a policy aimed at rapid integration of immigrants. The increasing legal security surrounding the residence of foreign immigrants—expulsion from the Netherlands after a stay of five years has become virtually impossible—and the effective recognition of the right to reunite families and to bring marriage partners over from abroad are part of such integration policies.

This strengthening of the legal position of the majority of an immigrant population can lead to considerable secondary migration on the part of the family members and marriage partners of those legally resident.

The scale of this secondary migration is dependent on the demographic structure of the families of the original migrants and the marriage cohorts of their children. This demographic structure is of particular importance in the early stages of a migration movement, in which first-generation migrants bring their families over and the children of those families recruit marriage partners predominantly or exclusively from the country of origin. The migration of Turks and Moroccans into the Netherlands in the period 1985-91 displays quite clearly the characteristics of this kind of secondary migration. The migration pressure in the countries of origin falls heavily on the possibilities for obtaining legal entry through secondary migration. For example, research at the local level has shown that the market value of legally resident young women is exceedingly high on the marriage market in the countries of origin.[8] In later stages, when the immigrant population, or at least the larger part of it, has been settled in the target country for some time and the number of generations increases (especially of those born there), adaptation to the host society will increase, thus altering the choice of marriage partners and ultimately leading to a decrease of immigration.

Immigrant populations and potential immigrants react to restrictive policy by embracing the remaining possibilities that still permit entry. Sometimes new restrictive measures are anticipated while they are being discussed in the political arena and are threatening to become reality.

Established immigrant populations function as a bridge not only for legal immigrants but also for illegal ones, by providing assistance in finding them shelter and work. Furthermore, there are a number of factors to be found at the collective level that generate migration; for example, the structure of particular institutions within the immigration group can lead to the transfer of specific types of immigrants, like imams or teachers. The structure of specific economic activities within the immigrant population can also operate as a pull factor for migrants, whether legal or not. An example is the Turkish clothing workshops in Amsterdam, in which an estimated 10,000 Turks, legal and illegal, are working.

Factors in the country of settlement and the effectiveness of policy

Whether the pressure for migration that we have outlined here actually leads to migration depends partly on the policy on admission. In principle, a strongly restrictive admission and expulsion policy, backed up with effective instruments and applied consistently, can exert a significantly limiting influence on immigration. In practice, however, in recent decades this has hardly ever occurred. In this context, three questions can be posed about policy designed to regulate migration: (1) Which factors exert an influence on the potential scope of policy? (2) What are the determinants that formally govern policy on admission and ex-

8. Muus and Penninx, *Immigratie van Turken en Marokkanen*, pp. 66-70, 77-80.

pulsion? (3) Which factors are responsible when a formally agreed restrictive policy is, in fact, applied very ambivalently or not at all?

The scope of policy. Migration-regulatory policy can affect only aliens. Nationals of the country of settlement are not the concern of such policy, and in the Dutch case, that also applies to the population of the Dutch Antilles and Aruba. As far as aliens are concerned, policy recognizes three grounds for admission: (1) international obligations, such as those applying to EC citizens and invited refugees; (2) Dutch economic interests; and (3) humanitarian considerations, such as family reunification, family formation, and asylum.

The state is evidently limited in its capacity to carry out a restrictive policy by the international obligations in the first category. As a result, labor migrants within the EC and, shortly, from other European states as well—the countries of the European Free Trade Association—cannot be included in regulations designed to slow down the pace of labor migration.

Regarding the economic interest of the Netherlands as a ground for admission, since the mid-1970s a political consensus has more or less obtained to the effect that the admission of labor has become undesirable in times of high unemployment, and this is especially true in the case of semi-skilled and unskilled workers. It is much less true for specific categories of labor, usually the highly skilled or specialized, and particularly for those who desire to enter under the auspices of an international business or institution: for such people permission to enter is possible.

For those who cannot avail themselves of these two sets of criteria, only humanitarian grounds are possible for legal entry to the Netherlands from outside the EC, which means, in practice, family reunification or an application for asylum. The scope for regulating secondary migration appears to be actually very limited, due to the fact that family unification and formation have become vested rights.

Thus an application for asylum is for many aspirant immigrants the sole remaining possibility for legal entry. Therefore, on the assumption outlined previously that the criteria upon which he or she is admitted are irrelevant to the potential immigrant, it is hardly surprising that the number of applications for asylum has risen sharply. Applications have risen so fast that all countries, including the Netherlands, have as their first priority to limit these numbers by fending off asylum seekers. Officially there is no question of meddling with the right of asylum itself, but nonetheless an attempt is made to dam the flow by introducing visa requirements and sanctions against those who transport people without valid papers. These are measures without justification in the sense that it is quite possible that a genuinely persecuted person might not possess a valid set of papers.

In addition, an attempt is made to distinguish between the genuine and the false refugees. The rising number of asylum applications has made differentiating the two more difficult. Furthermore, in a constitutional state, distinguishing between them implies all manner of opportunities for appeal, leading to drawn-out procedures. Although the percentage of asylum seekers finally recognized as refugees has continued to decline in recent years, there can still be problems concerning the execution of the agreed policy—deportation and expulsion—if the denial of the request for asylum comes after a long interval.

The scope of immigration policy is therefore much narrower than is often suggested, a point clearly manifested in the Dutch immigration figures for 1992. It is estimated that about a quarter of the rough total of 115,000 immigrants in that year were Dutch nationals returning from abroad; Dutch nationals from the Netherlands Antilles and Aruba counted for some 5 percent. Immigrants from member states of the EC made up a further 20 percent, which means that no less than half of the immigration was quite beyond regulation on the basis of current legislation and EC obligations. A further 20 percent of the immigration was accounted for by family reunification and formation from outside the EC, and this, too, fell almost entirely outside the scope of regulation, given current legal practice. That leaves just 30 percent of total immigration, of which about half consisted of asylum seekers.

In principle, a policy on emigration or return migration could complement an admission policy as part of a government's overall migration strategy; however, this element appears to hold only marginal significance in the Western European context, including that of the Netherlands. One reason is that evaluation studies of earlier examples of this type of instrument have shown return migration policy to have had little effect in the long term; second, a policy explicitly based on stimulating return appears to have a counterproductive effect on integration policies for legally resident immigrants.

Formal determinants of admission policy. Generally speaking, there is a connection in all the states of northwestern Europe between the labor market situation, on the one hand, and the degree to which restrictive admission to the country for purposes of work is devised and applied. This connection is not hard to explain, for the state has taken on the role of "gatekeeper"[9] and applies restrictions to labor migration according to the situation in the labor market. In practice, this has meant that most of the countries of northwestern Europe have granted entry for purposes of labor only on a highly selective basis since 1974, especially when dealing with the unskilled and semi-skilled.

Although this relationship is generally evident, it would appear that economic interest is by no means indivisible. Even in unfavorable periods in the business cycle, certain sectors continue to experience difficulty in recruiting unskilled and semi-skilled workers, which results partly from the nature, quality, and remuneration of the work in question and also from the fact that the social security of the unemployed is relatively

9. Gary P. Freeman, "Migration and the Political Economy of the Welfare State," *The Annals* of the American Academy of Political and Social Science, 485:51-63 (May 1986).

high. Sectoral economic interest of this sort can lead to the creation or continuation of illegal employment, especially when the supervisory institutions effectively turn a blind eye.

Political as well as economic factors exert an influence, as can clearly be seen in the case of postcolonial migration flows. But that apart, admission policy based on political grounds generally appears to work selectively. For example, the issue of who is eligible for refugee status, in terms of both time scale and numbers, is significantly related to the political, religious, cultural, or ethnic links that the refugees have or claim with the country of settlement. Such links appear to have an effect on admission policy for refugees and asylum seekers, influencing the extent of entry for certain categories.

The execution of policy. In addition to the scope of policy, the applicability of policy is also subject to a number of restrictions. In the first place, there are limits regarding the instruments that can be wielded. Inspection of the movement of people when they cross borders is the most important instrument of migration regulation, but it is an instrument that lacks efficiency. It is perfectly feasible to make inspections more thorough and so increase the efficiency, but one runs the risk of damage to other interests, like tourism, which benefit from a smooth passage at the border points. In any case, it is quite possible for someone to cross the border legally, as a tourist, for example, but thereafter to cease behaving like a tourist. Inspection of the domestic population is an alternative but

highly imprecise instrument, quite apart from the ethical and administrative problems. There seems to be a tendency toward operating checks "at the counters of the welfare state" as a further alternative, but this instrument requires an extensive leadtime for development. These limitations on the instruments of policy are increased by the fact that they must be carried out by police-type inspection organizations that have many other jobs to do and that must therefore establish priorities. In reality, illegal residence and illegal work are not given a high priority in the Netherlands in the range of assignments for the inspection organizations, and in situations of this kind, it is unlikely that measures to prevent illegal settlement will exert very much influence.

This is clearly shown by government policies relating to illegal work. Several official measures have been taken after public debate on this topic: sanctions for employers have been raised; employers are made responsible for the costs of removing the illegals from the Netherlands, and so on. But practice did not change: neither the number of search actions nor that of employers charged changed much—around 400 per year from 1988 to 1990. The number of illegal workers found did not change significantly—between 1250 and 1700 per year from 1988 to 1991. It all makes the impression of symbolic policy implementation. The low profile of policy implementation is publicly confirmed by the highest police officials in the big cities, stating that their priorities do not concern noncriminal illegals.

Second, applicability is limited by ethical and political or administrative confinements. Overrepressive execution or supervision clashes with moral and ethical principles or is seen as working against the aims of policy directed at legal residents. In this way, strict application of immigration and inspection policy can have undesired consequences for policy on ethnic minorities in general.

CONCLUSION

The West European states claim, as all other modern states, that they can regulate international migration according to their interests or humanitarian principles. We have been able to point out that they, in fact, exert only a limited influence.

In the first place, it is clear that those determinants of migration that are located outside the country of settlement can hardly be influenced in a direct sense, as is made clear by the attempts of Western European countries to reduce the tendency to emigrate in the countries of origin and to stimulate return migration. In the case of the factors that, in theory, should be subject to migration-regulatory policy, such as granting or refusing residence permits to foreigners, the effectiveness of such measures appears to be limited by the whole structure of the constitutional state, by conflicting interests within the receiving society, and by the impossibility of controlling all people who enter the country. Precisely because of the limitation of the scope of policy designed to regulate migration, the migrant population already present in the country of settlement exerts a great deal of influence on the subsequent development of the migration process. Ironically, to a large degree, this same population resulted from deliberate decisions to authorize foreign labor employment in an earlier period.

ANNALS, *AAPSS*, **534**, July 1994

Regional Economic Integration and Migration: The European Case

By HEINZ WERNER

ABSTRACT: Since the establishment of the European Economic Community (EEC) in 1957, economic and regional integration in Western Europe has been achieved. What consequences has this had for labor migration between the member states? What lessons are to be drawn from the EEC experience as to the effect of regional integration on unwanted migration? Would analogous results occur under the North American Free Trade Agreement (NAFTA)? The development of the European Communities (EC) shows that regional integration can attenuate socioeconomic disparities that induce people to migrate. Increased trade and welfare has had a leveling effect among EC states that has dampened migration. Trade exchanges and competition within the EC occurred more within industrial or product groups than between economic sectors. Thus adjustment to freer trade did not lead to the loss of whole industries and mass redundancies. But NAFTA differs from the EC in many respects. Although there are some similarities, the differences between NAFTA and the EC warn against the facile presumption that Mexico will go the way of Italy after ratification of NAFTA.

Heinz Werner, Ph.D., is an economist and senior research officer at the Institute for Employment Research, Nuremberg. His major fields of interest are European integration and the labor market, labor market policy, and migration. Previously he has held positions at the Economic Commission for Europe, Geneva; the Commission of the European Communities, Brussels; the Organization for Economic Cooperation and Development, Paris; and the International Labour Office, Geneva.

SINCE the establishment of the European Economic Community (EEC) in 1957, economic and regional integration in Western Europe has been achieved. What consequences has this had for labor migration between the member states? What lessons are to be drawn from the EEC experience as to the effect of regional integration on unwanted migration? Would analogous results occur under the North American Free Trade Agreement (NAFTA)? We can start to shed light on these questions by outlining the development of the EEC, which later developed into the European Communities (EC), and by presenting, in chronological order, some key economic data on integration.

The EEC was founded in 1957 upon the signing of the Treaty of Rome. Signatory states were France, the Federal Republic of Germany, Italy, Belgium, the Netherlands, and Luxembourg. In 1973, the United Kingdom, Ireland, and Denmark joined, followed by Greece in 1981 and Spain and Portugal in 1986. From the outset, the agenda of the EC has included the idea of fostering political community through socioeconomic integration. While Europeans differ on the ultimate and preferred nature of the European Union, this avowed goal clearly demarcates the EC from NAFTA.

In 1968, the customs union was completed. The customs duties and quantitative trade restrictions—for example, quotas—between the member states were abolished, and a common external tariff was introduced. Even if customs duties and quotas no longer exist, there are still many obstacles to the interstate exchange of goods and capital. These obstacles consist, for example, of technical standards for goods varying from country to country or of different currency regulations for movements of capital. The Common Market as striven for by means of European integration requires the realization of the four "basic freedoms," the unimpeded cross-border movement of goods, services, capital, and labor. It was therefore the declared aim of the EC Commission to reduce impediments that hamper transactions and bring about distortions of competition. It required harmonized and Community-wide policies, such as uniform trade and competition policies. Distortions of competition resulting from national non-tariff obstacles such as technical standards or national subsidies, which have not been coordinated throughout the Community, cannot be permitted. The objective of the EEC, therefore, goes far beyond the free trade area as striven for by the European Free Trade Association[1] or by the planned NAFTA.

The Single European Act of 1986 laid the foundation stone for the creation of the single European market by 1993. The abolition of barriers was envisaged as follows:

1. The European Free Trade Association (EFTA) was founded in 1960 on the initiative of the United Kingdom by a number of European countries that, in their economic integration in the form of a common market, did not wish to go as far as the EEC. For them a free trade area was sufficient. In the meantime, practically all the former member countries of EFTA have either joined the EC or have expressed their intention to do so.

— removal of checks on persons and goods at national borders;

— harmonization of standards and technical rules;

— allowing services to be offered everywhere in the Community on the same terms—including banks, insurance;

— harmonization of consumption taxes, particularly of value-added tax;

— Europe-wide invitations to tender for public orders above a certain financial level;

— extension of the freedom-of-movement ruling to persons not in gainful employment and facilitation of intra-Community mobility, for example, by mutual recognition of qualifications.

This ambitious program has largely been realized. Meanwhile all EC countries ratified the Maastricht Treaty for the creation of a European Union. From an economic point of view, the provisions for a European economic and monetary union are at the heart of this treaty. It is envisaged that, by 1999 at the latest, the transition to a uniform currency and to an independent European central bank committed to the aim of price stability will have taken place. Whether this schedule can be kept to is uncertain, as far as one can see at the present time, due to the turmoil in the monetary system and because of the still divergent financial and economic policies of the member states.

HOW DID EUROPEAN INTEGRATION DEVELOP?

In order to be able to assess the migration of labor between the member states of the EC, it is important to know how European integration has developed since the founding of the EC. How have trade and the international division of labor within the Community developed? Did trade act as a substitute for migration? Can convergent tendencies in terms of income or employment opportunities between the regions be seen that have reduced the pressure for migration between the EC countries?

The development of integration is shown by the following indicators: the trade links between the member states, the development of gross national products and of the interstate financial transfers to offset regional differences, and the availability of jobs or, rather, the lack of them—unemployment.

A look at Table 1, showing world trade relations, reveals that reciprocal trade between the EC countries—intra-EC trade—has constantly increased. From 1960 to 1973, the trade between the six founding countries, in terms of the share of overall trade, increased from 35 to 50 percent. This share stagnated until the mid-1980s and then rose to 60 percent by 1992.

Both periods of marked increase in intra-EC trade coincided with periods of relatively high economic growth. During these periods, trade obstacles were greatly reduced: by 1968 all customs duties between the member states had been abolished and a customs union with a common external tariff had been set up. The second period of comparatively high economic growth relates to the creation of the single European market: in 1987 the Single European Act came into force, of which the main

TABLE 1

TRADE OF EC ECONOMIES, 1960-90

Country	1960-67 World	1960-67 Intra-EC	1968-72 World	1968-72 Intra-EC	1973-79 World	1973-79 Intra-EC	1980-84 World	1980-84 Intra-EC	1985-90 World	1985-90 Intra-EC
Belgium and Luxembourg	37.5	64.8	42.8	71.2	48.9	71.2	61.5	67.0	60.8	71.7
Denmark	27.0	52.3	23.4	46.7	25.3	48.2	29.1	49.1	26.7	50.8
Germany (West)	15.9	44.8	17.6	50.9	20.4	50.3	24.8	50.5	24.9	53.1
Greece	12.7	50.6	12.7	53.4	17.6	47.3	19.5	48.1	20.8	60.5
Spain	8.1	47.8	9.2	44.4	11.2	41.3	14.4	39.3	14.4	56.0
France	11.0	45.8	12.5	57.2	16.6	55.0	18.9	53.9	18.6	61.9
Ireland	33.6	72.2	35.3	71.6	45.8	74.3	50.1	73.1	52.0	72.2
Italy	11.7	42.9	13.1	49.5	18.4	48.7	19.4	46.1	16.9	55.0
Netherlands	37.7	62.7	36.4	67.8	40.6	65.9	47.8	64.1	49.0	67.8
Portugal	19.8	48.3	20.3	49.6	22.2	50.2	30.1	50.1	32.5	65.1
United Kingdom	16.0	26.7	16.7	31.2	22.3	37.9	21.6	44.1	21.0	49.9
EC 12	8.8	45.0	8.3	51.9	10.2	52.6	11.5	52.2	9.8	59.8

SOURCES: Eurostat; Loukas Tsoulakis, *The New European Economy* (New York: Oxford University Press, 1993), p. 215.

NOTE: Figures for world trade as a percentage of gross domestic product (GDP) have been calculated by inserting country data for imports and exports of goods (SITC categories 0-9) in the formula: $\frac{\frac{1}{2} \Sigma (x \times m)}{GDP} \times 100$. Intra-EC trade is given as a percentage of total trade. For the member states, figures for world trade as a percentage of GDP include intra-Community trade; for the EC 12, intra-Community trade has been excluded.

part was the laying down of the legal requirements of the time schedule for the completion of the single market.

The relationship between trade and economic growth is not unidirectional; rather, they influence each other. The rapid dismantling of the internal customs duties and trade quotas between 1958 and 1968 and the setting up of the single market during the short time up to 1993 were easier to achieve under the favorable economic circumstances. Intensified international competition requires restructuring, which imposes work and capital costs and makes labor redundant. The cost of restructuring can, in terms of good economic growth, be compensated for by means of existing sales possibilities, and the labor made redundant can be employed in newly created jobs. Progress in economic integration is, therefore, rather to be achieved in times of economic prosperity. In this connection, Tsoulakis writes of a "virtuous circle,"[2] that is, the coinciding of a number of favorable factors: a good economic climate, which makes easier the acceptance of the agreements for the dismantling of trade barriers; and liberalization, which, in turn, leads to more trade exchanges and finally to more economic growth. Under poor economic conditions, competition-intensifying agreements are more difficult to achieve and the adjustment and restructuring processes necessitated by a transition period are more painful, as redundancies are not offset by newly created jobs elsewhere. Such fears were, for example, being expressed increasingly strongly as the date for the signing of NAFTA approached.

In a number of studies, it was ascertained that in the course of European integration, trade exchanges have developed more within industrial sectors and product groups (intra-industrial trade) than between industrial sectors (inter-industrial trade). This indicates an increased horizontal specialization within the economic sectors, that is, a diversification of the products within the sector rather than a division of labor in the form of production displacements. Production displacements would have led to adjustment problems such as the loss of whole production units and the associated redundancies.

The largely intra-industrial trade exchanges within the EC are accounted for in the following way:

The existence of similar and therefore competitive, as opposed to complementary, production structures is clearly a necessary condition for intra-industry specialisation to arise. If there is also some similarity of demand conditions among the member countries, reflected in overlapping tastes, and if goods are produced with economies of scale, so limiting the amount of product diversity that domestic producers can accommodate profitably, there will be an incentive to horizontal specialisation within industries in order to benefit from the economies of large-scale production.[3]

The situation has changed somewhat with the accession of new members to the Community. The EC is

2. Loukas Tsoulakis, *The New European Economy* (New York: Oxford University Press, 1993), p. 29.

3. Peter Robson, *The Economics of International Integration* (London: Unwin Hyman, 1987), p. 42.

TABLE 2
DIVERGENCE OF GROSS DOMESTIC PRODUCT
PER CAPITA IN EC COUNTRIES, 1960-93 (EC 12 = 100)

Country	1960	1970	1980	1990	1993
Belgium	97.5	101.1	106.4	104.9	106.2
Denmark	115.2	112.2	105.0	105.8	107.5
Germany (West)	124.3	118.6	119.1	117.6	116.4
Greece	34.8	46.4	52.3	47.5	47.8
Spain	58.3	72.2	71.7	75.4	77.2
France	107.7	112.7	113.9	110.0	111.9
Ireland	57.2	56.1	60.2	69.0	71.6
Italy	86.6	95.5	102.5	102.8	104.0
Luxembourg	155.3	138.4	115.6	127.2	129.8
Netherlands	116.8	114.1	109.2	102.4	102.6
Portugal	37.2	46.9	52.7	53.7	58.1
United Kingdom	122.6	103.5	96.4	100.5	96.2
EC 12	100	100	100	100	100
Standard deviation	36.6	29.1	24.4	24.3	23.8
United States	182.5	158.4	146.0	139.0	136.7
Japan	54.1	88.8	96.5	112.7	118.1

SOURCE: Commission of the European Communities, *European Economy*, no. 54 (Brussels: Commission of the European Communities, 1993), p. 206.
NOTE: Per capita GDP is given at current market prices per head of population and in purchasing power parities. The figures for 1993 are estimates.

now divided into a north with a per capita gross domestic product (GDP) above the EC average and a south—Greece, Portugal, Spain, southern Italy, and Ireland—with a below-average GDP per capita. This has tended to give relatively greater importance to inter-industry specialization associated with exploitation of comparative advantage. In turn, such specialization may be causing more adjustment problems than past integration.[4]

Further indicators of economic integration that are of interest in connection with migration movements are the development of incomes across the member states and the

4. André Sapir, *Regional Integration in Europe*, Economic Papers no. 94 (Brussels: Commission of the European Communities, 1991), p. 11.

availability—or lack—of jobs. Migrations of labor depend to a large extent on income differences between regions/countries and job opportunities.

In Table 2, as a proxy for income, the development of per capita GDP in the 12 EC countries is shown in relation to the EC average. The table shows that per capita GDPs of the EC countries have converged. As a measure of this convergence, in the last line the spread from the mean value (standard deviation) is shown. The decrease in values from 1960 (36.6) to 1993 (23.8) means a lower spread around the EC average.

Such global average figures do, however, conceal differences between the regions within the EC countries. These differences can be considerable. In Italy, the north-south gap is

TABLE 3
UNEMPLOYMENT RATES IN EC COUNTRIES (Annual averages)

Country	1971-80	1981-90	1992
Belgium	4.6	10.7	8.2
Denmark	3.7	7.6	9.5
Germany (West)	2.2	6.0	4.5
Greece	2.2	7.1	7.7
Spain	5.4	18.5	18.0
France	4.1	9.2	10.1
Ireland	7.7	15.7	17.8
Italy	6.1	9.5	10.2
Luxembourg	0.6	2.5	1.9
Netherlands	4.4	10.2	6.7
Portugal	5.1	7.1	4.8
United Kingdom	3.8	9.7	10.8
EC 12	4.1	9.6	9.5
United States	6.4	7.1	7.3
Japan	1.8	2.5	2.2

SOURCE: Commission of the European Communities, *European Economy*, no. 54, p. 200.

particularly clear: Lombardy, in the north, has a per capita gross national product that is 37 percent above the EC average, while that of Calabria, in the south, is 44 percent below the EC average. Similar large differences between the highest and the lowest incomes in the regions of the member states occur in other countries. For example, West Germany ranges from 83 percent above average to 19 percent below average; France, from 67 percent above to 23 percent below; the United Kingdom, from 54 percent above to 23 percent below; the Netherlands from 34 percent above to 37 percent below; and Belgium, from 64 percent above to 22 percent below average.[5]

5. Figures are taken from Regio, the data bank of the Commission of the European Communities. To allow comparisons between regions, purchasing-power parities are calculated that express for each country the price of an identical volume of goods and services.

Another major indicator of regional welfare besides GDP relates to employment or, rather, the lack of it—unemployment. In 1975, the Community had an unemployment rate of 3.5 percent. By 1985, those out of work in the EC 12 amounted to 15 million, producing an unemployment rate of 10.8 percent. The situation improved up to 1990—8.3 percent— to worsen afterward. In 1992, the unemployment rate rose to 9.3 percent. With the exception of Germany and Luxembourg, the unemployment situation is more serious for the young and for women: in 1992 the unemployment rate for young people was 18.2 percent and for women, 11.2 percent.

Of course, the countries and regions of the Community are not affected evenly by unemployment. There are considerable differences between countries (Table 3). In general, the employment problem tends to exacerbate GDP inequalities, although a strict generalization must be avoided. The regional pattern of unemployment is not one that follows a simple core-periphery model. Regions with traditional industries that were radically restructured or even eliminated during the 1970s and 1980s also suffered very high rates. The relatively high rates recorded in the northern-central United Kingdom as well as areas like the West Midlands (12.4 percent in 1987) are testament to this fact. Elsewhere, patches of high unemployment can be found in the geographical center of the Common Market in regions like the Nord-Pas-de-Calais in France (14.0 percent) or Wallonia in Belgium (14.4 percent).[6]

The differences between low-income and high-income regions continue to persist over time. The economic regional differences can even intensify in the course of integration processes as, due to the disappearance of obstacles, competition is intensified. Thus the already competitive countries and regions are strengthened, and the competitively weak, mostly peripheral regions fall even further behind. In order to offset regional differences, the European Regional Development Fund was set up in 1975. The effect was small, however, since the funds provided were low and were scattered over too many regions.

With the creation of the single European market, the European Communities Commission became aware of the danger of the regions drifting apart and emphasized the necessity for countermeasures in the white paper on the completion of the single market.[7]

In 1988, various EC funds—a regional fund, an agricultural fund, a social fund—were brought together to form the structural fund, which concentrated on the less developed regions or on certain aims, such as the combating of youths' unemployment or long-term unemployment. At the same time, the funds provided were considerably expanded. In 1992, they reached almost ECU20 billion (1 European Currency Unit = US$1.3). By 1999, this amount is expected to have almost doubled. Thus they are no longer a *quantité négligeable*. In 1992, capital from the structural fund already made up 28 percent of the EC Commission's budget, and for countries such as Portugal, Greece, or Ireland, it meant several percent of their national products.

To sum up, it can be stated that tradewise in the European Community, a high degree of integration has been reached. The trade relations between the member states have become more intensified. Trade exchanges and competition took place less between economic sectors than within the industrial or product

6. Figures refer to 1987 and are taken from Mark Wise and Richard Gibb, *Single Market to Social Europe* (New York: John Wiley, 1993), p. 208.

7. "EC integration, by increasing the possibility for human, material and financial resources to move without hindrance towards the most economically attractive regions, could lead to an increase in regional disparities." Commission of the European Communities, *Completing the Internal Market*, White Paper from the Commission to the European Council, 1985, p. 8.

groups. Such a development results from the integration of countries with roughly comparable levels of economic development. Increased trade resulted from the specialization of products within industries rather than as a consequence of a division of labor in the form of production displacements. Production displacements would have ruined whole industrial units and caused mass redundancies. The ensuing unemployment would have acted as a potential incentive to migrate. This migration pressure did not in general occur.

As to incomes, seen across the member states in terms of per capita national product, they show a convergent tendency, although regional differences within the member states still are considerable. These persisting or even increasing gaps between low-income and high-income regions within member states tend to contain potential migration flows within individual member states and tend not to induce workers to migrate across national borders. Employment, another indicator of welfare and a factor in migration, did not live up to expectations: a continuous overall increase in unemployment can be observed.

MIGRATION OF LABOR
IN THE EC: THE EFFECT
OF FREE MOVEMENT

Free movement of labor, that is, the opportunity to look for employment in another EC country and to hold it just as any national of that country, has been a reality for the six founding members—France, Italy, the Federal Republic of Germany, Belgium, the Netherlands, and Lux-

embourg—since 1968.[8] It now applies to all 12 member countries. Thus it is one of the major achievements of European integration.

When free movement of labor was being discussed in the 1960s, there were fears that Italian workers would flood the labor market.[9] At that time, Italy was the major European emigration country. But the overflow of Italian workers did not occur. The employment of Italian workers in the EC did, in fact, increase, but the growth in Italian migration between 1962 and 1972 was below the average for EC members as a whole.

Nor did the accession of the United Kingdom, Ireland, and Denmark in 1973 prompt a wave of migration, and this was also the case with full free movement of labor for Greek workers in 1987. There is no reason to expect developments with Spain and Portugal to be any different; the transition period to full free movement of labor for these states expired on 1 January 1993.

Table 4 shows the development of foreign populations and foreign worker populations in the EC member states. It can be seen that the employment of EC workers remained

8. Free movement of labor in the EEC Treaty means the "abolition of any discrimination based on nationality between workers of the Member States as regards employment, remuneration and other conditions of work and employment."

9. Cf. R. Penninx and P. Muus, "No Limits for Migration after 1992? The Lessons of the Past and a Reconnaissance of the Future," *International Migration*, no. 3, p. 373 (1989); Heinz Werner, "Freizügigkeit der Arbeitskräfte und die Wanderungsbewegungen in den Ländern der Europäischen Gemeinschaft," *Mitteilungen aus der Arbeitsmarkt- und Berufsforschung*, no. 4, p. 339 (1973).

TABLE 4
FOREIGN POPULATION AND FOREIGN EMPLOYEES IN EC COUNTRIES (In thousands)

Foreign Population, Foreign Employees	Year	Belgium	Denmark	Germany (West)	Greece	Spain	France	Ireland	Italy	Luxembourg	Netherlands	Portugal	United Kingdom
Foreign population total	1975		94	4.090	70	165	3.442					109*	
	1980	879*	100	4.453	98	183			211*	96*	473	80	1.682*
	1985	898	108	4.379	106	242	4.061	79		99	559	87	1.700
	1986		117	4.513	121	293				98	553	90	1.736
	1987			4.241	155	335					568	94	
	1988	859	136	4.489	173	398		84	407§		592	101	1.852#
	1989	869	142	4.846	172	408		79	434‖		624	101	1.894**
	1990	881	151	5.242‡	184	408	3.597	81	490	117	642	108	2.476††
	1991	905	161	5.343				88	781	115	692		2.429
of which: EC countries	1975			1.616	19	93	1.860						
	1980	598*	25	1.503	30	108			79*	89*	168	21	712*
	1985	584	26	1.357	34	142	1.566	65		93	173	23	729
	1986		27	1.365	38	170				91	162	24	754
	1987			1.240	46	193					160	25	
	1988		27	1.276	50	231		66	90		157	27	828#
	1989		27	1.325	50	241		62	100		160	29	879**
	1990		27	1.422‡	54	241	1.312	63	130	106	163	29	873††
	1991		28	1.439				69	149	103	169		782
of which: non-EC countries	1975			2.474	52	72	1.582						
	1980	281*	75	2.950	68	75			132*		306	59	971*
	1985	314	82	3.022	74	98	2.495	14		6	386	64	971
	1986		91	3.148	83	122				7	391	66	982
	1987			3.000	109	140					408	69	
	1988		109	3.213	123	166		17	206		435	74	1.025#
	1989		115	3.520	122	167		17	236		464	72	1.015**
	1990		124	3.819‡	130	167	2.285	18	361	11	479	79	1.603††
	1991		133	3.904				19	632	13	524		1.647
Foreign employees total	1975	230	41	2.091	25		1.900	13	10	49	113		791
	1980	213	39*	2.041		59	1.208*				190	26*	833*

	1985	187	39	1.555	24		1.260	20	57[†]	53	166	31	821
	1986		43	1.547	24		1.173	21		55	169		
	1987	177	46	1.557	25		1.131	20		59	176	33	
	1988	179	47	1.577	24		1.160	22		64	176	35	982
	1989	196	47	1.646	22	50	1.203	20		71	192		
	1990		47	1.740	23	63		21	381	78	197	37	751
	1991		47	1.842	30	76		24	234	87	214	40	704
	1992		45	1.967		168			309	92			
of which: EC countries	1975	174	14	849			1.045			46	59		347
	1980	159	11*	732	5	31	653*				84		406*
	1985	141	12	520	6	28[†]	640	17	14[†]	50	76	7	398
	1986		12	498	7		590	16		52	88		
	1987	130	13	484	7		569	16		56	83	8	
	1988	131	13	473	6		568	18		61	85	10	410
	1989	141	13	483	7	24	579	16		67	88		
	1990		13	493	9	30		16	50	74	90	8	347
	1991		13	497	18	36		19	44	81	92	8	333
	1992		13	476		39			45	87			
of which: non-EC countries	1975	56	27	1.242			855			3	55		444
	1980	55	28*	1.309	19	28	555*				106		427*
	1985	46	28	1.036	18	29[†]	620	4	43[†]	3	90	24	423
	1986		30	1.048	18		583	4		3	92		
	1987	47	32	1.074	18		562	4		3	95	26	
	1988	49	35	1.104	17		593	4		3	93	26	572
	1989	56	34	1.163	15	26	624	4		4	103		
	1990		34	1.247	14	33		5	332	4	109	29	404
	1991		35	1.346	12	40		5	190	5	122	32	371
	1992		33	1.491		129			264	5			

SOURCE: Eurostat.

*1981.

†1983.

‡30.9

§Including 111.167 people of unknown nationality.

||Including 97.911 people of unknown nationality.

#Average 1986-88.

**1987-89.

††1989-91.

stagnant or even dropped. How can the generally declining migration of labor between the EC countries be explained? This question will be approached by presenting some theoretical considerations on the determinants of labor migration before we sum up our findings.

DETERMINANTS OF LABOR MIGRATION

Economic theory provides two hypotheses concerning why workers move. According to integration theory,[10] the creation of a single market generates additional welfare effects by enabling labor to move to where it is most productive. The theory argues that a shift occurs from less productive to more productive jobs until marginal productivity and hence pay (for the same work) are in alignment within the area of integration. Prerequisites to this are, of course, that labor is mobile, that workers are informed of the job opportunities in other countries, that no other constraints on migration exist in the narrow sense—work permits, residence permits—as well as in the broader sense, such as recognition of qualifications, cultural differences, living and housing conditions, and language.

In contrast, classical foreign trade theory proceeds from the immobility of labor between states. The differences in production factor endowment —mineral resources, capital, technology, labor—are balanced out by means of trade, which raises prosperity. Each country concentrates on producing those goods for which it has a comparative advantage over the others, that is, those which it can produce more cheaply (the Heckscher-Ohlin theorem). According to this theory, trade relations induce a division of labor in line with the comparative production advantages between countries. From this standpoint, labor migration is thus unnecessary. Trade is a substitute for labor migration. Apart from that, capital is more mobile than labor.

To better understand the migration process, it is useful to discuss the mobility of labor between countries of different levels of economic development and of similar levels of industrialization.

Up to the beginning of the 1970s, most European industrialized countries pursued a comparatively liberal policy toward immigrant labor, when there was a corresponding need for labor. Obviously, when the receiving country adopts such an immigration and employment policy and there is a pronounced differential between levels of industrialization and employment and earnings prospects in the receiving and sending countries, the influx from the less developed countries will persist; in fact, it will grow. Böhning has called this the "self-feeding process of migration."[11]

10. Robson, *Economics of International Integration*, p. 65; Thomas Straubhaar, "Labour Migration within a Common Market: Some Aspects of EC Experience," *Journal of Common Market Studies*, p. 46 (Sept. 1988); George Borjas, "Economic Theory and International Migration," *International Migration Review*, no. 3, p. 457 (1989).

11. W. R. Böhning, *Studies in International Labour Migration* (London: Macmillan Press, 1984), p. 68 ff.

This self-feeding immigration is engendered by two factors. At the beginning of the immigration, the foreign workers take on jobs that are already unattractive to nationals. After a certain period, they obtain jobs that indigenous workers leave for status or prestige reasons. As it is easy to get foreign workers, new foreign workers replace foreign workers in jobs that the latter now find socially undesirable. For nationals, therefore, the employment of foreigners affords them greater vertical mobility. On the other hand, another cause of self-feeding immigration is that foreign workers tend to fetch their families, friends, and acquaintances to the receiving country. A migration push will continue to exist as long as there are enormous wage disparities between the receiving country and the country of origin. This cannot in principle be excluded even for a saturated labor market, as evidenced by the influx of emigrants from non-member states or economic refugees to the EC.

The considerations just described will gain new relevance in the context of the opening of the borders toward the Eastern European countries. It is clear from past migration experience that significant numbers of people could move from Eastern Europe in search of work in the Community and other countries if they become free to do so.

All the investigations conducted so far on voluntary migration indicate that a major determinant is the differential in economic development and hence earning opportunities. Between countries of similar levels of development, the pressure to migrate for economic reasons is low. In the course of the integration process, an alignment of economic development and, therefore, pay can be expected. Thus a major migration impulse—income differentials—will further diminish. The prosperity gap has also been lessened by increased trade between the EC countries.

To sum up, cross-border labor migration between EC countries has not increased.[12] Trade has substituted for migration. Intra-industry trade, a characteristic feature of European integration, as mentioned earlier, risked less the loss of whole industry units—and hence jobs—in favor of other countries. Furthermore, capital is more mobile than labor and can therefore act as a substitute for migration. Migration thus does not behave complementarily to trade relations between the EC countries.[13] Classical foreign trade theory is confirmed here. This, of course, does not rule out that here and there sectoral or qualification-related gaps can emerge between countries that then generate a migration potential. This may result in movements of specialists, managers, or other highly skilled manpower but not in large-scale migration.

12. The mobility of labor between EC countries thus declined along with the regional mobility within the EC countries. Cf. W. Karr et al., "Regionale Mobilität am Arbeitsmarkt," in *Mitteilungen aus der Arbeitsmarkt- und Berufsforschung*, no. 2, pp. 197 ff (1987).

13. Thomas Straubhaar, *On the Economics of International Labour Migration* (Bern and Stuttgart: Verlag Paul Haupt, 1988), pp. 127 ff.

WHAT TYPE OF
MIGRATION IN A SINGLE
EUROPEAN MARKET?

Twenty years ago, most Community member states experienced immigration of unskilled or semi-skilled migrant workers from outside the European Community, filling up the great shortages at the lower end of the labor market. However, employment and the demand for labor have changed radically since then: the number of vacancies for the least qualified workers is much lower; unemployment among them is disproportionately high. The presence of large numbers of unemployed nationals, citizens both of the European Community and from outside and with low levels of skills, means that even if demand for labor were to increase, provisions for it could easily be made without immigration.

In addition, certain general conditions have changed. Owing to their declining demographic trends—apart from Ireland and Portugal—and continued industrialization, the outlying countries of the EC that have served so far as labor reservoirs for the European industrialized nations will in the future need more workers themselves. Some countries, such as Italy, Spain, or Greece, are already drawing large numbers from the labor force of third countries, particularly from those in Africa and Asia.[14] For example, 1 to 1.5 million foreigners are estimated to be living in Italy, mostly illegally. With the opening of the borders of the East

14. Cf. Organization for Economic Cooperation and Development, *SOPEMI Reports* (Paris: Organization for Economic Cooperation and Development, annually).

European states, migration pressure will not only come from the developing countries but will also considerably increase from the East European countries.

As stated earlier, migration streams are strongly determined by different levels of income between the home country and the immigration country. But the emigration push does not solely depend on the absolute difference between income levels in the country of origin and the target country. The relative level of pay in the country of origin is important as well. If an income is socially acceptable in—commensurate with—the conditions at home, it may be assumed that the threshold to emigrate will be higher; that is, the absolute earnings differential could widen without necessarily causing labor to migrate. With increasing industrialization in the peripheral countries of the EC, economic development and pay in the EC countries have leveled out. Thus the threshold for economic migration to another country may be crossed in only some sectors or skill levels.

Based on the foregoing, it should be clear that, even after the completion of the single European market, there is no reason to expect spectacular migration of labor between current EC member states. But partial imbalances for certain groups of workers may arise and additional, economically motivated migration could occur.

Such migration could come about because specialists, managers, technicians, and other highly qualified labor will be in demand in all EC countries and are expected to move

TABLE 5

**FOREIGN EMPLOYEES IN THE FEDERAL REPUBLIC OF GERMANY
BY OCCUPATIONAL QUALIFICATION, 1977-92 (Indices 1980 = 100)**

| | Foreign Employees | | | | | |
| | Total | | | EC nationals | | |
Level of Qualification	1977	1987	1992	1977	1987	1992
Trainees	87	157	292	92	82	93
Employees with low qualification	96	74	94	103	62	60
Employees with middle-level qualification	93	87	109	94	78	82
Graduate employees	86	98	122	84	96	115
Total employees	95	80	102	100	67	67
Absolute numbers (in thousands)	1,889	1,589	2,036	730	492	494

SOURCE: Bundesanstalt für Arbeit.

across borders more frequently. This development is due to the globalization and internationalization of companies. Judging from data for the Federal Republic of Germany, the hypothesis of more migration of highly qualified workers can be confirmed (Table 5). Whereas overall employment of EC nationals has gone down, employment of graduates from EC countries has risen almost throughout, although the level is still quite low. This phenomenon, incidentally, is not confined to the EC countries; it can be observed worldwide.[15]

A survey of multinational companies in the EC[16] commissioned by the Commission of the European Communities proves that "Euro-executives" are more and more appreciated. These are either nationals with experience abroad or from the EC countries. A stay abroad is increasingly considered desirable and supported by companies as one stage in a successful career. This practice of going abroad is bringing about a highly qualified, internationally mobile group that is linguistically, technically, and culturally flexible. The members of this group are still small in numbers now, but they will be increasingly in demand by companies acting internationally.

Migration could also take place because regional economic areas near the borders will become more tightly merged. Certain Euroregions could develop where national frontiers will increasingly forfeit their separative function. Commuting between a residence and a workplace that are in separate countries could expand here. This is true, for instance, for the Franco-German border, where such commuting has increased.

Workers in border areas are particularly fast to react to changes in the neighboring country. In addition,

15. John Salt and Allan Findlay, "International Migration of Highly Skilled Manpower: Theoretical and Development Issues," in *The Impact of International Migration on Developing Countries,* ed. Organization for Economic Cooperation and Development, Development Centre (Paris: Organization for Economic Cooperation and Development, 1989), pp. 159 ff.

16. Ulrich Walwei and Heinz Werner, "Europeanizing the Labour Market: Employee Mobility and Company Recruiting Methods," *Intereconomics,* pp. 3-10 (Jan.-Feb. 1993).

many of the obstacles that play a role in migration across borders do not apply to these workers or are less important: normal surroundings, including housing, need not be changed, children can continue on in the national school system, the spouse can keep his or her employment, language problems are relatively minor, because of the proximity of the border.

Migration of a particular sort can be found in temporary exchanges in education and on-the-job training, study courses abroad, business travel, and the like. These will increase, and they will not necessarily mean a permanent change of residence. Such stays abroad need not be recorded statistically and are therefore difficult to quantify. Nevertheless, it seems certain that they are increasing, because they are connected with the internationalization of business firms. They are a modern form of or a substitute for the traditional migration of labor. A number of programs of the Commission support such exchanges financially.

THE BIG QUESTION:
THE FUTURE OF IMMIGRATION
FROM EASTERN EUROPE
AND THE THIRD WORLD

Almost all Western European countries have experienced a dramatic surge in the number of people seeking asylum in recent years. In 1974, regular recruitment of foreign workers was drastically lowered in the wake of the oil price shock and the poor labor market situation. Even today there is a more or less stringent freeze on hiring foreign workers from outside the EC. Only reunification of families and certain exceptions were permitted, if no suitable labor was available on the national labor market. Access to the rich countries was possible only when applying for asylum or by staying illegally. The Geneva Convention for Refugees protects those who are suffering political persecution but not those attracted to the richer countries because of the economic plight of their home countries—the so-called economic refugees. Determining and verifying whether or not there is real political persecution in an individual case is difficult and takes time. Applicants rejected after many years are frequently allowed to stay on for humanitarian reasons.[17]

The pressure of this migration will not stop. If checks of people at the common borders of the EC countries are abolished, a uniform type of control at the outside borders has to be established. Otherwise, economic refugees could gain access to the EC at the easiest point of entry and then apply for asylum in another country or reapply if their original application had been rejected. This is why policies regarding visas and asylum must be uniform throughout the EC. Policies regarding aliens and asylum seekers are still, however, considered to be strictly national affairs.

The transformations in Eastern Europe and the opening of the borders were political events of major significance. Compared to the Western industrial countries, the East European countries are poor. Their

17. In the Federal Republic of Germany, 440,000 persons applied for political asylum in 1992. Even if the application is rejected, most of them are allowed to stay.

economies are not structured as those that have been formed under the competitive conditions of free market economies. Restructuring will take time and money, neither of which these countries possess.

For the time being, investment from outside will not be high enough to assure rapid economic progress. Proceeds from exports will be minor for some time, because low productivity and poor quality standards prevent East European exports from being really competitive. Industries that might still be competitive—such as agriculture, textiles, or steel—meet resistance when demanding an opening of the EC markets. The counterparts of these industries in the EC either are subsidized or are themselves having problems.

At any rate, high unemployment can be expected in the course of the restructuring process. For lack of funds, unemployment benefits will not be any compensation for wages lost during the foreseeable period of mass unemployment. Therefore these countries will experience strong pressure for emigration. The consequences of this pressure depend, among other things, on whether the people perceive any improvement in the near future in their own country.

REGIONAL INTEGRATION AND UNWANTED MIGRATION: WHAT INSIGHTS?

It seems clear from EC history that regional integration can attenuate socioeconomic disparities that propel people to emigrate. Over time, regional integration through increased trade and welfare has had a leveling effect among EC states that has dampened migration. Expectations of massive migration from poorer areas northward to more advanced regions in other member states generally were not borne out. Freedom of labor movement has not resulted in massive migration between EC member states, nor is there any reason to expect this situation to change. Indications are that movements of highly skilled workers between EC member states will continue to grow while the migration of low-skill workers between member states will stagnate or decline.

Regional integration in the EC case has generally taken place between economies at roughly similar stages of development. But within countries, considerable differences between regions can exist. Where these regional disparities persist, they often foster large-scale migration, but much of this has remained within member states, as in the case of southern Italians migrating to Milan or Turin. The pattern of trade exchanges and competition taking place more within industrial or product groups than between economic sectors meant that adjustment to freer trade generally did not ruin whole industries and cause mass redundancies.

NAFTA differs from the EC in important respects. The Mexican economy is dwarfed by the United States and there are large gaps in development and wages between the United States (and Canada) and Mexico. NAFTA is more comparable to the European Free Trade Association than to the EC in that there is no explicit project of fostering political community, which would also require the transfer of funds from richer to poorer countries, as has been the case in the EC. Nor is there an analogous provision for freedom of labor mobility between the NAFTA countries. It has not been an explicit aim of the EEC or EC to prevent unwanted migration.

The EC faces an enormous challenge in controlling immigration from the South and from the East. There is a rough analogy between the challenge faced by the EC and the situation confronted by the United States and Canada. This shared dilemma makes reflection on the history of EC regional integration and its effect on international migration timely, but the many differences between the two contexts warn against the facile presumption that Mexico necessarily or quickly will go the way of Italy now that NAFTA has been ratified.

ANNALS, *AAPSS*, **534**, July 1994

Helping Migrants to Stay at Home

By W. R. BÖHNING

ABSTRACT: The relatively new but growing phenomenon of international migration pressure is documented and explained by reference to the widening income and trade gap between middle-income emigration and high-income immigration countries as well as by reference to the crucial role of networks. The three main international instruments for helping emigration countries to generate employment and income faster than in the past are then reviewed—trade expansion, foreign direct investment, and official development assistance. Trade is shown to have bypassed most emigration countries; growing protectionism does not augur well for the future. Foreign direct investment, similarly, has mostly taken the form of an exchange between rich countries or of inflows into Pacific Rim countries. Official development assistance is increasingly looked at as an option to be exploited for the purpose of reducing migration pressure. There are problems, of course, and little besides lip-service to date. An International Labour Office initiative to have emigration countries, immigration countries, and multilateral organizations collaborate is a promising approach to mobilizing increasingly scarce aid funds.

W. R. Böhning was trained as a political scientist at the Free University of Berlin but became an economist during his five years at the University of Kent at Canterbury before joining the International Labour Office (ILO) in Geneva, Switzerland. His publications include The Migration of Workers in the United Kingdom and the European Community *(1972);* Black Migration to South Africa *(editor, 1981); and* Studies in International Labour Migration *(1984). His current position with the ILO is as chief of the Migration and Population Branch in the Employment and Development Department.*

A DAM Smith's dictum that man is of all the most difficult luggage to transport would sound incredible to Immigration and Naturalization Service officials along the Rio Grande, to border guards at Germany's Neisse River, or to immigration officials in Tokyo's Narita Airport, who never before had to cope with so much "luggage" and so many ingenious modes of transport. From their questioning as to the foreigners' motives, they would conclude that a little help given to the impoverished seeking entry would go a long way to make them stay at home.

That judgment is at heart correct but very difficult to put into practice with lasting effect because it goes beyond help extended to individuals. It involves crucially the context and structures that make people move, apparently inexorably, from poor to rich countries.

This will be the subject of this article. I shall illustrate several arguments in simple graphical form by reference to countries that are typical of those that, in the last thirty years or so, have seen many of their ordinary laborers and well educated move abroad for economic reasons. I shall leave aside typical refugee-producing countries, such as Sri Lanka or Sudan, because I am increasingly convinced that financial or technical assistance does not lend itself to tackling the root causes of refugee outflows—ethnic tensions, highly autocratic or dictatorial regimes, elitist economic policies, and so on.[1] I shall

also leave aside major emigration countries such as Egypt, Pakistan, or Indonesia whose citizens move primarily to countries such as Saudi Arabia or Malaysia; I shall do so because the latter are not considering promoting the more rapid development of their emigration partners through special measures in their favor.

The countries used for the purpose of illustration are Colombia, the Philippines, Morocco, and Turkey. Colombia and the Philippines are major source countries of immigration into the United States. (Mexico will be disregarded because it is an overstudied case and because it forms part of the North American Free Trade Agreement, a trade relationship from which other migrant-producing countries will not benefit.) Morocco and Turkey are major source countries for immigration to France and Germany, respectively, but also to other European countries.

---

1. In 1991 the International Labour Office (ILO) and the United Nations High Commissioner for Refugees (UNHCR) commissioned a series of regional and country case studies to explore whether development aid could be structured and targeted in such a way as to make it unnecessary for people to expatriate themselves on economic or political grounds in one or two generations hence. UNHCR's researchers came up with very little in that context—not because they were short of ideas but because refugee-producing situations, while they may ultimately be calmed by economic growth with equitable income distribution, are intractable in the face of economic remedies that can be provided by official development assistance. For a list of these studies and a summary of the discussions to which they gave rise, see *Joint ILO-UNHCR Meeting on International Aid as a Means to Reduce the Need for Emigration, Informal Summary Record* (Geneva: ILO and UNHCR, 1992). A selection of the studies can be found in W. R. Böhning and M. L. Schloeter-Parades, eds., *Aid in Place of Migration?* (Geneva: ILO, 1994).

What is striking about these and other typical migrant-sending countries is that they are, in World Bank parlance, middle-income countries. For reasons that no doubt have to do with geographical and cultural proximity or ease of economic penetration and relationships, today's major emigration countries are rarely among the poorest countries of the world, just as emigrants from them come disproportionately from low- or middle-income households rather than from the very poorest families.[2] That being said, more and more nationalities turn up in rich countries, as revealed, for example, by recent European amnesties.[3] Their countries of origin could not yet be qualified as major emigration countries, but one single person can start a network that may expand and defy immigration restrictions.

MIGRATION PRESSURE

The economic parameters of the world have changed dramatically in the last several generations. While it was once necessary to send out recruiters from, for example, Johannesburg to Mozambique or from the southwestern United States to Mexico or from London to Barbados or from Frankfurt to Turkey to entice sufficient numbers of people to turn

the wheels of capitalist economies, today more foreigners are knocking at advanced countries' doors than these countries are willing to admit. Demand pull has been replaced by supply push. "Migration pressure" is the term coined to characterize the new situation.

The term is suggestive but controversial as to its scientific validity[4] and difficult to measure.[5] Put most simply, emigration pressure is embodied in the number of nationals who have taken steps to leave for (employment) abroad in excess of those who, legally or illegally, have already managed to do so. Immigration pressure is the mirror image: the number of non-nationals who have taken steps to enter (for the purpose of employment) in excess of those who have been admitted legally or who have made it into the country illegally. I have put the employment reference in parentheses to indicate that not all migration pressure is of a purely economic nature even where one focuses on economic migration streams; family reunification can be an important component of migration pressure. One should also note that the concept is cast in terms of concrete steps rather than intentions. Lots of people in sub-Saharan Africa or Central and Eastern Europe tell interviewers about their desire or intent to leave for richer

2. By contrast, among refugee-producing countries are several of the world's low-income countries, and among refugees from African or Asian countries one frequently finds the poorest of the poor. The refugees who reach Europe or North America, however, come disproportionately from relatively well-off households.

3. Just over 100 nationalities turned up in the Italian regularization of 1987. Four years later, 184 nationalities were registered in another amnesty.

4. See G. Tapinos's contribution in C. B. Keely and G. Tapinos, *Two Views on International Migration*, Working paper (Geneva: ILO, 1992).

5. See P. V. Schaeffer's and Th. Straubhaar's contributions in W. R. Böhning, P. V. Schaeffer and Th. Straubhaar, *Migration Pressure: What Is It? What Can Be Done about It?* Working paper (Geneva: ILO, 1991).

countries, but relatively few actually take steps to that end—the distinction matters.

Emigration pressure can be documented in, for example, the Philippines and Turkey. Filipinos, initially recruited for Hawaiian plantations, took advantage of the 1965 U.S. Immigration Act and the employment opportunities in Persian Gulf states after the oil price rises of the 1970s. Today, over 1 million are active abroad, but at home the queue is getting longer. One-quarter of the Filipinos who aspire to work abroad actively search for an opportunity to do so,[6] which comes to 2.2 million people. In Turkey, emigration was practically unknown until the second half of the 1950s. Nowadays, 2 million Turks labor abroad, and another million remain registered with the Turkish Employment Service to that end.[7] An International Labour Office survey of key informants in Turkey found that, in 1989, 20-50 percent of Turkish men aged 20-35 would emigrate if they could. This would add up to 7 million persons if one were to put the proportion at 33 percent.[8]

Immigration pressure can be measured in the case of the United States by the length of the queue under individual preferences and by the apprehension statistics of the Immigration and Naturalization Service—the queues keep growing and

the number of apprehensions, rising. In Western Europe, the immigration pressure has manifested itself in the last ten years or so through increasing numbers of persons claiming refugee status who were not, in fact, politically persecuted, as is evident from the drop in the rate of status decisions in their favor—now well into single-digit figures in many countries. As Western Europe did not generally want to admit primary labor migrants, the asylum detour represented the easier way into a country. This door is now becoming more firmly guarded.

But why are middle-income countries experiencing high emigration pressure and industrial countries, growing immigration pressure? Is this a passing or a lasting phenomenon? The answers to these questions are not difficult to find. They can be inferred from Figure 1.

Even though individual migrants state a variety of economic or personal reasons for leaving their country, the idea of earning more income dominates and decisively influences the choice of destination. To earn more income, a Filipino cannot usually turn to Papua New Guinea but has to set his sights on Japan, Saudi Arabia, Spain, or the United States.

Average income calculated as gross national product (GNP) per capita, albeit an imperfect indicator, is a useful approximation to visualize the income gap that is the key motivation of economic migrants.[9] The citizens of all the world's middle-income countries today enjoy 11 percent of the average GNP per capita of

6. *Social Weather Bulletin* (Manila) (Jan. 1991).

7. F. Uygur, *Foreign Aid as a Means to Reduce Emigration: The Case of Turkey*, Working paper (Geneva: ILO, 1992), p. 35.

8. See Philip L. Martin, *The Unfinished Story: Turkish Labour Migration to Western Europe* (Geneva: ILO, 1991), p. 94.

9. The data on GNP per capita (current US$) are drawn from World Bank statistics.

FIGURE 1

INCOME GAP: COLOMBIA, PHILIPPINES, MOROCCO, AND TURKEY

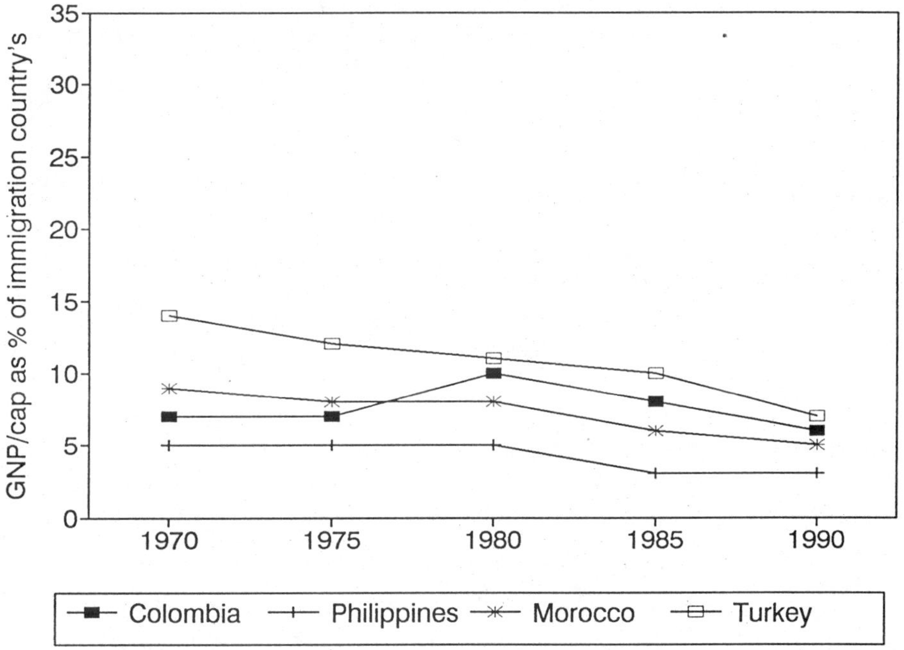

SOURCE: World Bank statistics.

NOTE: The data on gross national product per capita (in current U.S. dollars) are expressed as a percentage of U.S. GNP in the case of Colombia and the Philippines, French GNP per capita in the case of Morocco, and German GNP in the case of Turkey.

France, Germany, and the United States combined, compared with 14-15 percent ten or twenty years earlier. They have good reasons for wanting to join them, and more reasons today than a generation ago.

Adjusting current GNP by currencies' purchasing power—US$1 buys more goods and services in a poor country than in a rich one—would reduce the income gap considerably, as Table 1 indicates. However, the 1:5 difference in the case of Colombia versus the United States and the difference in the case of Turkey versus France and Germany is evidently too large to induce Colombian and Turk-ish citizens to stay at home. If intra-European migrations are anything to go by, the differential has to narrow to 1:3 or 1:2 for mass movements to turn into more individually driven phenomena,[10] where freedom to choose is a reality and noneconomic factors holding people back become more important.

10. See W. Molle and A. van Mourik, "International Movements of Labour under Conditions of Economic Integration: The Case of Western Europe," *Journal of Common Market Studies*, 26(3): 317-39 (1981); W. R. Böhning, *Mediterranean Workers in Western Europe: Effects on Home Countries and Countries of Employment*, Working paper (Geneva: ILO, 1975).

TABLE 1

CURRENT GROSS NATIONAL PRODUCT PER CAPITA AND REAL GROSS DOMESTIC PRODUCT PER CAPITA: ABSOLUTE AMOUNTS AND PROPORTION OF EMIGRATION COUNTRIES' INCOME TO IMMIGRATION COUNTRIES', 1990 (U.S. dollars)

	Colombia	Philippines	Morocco	Turkey
Gross national product per capita	1,260	730	970	1,640
as percentage of U.S., French, or German gross national product per capita	6	3	5	7
Real gross domestic product per capita (purchasing power parity)	4,237	2,303	2,348	4,652
as percentage of U.S., French, or German real gross domestic product per capita	19	11	13	26

SOURCE: World Bank statistics; United Nations Development Programme, *Human Development Report 1993* (New York: Oxford University Press, 1993).

The downward-sloping lines in Figure 1 demonstrate the widening income gap between middle-income emigration and high-income immigration countries. Widening means that emigration pressure should be growing rather than subsiding—which is exactly what Immigration and Naturalization Service personnel at the Rio Grande, German border guards, and Japanese immigration officials observe. Purchasing-power comparisons over time might render such a judgment more complex.

What neither average GNP nor real gross domestic product comparisons catch is income distribution and the dynamic role of migration networks and chains, which facilitate and sustain flows when economists' static or time-period comparisons would expect migration flows to ebb. Migration networks, which derive from existing migrant populations and agents or even smugglers, may be more important than income differentials. After all, there are several countries—such as Angola or Laos—where workers earn 1 percent or less of what their fellow workers in rich

countries earn. Yet there is no migration pressure from them because there are no networks. Where significant income differentials are linked by networks, flows occur and are difficult to stop administratively.

What can be done to reduce the attractiveness of temporary or permanent emigration? Economic growth yielding sufficiently productive employment opportunities is the evident answer. That task is, in the first instance, the responsibility of the emigration countries themselves. Despite sometimes very sound policies and respectable growth rates, which are, however, decreasingly employment-intensive,[11] the task of closing the gap seems to be beyond many emigration countries' capacities. Support has to come from the outside to help them achieve that goal. Three key international measures are available—trade, foreign direct investment (FDI), and official development assistance (ODA)—and they will be examined briefly in turn.

11. See United National Development Programme, *Human Development Report 1993* (New York: Oxford University Press, 1993).

FIGURE 2
TRADE GAP: COLOMBIA, PHILIPPINES, MOROCCO, AND TURKEY

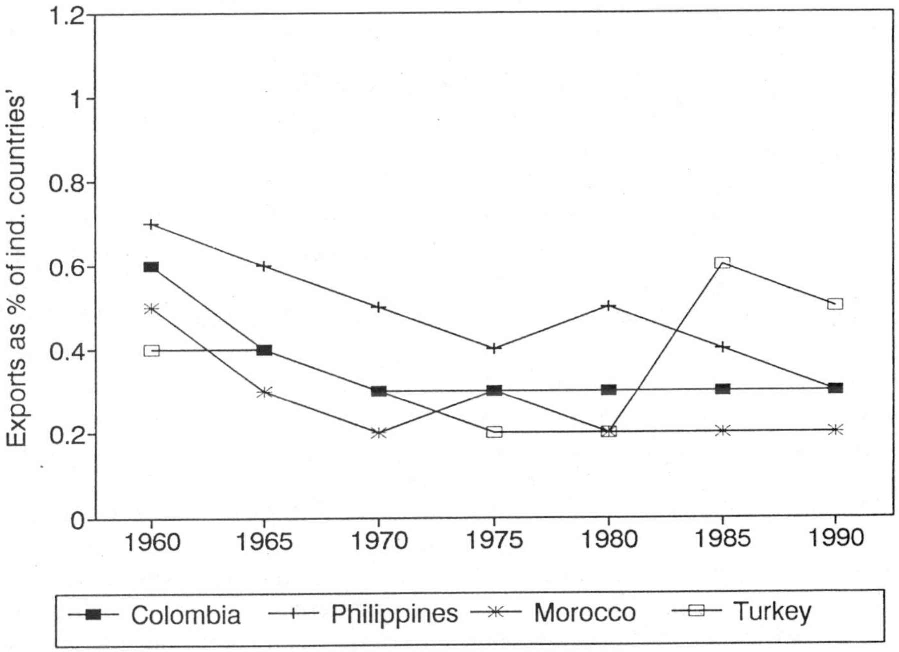

SOURCE: The statistics on countries' exports are from *International Financial Statistics* (International Monetary Fund).

NOTE: The statistics on countries' exports are calculated as a percentage of all industrial countries' exports.

TRADE

Trade expansion, as the U.S. Commission for the Study of International Migration and Cooperative Economic Development emphasized, "is the single most important long-term remedy."[12] The trouble with international trade is that governments exercise a great deal of control

12. Commission for the Study of International Migration and Cooperative Economic Development, *Unauthorized Migration: An Economic Development Response* (Washington, DC: Commission for the Study of International Migration and Cooperative Economic Development, 1990), p. xv.

over it, chiefly to protect politically powerful domestic producers and workers, and this mainly in respect of employment-intensive products that would be of greatest benefit to emigration countries. The example of the Florida sugar growers is sufficiently well known not to be retold here. Polish beef and steel, Tunisian textiles, Mexican tomatoes or strawberries, among others, could be added to the list of migration-promotion products controlled by rich countries.

Of course, international trade has expanded tremendously since World

War II. But it expanded more rapidly among Organization for Economic Cooperation and Development (OECD) countries than between them and their low- or middle-income trading partners. As Figure 2 demonstrates, Colombia, Morocco, and the Philippines commanded in 1990 merely half the market share of industrial countries that they did thirty years earlier.[13] Only Turkey fared relatively well after democratization and liberalization in the early 1980s.

To narrow the trade gap and thereby reduce migration pressure, immigration countries must enable emigration countries to export an increasing share of goods and services to them. But not only has the secular trend generally gone in the wrong direction, but recently "trade protection in OECD countries became more widespread, especially in sectors where developing countries have a distinct comparative advantage."[14] This, says the OECD, "discourages new investment in the export sector" and "has

contributed to increase the demand for low-cost migrant workers."[15]

The U.S. commission's view has actually been borne out in Pacific Rim countries—the Republic of Korea, Malaysia, Singapore, Taiwan, as well as Hong Kong—but the general picture is bleak. Even while Turkey marginally increased its international market share, strong population growth nullified much of its trade performance, as a comparison of Figures 1 and 2 indicates. Whereas middle- and low-income countries would need to capture a growing share of the profitable export market, they actually have to contend with a decreasing proportion due to factors over which they have no control. The expansion of trade is, as long as one can see ahead, not likely to be the international instrument that would decrease most countries' emigration pressure.

FOREIGN DIRECT INVESTMENT

FDI basically takes two forms— tariff-hopping investments aiming to supply local markets, and investments for export purposes. Tariff hopping makes sense with large and growing markets, which some middle-income countries, such as Mexico, can boast of but not by any means all of them. Export-oriented FDI has been Japan's strategy toward Pacific Rim countries, with notable success. In effect, domestic policies coupled with Japanese FDI have led to a situation where former emigration countries, such as the Republic of Korea,

13. The statistics on countries' exports have been culled from *International Financial Statistics* (International Monetary Fund) and calculated in Figure 2 as percentage of all industrial countries' exports. The latter earned about three-quarters of the world's export dollars in 1960, only 1 in 2 dollars when oil prices rose in the 1970s and early 1980s, but by 1990 their market share had crept back to 74 percent.

14. Organization for Economic Cooperation and Development, Development Cooperation Directorate, "Development Challenges, Development Cooperation and Migration," OECD document GD 93(39) (Paper for the "Conference on Migration and International Cooperation: Challenges for OECD Countries," Madrid, Mar. 1993), p. 17. This paper summarizes both tariff and nontariff impediments inflicted on developing countries recently.

15. Ibid., pp. 18 and 19, respectively.

FIGURE 3
**FOREIGN DIRECT INVESTMENT, NET:
COLOMBIA, PHILIPPINES, MOROCCO, AND TURKEY**

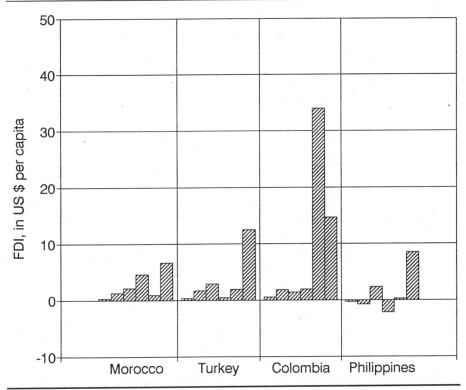

SOURCE: Data from *International Financial Statistics* (International Monetary Fund).
NOTE: For each country, the first bar relates to 1965, the second to 1970, the third to 1975, the fourth to 1980, the fifth to 1985, and the last to 1990. The data are in current U.S. dollars. These are net FDI figures; a minus sign indicates net outflows of FDI from the country.

Malaysia, and Taiwan, have experienced both high growth and labor shortages leading to demand-pull immigration. Greece, Italy, Portugal, and Spain have similarly turned from emigration into immigration countries.

The general picture of FDI's migration-reducing potential is not as sanguine as these somewhat special examples suggest. Figure 3 shows the amount of FDI per citizen of the selected typical emigration countries. These amounts, not surprisingly, are small, while the marginal cost of creating one workplace in those countries runs into tens of thousands of dollars. Colombia comes out highest with US$34 per capita in the mid-1980s; the Philippines lost FDI during much of the last 30 years.

It is instructive to compare these amounts with those received by Pacific Rim countries. Malaysia's net receipts per capita went up from

US$68 in 1980 to US$130 in 1990, Thailand's from US$4 in 1980 to US$41 ten years later, and Singapore's from US$471 in 1980 to US$1237 during the same period.

The full story about FDI is similar to the tale about trade. FDI has disproportionately favored traditional industrial countries or, indeed, the new industrial economies of the Pacific Rim. At the end of the 1960s, some 30 percent of FDI went to the developing countries, but by the mid-1980s their share had dropped to 25 percent and by the end of the decade, to 17 percent. The explanation lies in a mixture of small, unprofitable markets in sometimes unwelcoming and sometimes politically unstable countries, on the one hand, and better prospects in the United States, the European Economic Community, or Japan, on the other. The last few years, however, suggest a reversal of this trend, with an increasing share of FDI being directed to developing countries.

FDI, then, is as much or as little an instrument to induce economic migrants to stay at home as is international trade. While the secular trend is not entirely clear, middle-income countries need to render themselves as attractive as possible to receive the kind of tariff-hopping or export-oriented FDI that would help them to grow faster and employ more of their citizens.

Unfortunately, the problem with FDI is that immigration countries' governments have practically no control over either the amounts or the destinations of FDI. Both are in the hands of the private sector, which will decide by return-on-capital criteria rather than socially desirable considerations such as the reduction of migration pressure. Even state-controlled enterprises of OECD countries would not accept governmental directions on where to invest.

OFFICIAL DEVELOPMENT ASSISTANCE

This leaves us with ODA, over which governments exercise full control. The picture here is quite impressive as far as the volume of ODA is concerned, which exceeded US$50 billion in recent years. Figure 4 shows ODA for three middle-income emigration countries in per capita amounts on the same scale as Figure 3 for FDI. The per capita U.S. dollar receipts are at a level similar to FDI in the case of Colombia; they are not negligible in the case of the Philippines; and they dwarf per capita FDI amounts in the case of Morocco.

The problems with ODA are severalfold, however. First is its use. As a child of the Cold War, much ODA has been allocated for military purposes, but that component, it is hoped, will now decline. Development aid consists partly of technical advice, partly of grants, partly of loans that have to be repaid, and part of it tends to be tied to supplies from rich countries. Respectable economists continue to doubt the beneficial impact of ODA, arguing that low- and middle-income countries were less constrained by scarcity of financial capital than generally assumed and that aid reduced "the domestic rate of savings" and encouraged "capital flight by lowering the real rate of interest and tem-

FIGURE 4
DEVELOPMENT ASSISTANCE:
COLOMBIA, PHILIPPINES, AND MOROCCO

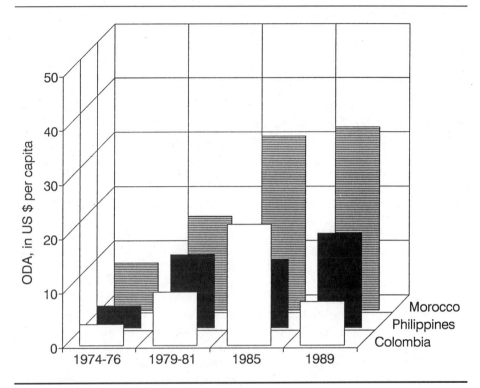

SOURCE: Data from United Nations, *Statistical Yearbook* (New York: United Nations, various years).

NOTE: The data are in current U.S. dollars, calculated per head of the population of the receiving country. Comparable statistics for Turkey are not given in the source because Turkey is an OECD country.

porarily appreciating the exchange rate."[16]

Be that as it may, it does not have to be the same in the future. ODA, whether in the form of technical assistance or untied capital infusions, could be structured and targeted with a view to reducing international migration pressure.

For the last several years, Western European governments and OECD, European Economic Community, or Council of Europe meetings have many times called for international aid to be used to stem migration flows. The Canadian government has given it some thought.[17] Japan, too, is

16. K. Griffin and T. McKinley, *Towards a Human Development Strategy*, Human Development Report Office Occasional Papers (New York: [United Nations Development Programme], 1993), p. 68.

17. See M. Brem and Ph. Rawkins, *Development, Assistance, Migration and the Cana-*

interested in the idea. By contrast, neither Australian nor U.S. officials have seriously considered putting the issue on the policy agenda—Australia apparently because it still feels sufficiently far removed from migrant-producing countries, and the United States probably because it pursues a relatively open immigration policy and presumably hopes that the North American Free Trade Agreement will eventually render Mexico more attractive to Mexicans.

What is striking in vociferous Western Europe is how much has been said and how little has been done about using ODA for stay-at-home development. The OECD held two major conferences—in Rome, in April 1991, and Madrid, in March 1993— yet the Italian Ambassador to Tunisia had to confess in his Madrid address that nothing concrete had been done to implement the call for "cooperation in place of migration" in the interval between the two conferences.

An International Organization for Migration (IOM) seminar on migration and development took place in Geneva in September 1992.[18] It sprang from the rather narrow and dated idea of identifying how migration movements themselves could be organized to foster development—an idea that is not a priori groundless if looked at solely from the static perspective of countries of origin. But it does not take into account that planned demand-determined immigration flows tend to help migrant-receiving countries more than sending countries, that is, they widen rather than narrow the gap between them.

AN ILO INITIATIVE

The International Labour Office, having commissioned a study in the late 1970s on trade in place of migration,[19] became involved in the "aid in place of migration" debate in 1991 when it launched, in association with the United Nations High Commissioner for Refugees, studies that sought to identify the scope and limits of ODA in enabling emigration countries to generate employment and income more rapidly than in the past. These were mainly country case studies and thus were closer to reality than previous work. The discussions to which they gave rise at a joint ILO-UNHCR meeting in Geneva, in May 1992, were revealing of both the enthusiasm and the skepticism that surround this debate.[20] The enthusiasm was most evident among European governments, both governments of Western Europe's main immigration countries and governments of Central and Eastern European countries undergoing transition to market economies. Skepticism was aired by a number of researchers, not so much on grounds of the inherent problems of promoting employment creation but based on ODA's track record and anticipated decline. Several governments of middle-income emigration countries similarly pointed

dian Agenda: Linking Policy, Programmes and Actions, Working paper (Geneva: ILO, 1992).

18. See the special issue of International Migration, 30(3-4) 1992.

19. See A. Hiemenz and K. W. Schatz, Trade in Place of Migration: An Employment-Oriented Study with Special Reference to the Federal Republic of Germany, Spain and Turkey (Geneva: ILO, 1979).

20. See fn. 1.

to their receipts of remittances, going into billions of U.S. dollars—indeed, exceeding the concessional aid flows in toto—while they were not confident that more ODA or the right kind of ODA would be forthcoming in future years.

It was clear to the ILO that more of the same, let alone less of it, would not be the key to using ODA to decrease emigration pressure. It was also clear that ministerial speeches were not the most promising way to set in motion desirable changes. As a result, a different approach, a bottom-up approach, was launched, and the Maghreb's three major emigration countries—Algeria, Morocco, and Tunisia—were focused on because they were prepared to give it a try.

What does the new approach consist of? First, it seeks to involve, from the beginning and throughout the process, development practitioners of both concerned immigration countries and the emigration countries willing to try out the new idea. Second, it strives to organize all interested immigration countries and relevant multilateral organizations in such a way that they put their minds and means together to come to a division of labor on agreed programs of action rather than to continue sprinkling aid here and there in response to needs whose origins are not always clear and which may have nothing to do with the generation of employment and income for the emigration country in question.[21]

After preliminary discussions between development and employment specialists from Belgium, France, Germany, Italy, Spain, and several international organizations, on the one hand, and from Algeria, Morocco, and Tunisia, on the other, general proposals were prepared by Morocco and Tunisia and were examined by European and international experts during national workshops in each of these two countries in the autumn of 1993. (An Algerian workshop had to be postponed due to the current developments in that country.) The revised and greatly more specified proposals of Morocco and Tunisia will be submitted to decision makers for funding or technical support at a donor meeting at the ILO in 1994.

21. Cooperation between donors is also necessary to avoid ODA activities that actually encourage emigration pressure, such as when training courses are set up and staffed with trainers from European countries and turn out workers whose skills may not be in demand in the Maghreb countries for the foreseeable future but prove marketable on the other shore of the Mediterranean Sea.

Book Department

INTERNATIONAL RELATIONS AMD POLITICS

BIENEN, HENRY S. and NICOLAS VAN DE WALLE. *Of Time and Power: Leadership Duration in the Modern World.* Pp. xiv, 215. Stanford, CA: Stanford University Press, 1991. $25.00.

This thin volume is, at the authors' own insistence, a study in the use of statistical theory; at their urging, it should not be read as a foray into political analysis. But despite this repeated admonition, Henry Bienen and Nicolas van de Walle would ask the community of political science scholars to give serious attention to their findings, conclusions that focus on the length of time in high political office of presidents and prime ministers, kings and military rulers. Their study examines the passage in chronological time of more than 2000 leaders, representing every continent, from a period midway into the nineteenth century to 1987. The ambitiousness of this effort is recorded in the approximately 80 pages of tables enumerating how many years each leader spent in power, whether they came to power through constitutional or nonconstitutional means, how they left office, whether they were civilians or members of their armed forces, and, finally, which among them returned to serve yet another term.

It must be noted that Bienen and van de Walle do not examine the question of succession, nor do they dwell on issues of legitimacy or how influence is manifested and power demonstrated. Rather, the scant 106 pages of narrative aim at explaining the character of the study, the methodology chosen, and the significance of the data they have collected and sifted. This study, in spite of all the data provided, is nevertheless little more than raw material for students concerned with the broader and deeper issues of political tenure.

Leadership skills, for example, are not investigated, the authors arguing that such material does not yield to quantification and would be better pursued through more traditional political analysis. Bienen and van de Walle, however, believe event-history, their choice (they reject multivariate regression techniques as unsuitable to their purpose), is a useful approach and does yield to statistical methods. The coding of executive leaders was a significant factor in the approach taken because it often became necessary to shift attention from a president to a prime minister or from a formal leader to an informal one. The strategy adopted by the authors was obviously daunting, and, as such, they knowingly exposed themselves to challenges, albeit criticism, that question the methodology employed, the introduction and selective use of data, and, more obviously, some of the conclusions they draw from their exhausting sample.

One illustration of the problem can be cited three-fourths through the narrative, where the authors discuss leaders and the subject of risk. They note that their findings indicate a lower level of risk for leaders coming to power in the 1970s than those who did so in the 1960s. They also state in the same paragraph that the new states created after World War II had lower leadership turnover than in European countries, where stability had actually increased. Turnover therefore is not a measure of stability.

Bienen and van de Walle find their explanation for such observations in the age of leaders, which they insist is "positively" correlated with risk, that is, older leaders become more vulnerable. They also stress that, contrary to conventional wisdom, military leaders face no higher risks than do civilians. In fact, they argue, once military leaders have entered power "unconstitutionally" and, it is assumed, consolidate their power or gain popular acceptance, their risk of losing office is lower than that of the civilians measured. It is also stated that there are higher risks for leaders in Latin America, North America, Europe, and Australasia than in Africa, the Middle East, and Asia.

The reader's need for something more than quantified data is obvious when such findings are considered along with, for example, the assassination of Sheikh Mujibur Rahman in 1975, the murder of Mohammad Daud in 1978, and the execution of Zulfikar Ali Bhutto in 1979, all relatively young men who came to power in the 1970s. In addition, although the authors do not ignore the differences between political systems, they do not satisfy the reader that the matter of risk can not only be reduced to a cipher, but that it can be studied without reference to the diversity of and disparity between political cultures.

We should know something about the conditions and the issues that lead to the demise of original leaders, who the authors suggest show greater capacity for long-term rule. There must be more detail on successor leaders and why they are judged greater subjects for risk. Moreover, while external factors are noted, they, too, are passed over as less than germane to the study. What then can one cite about the fall of Nkrumah or the demise of Sukarno, let alone the collapse of the Shah of Iran or the forced resignations of Ayub Khan and Yahya Khan and the assassinations of John Fitzgerald Kennedy and Indira Gandhi, which cut across all categories and demand elaboration, not simply a somewhat arbitrary categorization?

It is difficult to accept the authors' argument that the character of leaders is more important than socioeconomic considerations in putting leaders at risk. By the same token, the idea expressed that some countries are more easily governed than others demands more rigorous content analysis. In the absence of such efforts, Bienen and van de Walle can only cite the obvious, such as that monarchs generally rule longer (p. 91) or that dictators do not yield power willingly (p. 93).

In sum, this book is a methodological innovation, not substantive political inquiry and analysis. The reader will find an emphasis on personality without exploration of its dimensions. Bienen and van de Walle raise the issue of constitutionalism, but they do more to skew constitutional theory than to clarify what is meant by constitutional structure and behavior, let alone constitutional and unconstitutional entrance or exit. At no point, for example, do they treat the subject of constitutionalism in the context of limited government.

The problem for me, and I would assume for others as well, is that given the need to reduce the available data to specific categories and numerical features, the conclusions presented are less valuable for political insight than they are as statistical exercise. Moreover, Bienen and van de Walle seem to prefer it that way. Perhaps a more modest title would have better focused the reader's attention; it certainly could have established the limits of expectation.

LAWRENCE ZIRING

Western Michigan University
Kalamazoo

JOHNSTON, RICHARD, ANDRÉ BLAIS, HENRY E. BRADY, and JEAN CRÊTE. *Letting the People Decide: Dynamics of a Canadian Election.* Pp. x, 316. Stanford, CA: Stanford University Press, 1992. $37.50. Paperbound, $12.95.

Letting the People Decide presents an interesting and well-written account of the Canadian party system, anchored as it was in 1988 by the governing Progressive Conservative (led by Brian Mulroney), Liberal (led by John Turner), and New Democratic organizations. The authors examine issues, leaders, and media influences in this free-trade election using data from their rolling cross-sectional survey as well as from public opinion polls and media studies. The data are presented clearly and help to document the bases for another Conservative majority. Readers learn that Turner's debate performance plus the anti-free-trade argument citing danger to Canada's social programs were significant during the early stages of the campaign. As time passed, however, pro-free-trade advertising and doubts nurtured by the Conservatives about Turner's competence helped to turn the tide.

The authors make a number of important contributions in this study. They presage major ongoing tensions in the Canadian party system, notably the entrance of new organizational players. They acknowledge the reality and diversity of media influences, and they address Quebec's distinct responses to party leaders as well as political issues. Finally, they emphasize the substantive importance of election campaigns, underlining the role of party strategies.

One dimension of the 1988 campaign that is neglected involves pro- and anti-free-trade interests; the book refers to this phenomenon as a "striking intrusion of third-party advertising." Because they challenged older partisan models of electoral competition, the interventions of the Pro-Canada Network, the Canadian Alliance for Trade and Job Opportunities, and other groups on both sides of the trade debate were crucial. These coalitions operated within a polarized ideological environment that set neoconservative market solutions and continentalism on one side, against interventionism and nationalism on the other. Giving some voice in the book to unorganized citizens and organized groups, rather than only to party leaders and their strategists, would have revealed much of this decision-making context.

It is notable that *Letting the People Decide* ignores women, women's groups, and social movements generally. Poll data from 1988 indicated, among Canadian women, approximately 20 percent less support for free trade and considerably lower support for Prime Minister Mulroney, parallel with President Reagan's gender gap in the same period. English Canadian women's groups have strongly opposed free trade since 1985. The inclusion on p. 95 of abortion and child-care items in a factor analysis pool suggests the need for some attention to gender, since readers could mistakenly conclude that these issues emerge and organize along traditional territorial or class lines.

Questions of context and agency can be addressed in survey research, including analyses of the next Canadian election. By setting a high standard in many areas, *Letting the People Decide* challenges empirical scholars to take them on.

SYLVIA BASHEVKIN

University of Toronto
Ontario
Canada

MOYNIHAN, DANIEL PATRICK. *Pandaemonium: Ethnicity in International Politics.* Pp. xvii, 221. New York: Oxford University Press, 1993. $19.95.

In 1931, Heidegger's antipode at Heidelberg, Karl Jaspers, who lived just a few houses away from the former residence of Hegel, published *Die geistige Situation der Zeit*. During the Cold War, their student Hannah Arendt wrote on the human condition. With the Cold War over, these significant works are now complemented on a high level by the book under review. It is a sequence to the author's previous studies on ethnicity, *Beyond the Melting Pot: The Negroes, Puerto Ricans, Jews, Italians, Irish of New York* (1964) and *Ethnicity: Theory and Experience* (1975), studies done in collaboration with Nathan Glazer. An elaboration of the distinguished 1991 Cyril Foster Lecture at Oxford University, *Pandaemonium* crowns these studies. Due to events during the past years, it shows convincingly that Moynihan, for a long time considered a lonely and often disliked voice on account of his emphasis on ethnicity and its power, has been right all along.

Disturbed by the riots in the 1960s, I and many others for a long time saw the Soviet Union as a solid block, a serious danger to the West. Moynihan stood almost alone in predicting its demise owing to ethnic conflicts. That demise has become evident since the fall of the Wall, a fall that prompted Leonard Bernstein to conduct Beethoven's Ninth Symphony in East Berlin, replacing the Ode to Joy with an ode to freedom. Ever since, the risk involved in that replacement has become increasingly obvious. More and more ethnic groups have claimed their right to self-determination, an idea advanced by Woodrow Wilson. It has become evident that conquest of, and dominance over, ethnic groups as well as Schiller's hope that all men would be brethren, shared in one way or another by Marx and others, cannot quell the desire of such groups to emphasize their own particular character and to assert their respective ways of life.

This has been the most obvious in the former Soviet Union and Yugoslavia. But Moynihan's comprehensive and well-documented study shows that it can be found all over—in Africa, Asia, Europe, and Latin America. Moreover, ethnicity plays a role not only in international politics but also in national politics. Well-established nonimmigration democracies such as Austria, France, Germany, and Great Britain have become aware of it, as has an immigration country like the United States. Recent riots in Los Angeles have demonstrated it, as have the books *The Disuniting of America: Reflections on a Multicultural Society* (1991), by Arthur M. Schlesinger, Jr., and *Two Nations: Black and White, Separate, Hos-*

tile, Unequal (1993), by Andrew Hacker. One can see in Moynihan's work a confirming sequence of these studies. It is hoped that it will find a broad audience, for it points to serious problems in liberal democracies and is sobering in its warning that the expectancy that after World War II there would be an eclipse of ethnicity was mistaken. Certainly, the fluent, readable style of the book justifies expectations of such an audience.

Moynihan's warning is not without hope. Freud's sad comment that what he learned as a boy in his history classes was that ethnic groups annihilate each other need not, according to Moynihan, be affirmed. For him, ethnic cleansing is not inevitable because the dynamics of ethnic conflict can be moderated through an understanding of the basic value of ethnic pride, a pride in belonging that to me, probably in line with Heidegger, warrants protection as a human right.

GOTTFRIED DIETZE

Johns Hopkins University
Baltimore
Maryland

TUCKER, ROBERT W. and DAVID C. HENDRICKSON. *The Imperial Temptation: The New World Order and America's Purpose.* Pp. 228. New York: Council on Foreign Relations Press, 1992. $22.50. Paperbound, $14.95.

LUNDESTAD, GEIR. *The American "Empire" and Other Studies of U.S. Foreign Policy in a Comparative Perspective.* Pp. 214. Oslo: Norwegian University Press; New York: Oxford University Press, 1991. $29.95.

After nearly a half-century of Cold War politics filled with circumscribed rationales on American foreign policy and narrowly defined debates on alternative directions, the current atmosphere of discussion is refreshingly open and exciting.

What should be borrowed, saved, or discarded from the bipolar era to structure peace in the New World Order? Among the darker questions emerging in this environment is whether a unipolar system signals the dawn of the age of American imperialism at the expense of the long-anticipated Age of Aquarius. The implicit assumption is that continued U.S. policy practice, with its particular brand of realism and status quo ideology buried in the rhetoric of morality and universalism, will promote just that.

This pair of books, despite differences in emphasis and intended audiences, addresses this critical issue by exploring how the United States dominates the world. On their titles alone, these books are telling: empires are customarily looked upon as illegitimate forms of governance, and the notion of imperialism has been recently politicized to denote improper, even villainous behavior. By strict definition, though, an empire is a state substantially larger than others in territory, resources, global issue involvement, recognition, and sense of duty to the entire international system. This portrays the current role of the United States accurately. The focus in these studies is this: Will American foreign policy play up the negative features of power by exerting coercion and control over sovereign states, leading to charges of empire rule? Or will decision makers develop the positive face of domination expected of a country that has acquired an empire (by default or invitation or design) and is therefore obligated to govern the world community responsibly?

Tucker and Hendrickson organize their study around large topics: part 1, "America's Road to the New World Order"; part 2, "The Gulf War: An Autopsy"; and part 3, "American Security and National Purpose." Essentially, though, the twenty short chapters highlight their basic argument with the Bush administration. These leaders acted unwisely, they assert, by missing the opportunity brought about by the end of the Cold War to exercise restraint and civility, and the consequence was the Gulf war, a mistake drawn from misinterpreting moral responsibility that should have been undertaken. Criticism is sweeping and deep, yet with Bush out of office, the case seems to lose its bite, striking one as oddly outdated. This is sad, for the analysis deserves an airing. Perhaps the proper venue for such heated, reasoned evaluation would have been a journal rather than book format, if the authors intended to encourage debate on current issues.

Here is what they say: The Cold War finale "dramatically broadened" the decision latitude for American foreign policy, and unfortunately, the U.S. administration opted to follow a dangerous path, succumbing to imperial temptations by an overexertion of military force to silence aggression. They see this behavior as evidence of a "Faustian bargain": The United States has a pathological attitude toward the use of force that requires massive use of American firepower and speedy withdrawal from the scene of destruction, unaccompanied by any sense of responsibility. This is not acceptable, for it offends the dictum that war is but a means to a peaceful end. Following a clinical examination of U.S. Gulf war policies—the best arguments for diplomatic and political solutions are found here, along with sensible points about physical reconstruction and regime replacement in Iraq—Tucker and Hendrickson finish off with some general questions about the original understanding of American security and how this was altered in recent times.

Although their final word is pessimistic, suggesting that current U.S. policies have betrayed the nation's purpose and prefigure the end of American history, there is a hope expressed that the imperial temptation will be resisted. This rests on the belief that American power can be used differently if we recapture our exceptionalism. "We have forgotten some of the very elements of our political order that were intended to make us exceptional," they write.

With all of these blanket conclusions and warnings, it is helpful to turn to Lundestad, who provides some balance. This work is also flawed by datedness and suffers from discontinuity between chapters, but the commentary gives some distance to the mainstream assessments drawn by Americans about what is right or wrong. Lundestad, a Norwegian, consciously brings a European perspective to his subject. There are four chapters, three of them published before. The four are "Moralism, Presentism, Exceptionalism, Provincialism, and Other Extravagances in American Writings on the Early Cold War Years"; "The American 'Empire' 1945-1990"; "Uniqueness and Pendulum Swings in US Foreign Policy"; and "The United States, Great Britain and the Origins of the Cold War in Eastern Europe."

Lundestad is skeptical about claims of American exceptionalism; he states, "To many Europeans, what was unique about America was its uncanny ability to make the most inspiring idealism coincide almost perfectly with rather ordinary national objectives." He pleads for less moralism and less America-centered analysis and recommends greater focus on the interplay of international and local factors to explain the outcome of events involving U.S. foreign policy. Arguing that the Americans have exerted great influence in many cases, particularly post-World War II rebuilding, he also recognizes many situations where the superpower's control was limited, citing Eastern Europe, Vietnam, Iran, and Lebanon.

He asks for a two-sided appraisal when suggesting greater attention be paid to local factors: to remember that "locals tend to insist on the importance of the local scene, unless the outcome is unfavorable, when it is convenient to blame the outsiders," and that America's rule in local arenas often represented "empire by invitation," meaning local consent and support, since Washington was seen as the leader of the free world. The core of Lundestad's argument is a rather commonly held European perspective that these invitations turned sour · because as soon as the Americans had committed themselves economically, politically, and militarily, there was a growing tendency to complain about the strings attached to U.S. assistance. Once the benefits of the American presence were taken for granted, cries about interference became more vocal. On the whole, he concludes, American foreign policy has rested on firm principles, showing a balanced perspective on the use of power; the country has not been as dominant as conventional wisdom would have us believe. From this assessment, he is led to a conclusion exactly the opposite of Tucker and Hendrickson's, namely, that the passing of the Cold War means in all likelihood a diminished role for the military in regulating international politics.

As it happens, these books are talking to each other. Lundestad has the advantage of objectivity by cultural heritage and can temper the gloomy appraisal of Tucker and Hendrickson, who benefit, in turn, from their own commitment of purpose and dedication to policy improvement by virtue of their American nationality. Although these two works offer some interesting analyses, it is hard to see, from their glimpses of the huge landscape of past and future American foreign policy, any model for reform or mechanisms for opening a dialogue. Without subtlety, Tucker and Hendrickson have tried to be controversial in contributing their arguments to the discussion over the New World Order. To do this, they appear to be addressing the Republican Party, Bush voters, and Gulf war supporters. Lundestad wants to gather those European critics who have been jumping on American foreign policy for years and show them a voice of fairness and moderation. Will these scholars achieve their purpose of serious consideration by the opposition? The catchy titles of the books may ensure some interest, but beyond that, substantial impact on this vast terrain is probably unlikely. On second thought, we might want to check the pulse of the nation in ten years.

KAREN A. FESTE

University of Denver
Colorado

AFRICA, ASIA, AND
LATIN AMERICA

CALMAN, LESLIE J. *Toward Empowerment: Women and Movement Politics in India.* Pp. xxiii, 230. Boulder, CO: Westview Press, 1992. $45.00. Paperbound, $15.95.

PESTONJEE, D. M. *Stress and Coping: The Indian Experience.* Pp. 240. Newbury Park, CA: Sage, 1992. $32.00.

The authors of *Toward Empowerment* and *Stress and Coping* have focused on what they see as two serious social problems in India. Leslie Calman thinks that the growth of the women's movement after 1980 is a possible solution to the problem of violence against women. D. M. Pestonjee argues that stress is bad for one's health and offers solutions for individuals seeking ways to avoid stress. Calman portrays economic development and urbanization as the way women can seek liberation from tradition, while Pestonjee cites evidence that urbanization and economic development lead to increased stress.

India is one of the few nations of the world where a majority of the population is male. It has been shown that while first-born girl babies and boy babies both have the same infant mortality rates, the second-born female infant in a family of two or more girls has a mortality rate much higher than would be expected. Calman does not emphasize such statistics in her argument. Rather, her technique is rich ethnographic description of individual cases to show that in India, just as in the West, "underlying patriarchal socio-religious institutions relegate women to a secondary status."

Calman has written the ultimate politically correct book about India. I use "politically correct" as a compliment, because she has done a good job making her case, at least within the limits of her theory. Getting beyond boilerplate, Calman provides an excellent and well-written description of the problem that women face in India when they try to get jobs and move beyond the family. There is no talk of the modernity of tradition here. Tradition and even the family prevent women from becoming "horizontally organized." The growth of modern institutions is seen as necessary for empowerment. The word "anger" appears in the first paragraph of *Toward Empowerment* and pretty well sets the tone of the book.

Pestonjee's book, *Stress and Coping: The Indian Experience*, pulls together in one place the empirical knowledge of the causes and solutions of stress in India. Beginning with stress in ancient India (including the *Yogasutras* and *Bhagavad-Gita*), Pestonjee ends up with a book similar to an annotated bibliography with connecting dialogue. For many readers, *Stress and Coping* may well be more useful as a reference book.

What causes stress in modern urban India? A very interesting and previously unpublished dissertation is summarized to address this issue. Role stress is more severe among women, those with low income, and those who have to commute to work. The unmarried suffer more stress than the married, although large family size increases stress, too. Urbanization is associated with more stress than rural living.

Both volumes will probably be used as textbooks in specialized courses taught by the authors. For the general reader, Calman's volume provides a good background of recent political history and the women's movement in India, even if some may wonder if the solution to social violence in India is more westernization. Pestonjee's work will probably be consulted most by those who need a convenient and up-to-date summary of the empirical literature on stress in India.

GEORGE H. CONKLIN

North Carolina Central University
Durham

DABASHI, HAMID. *Theology of Discontent: The Ideological Foundations of the Islamic Revolution in Iran.* Pp. xxiv, 644. New York: New York University Press, 1993. No price.

Some fifteen years after the success of the Iranian Revolution of 1978-79, a plethora of literature has been published on that historic event. That this literature has been vastly unequal in quality and scholarship has only hampered our understanding of the precise historical, social, cultural, and political forces at work in the revolution's making. Amid this mounting scholarship, *Theology of Discontent* stands out as undoubtedly one of the most significant contributions to the study of the Iranian Revolution. Dabashi has written a book that is both insightful and thorough and yet quite modest in its central task: to decipher, from disparate and scattered essays, books, pamphlets, speeches, and tracts, the ideology of the Iranian Revolution.

The book concentrates on the life and the writings of eight revolutionary ideologues, four from secular backgrounds and four clerics. Al-e Ahmad, Shariati, Bazargan, and Bani-Sadr, all of whom were non-clerics, each in his own way sought to construct an ideological framework within which Islam could not only meet the challenges of modernity but also offer a political alternative to the hopelessly corrupt and destructive rule of the secular Shah Mohammad Reza Pahlavi. Through masterful and balanced use of rare and original sources, Dabashi demonstrates how these ideologues went about constructing a politicized Islamic ideology by relying on their specific fields of expertise as frames of reference. Al-e Ahmad, the explorer, both of himself and of Iran, tried to reignite the old Iranian passion for politicized religion. Shariati, the French-educated sociologist, sought to reconcile the central tenets of revolutionary Shiism, which he called "Alid Shiism," with those prevalent among the progressive European intellectual circles of his day. Bani-Sadr, the eternal student, theorized about Islamic economics, while engineer (*muhandis*) Bazargan highlighted the compatibility of a reinvigorated Islam with science and technology.

Politically active clerics did their own reinterpretations of core Shiite principles as well, legitimating an increasingly blunt opposition to the Shah's regime as mere adherence to the true essence of Islam. Here Dabashi concentrates not on the politically most consequential clerics —Ayatollahs Montazeri, Beheshti, and others—but rather on the most learned for whom political Islam became a central philosophical and ideological preoccupation. With different philosophical, and theological emphases and concerns, Ayatollahs Motahhari, Taleqani, Tabataba'i, and Khomeini went about meticulously reformulating the central premises of Shiism, which had previously become politically conservative and docile under the weight of the Pahlavi dictatorship.

The deceptively simple task that the book sets for itself, the reconstruction of

the Islamic ideology, is one of its greatest strengths. Dabashi refrains from such lofty attempts as, for example, placing the Iranian Revolution within a broader Shiite or Islamic framework or exploring the social and political causes of the revolution. Such tasks each require separate books in themselves. By concentrating on the evolution of the Islamic ideology, he is able to recount and reconstruct, in great detail, the intellectual evolution and erudition of his principal subjects and their accumulative significance for the revolution.

The tediously long length of the book —more than 500 pages of text—is more than made up for by an engaging writing style. The detailed citations, bibliography, and index all add strength to the serious scholarship that has gone into the writing of the book. For anyone seriously interested in the Iranian Revolution and in the main intellectual currents in contemporary Iran, *Theology of Discontent* is must reading.

MEHRAN KAMRAVA

Rhodes College
Memphis
Tennessee

HOLLAND, HARRISON M. *Japan Challenges America: Managing an Alliance in Crisis.* Pp. xiii, 233. Boulder CO: Westview Press, 1992. $24.95.

Harrison Holland is an experienced former diplomat who wants to warn Americans about the dangers of the emerging new era in the United States' relationship with Japan. His book includes brief accounts of Japanese ways of thinking and behaving and of current affairs including key binational relationships; two chapters on economic relations with the United States; plus one each on defense and political relations; a chapter on communications and rhetoric; and two chapters that look to the future.

The book takes up many of the issues that concern both Japanese and Americans today. How can Japan be induced to reduce its trade barriers and the surplus with the United States? Can the alliance be based on reciprocity or burden sharing? What is the proper balance between American pressure, Asian worries, and actual security concerns in defense policy? Will Japan assert itself internationally? Is there some way to avoid the poisoning of the U.S.-Japan relationship by all the harsh words used on both sides?

Holland does not answer all these questions—no one could—but he discusses them in an evenhanded and commonsensical way. The book is a solid introduction to U.S.-Japan relations for college students and general readers. The facts and viewpoints included will be generally familiar to specialists, but less familiar might be the views expressed by the more than 100 Japanese, from officials and experts to ordinary people, interviewed by the author in 1988-90. The many direct quotations give a good flavor of how these issues are perceived in Japan.

Holland's own view is cautiously optimistic. He worries about how quickly Japan can change and about the American proclivity to misunderstand and blame. Certainly there are many risks ahead. Still, the relationship has managed to get through many crises in the postwar era, and mutual interdependence has continued to grow. Responsible people in both Tokyo and Washington are well aware of how less pleasant the world would become if the United States and Japan cannot find ways to manage our inevitable conflicts.

JOHN CREIGHTON CAMPBELL

University of Michigan
Ann Arbor

EUROPE

DIUK, NADIA and ADRIAN KARATNYCKY. *New Nations Rising: The Fall of the Soviets and the Challenge of Independence.* Pp. vii, 292. New York: John Wiley, 1993. Paperbound, $14.95.

When it dissolved in December 1991, the Soviet Union was, in itself, a multicultural and multinational empire. It is now dissolving these imperial constraints and becoming, differentially, 15 independent nation-states.

Many in the United States, not excluding many government leaders, have found conceptual difficulty in this reality. We are reminded of George Bush's July 1991 lecture to Ukranians—in their own capital!—about the risks of "suicidal nationalism" in confronting Moscow. Most adult Americans have been victimized by our own systemic ideological hostility to being continuingly ignorant about the former union. Our foreign policy is only now beginning to deal with these lacunae. If the USSR was long a monolith for American strategists, it was in part because our media chose to depict it thus and public opinion accepted.

But the peoples of the Soviet Union were also imprisoned by an ideology devoted to maintaining ignorance of the union's cultural reality and its role toward the West. Moscow was the center for a co-opted political elite that drew its members from many regions of the union, but that had, with the passing of generations, itself become ignorant of the complexity of its empire. Mikhail Gorbachev could demonstrate his insensitivity toward regional nationalisms by means far more destructive than Bush's, since perfection of the Soviet authoritarian empire was his agenda's priority topic and his impatience with opposition often inspired his retaliation.

This volume deals with both sets of problems, although the former union's internal characteristics and tasks properly receive greater attention. To some extent, the importance of nationalisms, as disruptors of the central Soviet system, is overstated in chapter 1. But the politics of inequality, depicted in the second chapter, is a major issue in the present Commonwealth of Independent States. Czars as well as party apparatchiki had, for centuries, believed that Russians had an endowed right and duty to give the Eurasian empire identity, and one of the most provocative issues in the Russian constitutional convention of June 1993 was the resolution of this issue of non-Russians within the republic.

The following four chapters discuss Ukraine, the three Baltic states, the three Caucasus states, and the five Central Asian states. At least one of the authors visited many of these republics. Ukraine receives by far the best treatment; while a few pages seem almost excerpted from a Michelin guide, others report and analyze solidly if briefly the nature of Ukraine's values and political system, and its causes for contention with Moscow. The chapter on the Baltics is less successful, reporting a smattering of facts on three historic national systems that differ broadly. The Caucasus chapter's greater value is its introduction; its countries receive such varying treatment that the reader's understanding is not advanced greatly. The Central Asia chapter's introduction is strong and more formally academic than much of the book; its individual country treatments are, frankly, throwaways, with a disturbingly large number of references withheld for the concluding chapter.

Chapter 7, "Russians: Democracy or Empire?" offers fruitful chronicling, analysis, and conjecture. Intra-Russia political clashes, between progressive, reformist, pro-democratic President Boris Yeltsin and the many nationalist, imperi-alist, and economic quasi parties and groups to his ideological right, are placed in context. Personalities, groups, and positions are sketched helpfully. Nationalities receive less attention than might be expected. The reader is left in no doubt of the stakes at play in the clashes between Yeltsin and the neofascists who dominated the Congress of People's Deputies in 1993.

Chapter 8 offers conjectures and possibilities for the new tottery commonwealth and also for the relations of the West—and the United States—with this new continental country that is trying so hard to find internal agreement and stability.

Diuk and Karatnycky are competent observers, and one is academically prepared. The numerous faults of the book are thus often difficult to accept. Known authors are occasionally quoted, but their works are irregularly cited; there are no direct notations. Some sections of the discussion are so badly pieced together that they cry for competent editing. The quality of treatment varies so greatly that I feel that some portions should not have been printed.

On the other hand, the book seeks, currently and instantly, to fill a necessary place in the available literature. On the whole, it is a creditable effort.

PHILIP B. TAYLOR, JR.

University of Houston
Texas

HOLLIFIELD, JAMES F. *Immigrants, Markets and States: The Political Economy of Postwar Europe.* Pp. ix, 305. Cambridge, MA: Harvard University Press, 1992. $35.00.

Despite the subtitle, which implies a broad study of the political economy of post-World War II Europe, this book is primarily devoted to advancing James

Hollifield's thesis that liberal democracies around the world have since World War II developed political and social principles that are now so embedded in their political and economic decision making as to constrain them from statist efforts to regulate immigration. Basic to his analysis is the argument that the rights and privileges of citizens in the postwar world have become extended to noncitizens. He believes this has occurred because liberal norms and principles include human rights, which immigrants are using as an argument for their protection from the vagaries of the marketplace and from the arbitrary power of nation-states. Thus liberal democracies may try to regulate immigration according to the principles of sovereignty and national interest, but they are prevented from so doing because of increased emphasis in recent years on human rights. In other words, their own cultures and institutions have compelled the liberal states to modify or abandon statist policies of limiting immigration.

Hollifield then broadens his challenge to the traditional powers of the individual nation-state by arguing that if the European Community (EC) implements its plans under the Schengen Agreement to eliminate internal border controls among EC countries, "liberal constraints" will then come into effect at the regional level. "When rights such as freedom of movement are extended to citizens of the member states, can other members of these societies who are not citizens (only denizens) be denied equal protection?"

Since Hollifield defines North America, Europe, and Australia as the principal countries of immigration among the liberal democracies, his evaluation of the effect of "embedded liberalism" on U.S. immigration policy is interesting. He believes that rights-based politics originally intended to help African Americans obtain full civil rights have been extended to benefit immigrants. In his view,

"the United States has been compelled to live up to its liberal creed by the civil rights revolution, the growth of a hemispheric labor market, and by human rights activists who encourage immigration by individuals fleeing oppression from friendly regimes of the right, and not-so-friendly regimes of the left." As he sees it,

old notions of rights versus privilege, individual consent, national sovereignty, sovereign immunity, and other statist/realist conceptions of the relationship between the individual and the state have receded in favor of greater legal protection for the rights of groups and individuals. The judicial assault on the sovereignty and autonomy of the state has contributed significantly to the rise in the tide of immigration in the United States.

Looking into the future, Hollifield foresees that the "enclosure of the individual within national boundaries" will continue to weaken, and that immigration may be expected to increase dramatically, both from the former Communist countries of Central and Eastern Europe into the EC and more generally from the less developed countries in Central and South America, in Southeast Asia, and in Africa into the developed countries of the Organization for Economic Cooperation and Development (OECD) around the world. He looks forward to a new world order, based more than ever on liberal, rights-based principles, and foresees that immigration will become a more prominent feature of the international scene.

The startling feature of this whole book is its fervent conclusion that immigration is a defining characteristic of liberal democracy that will "change the concept of citizenship itself." Yet Hollifield's assumption that immigration will more or less automatically continue to increase and to erode the traditional concepts of citizenship and national control of movement across borders gives relatively little weight to the signs of significant political backlash against further massive immigration that have become increasingly visible in almost all the developed OECD countries around the world during the 1990s. His statement less than a year ago that, despite the flood of immigrants into Germany, "there is no sign of panic in German politics," and his bland assumption that "liberal pressures" would prevent, "in the German case, closing the refugee valve [through] a change in the Constitution (Basic Law)" contrast sharply with the fact that only a few months later the German government did take that very action.

In France, the opposition to the EC's Schengen Agreement has grown sharply, and the Balladur government has adopted strict new measures to curb immigration and easy acquisition of French citizenship. In Australia and the United States, the immigration debate is regularly featured on the television talk shows, in magazines with varying political views, and on the front page of national newspapers. Hollifield's optimistic assumption that increases in immigration are inevitable, and his dismissal of political opposition to past immigration policies as confined to marginal groups of right-wing extremists in France and Germany and to "nativists" in the United States, seem out of focus in light of current developments in the democratic countries. His assessment that it is impossible for liberal democracy to control immigration may well be under increased challenge in the near future.

How he will respond to changes in the immigration policy of developed democracies that conflict with his theses will be interesting. In the case of Japan, where the foreign worker population has been growing, his comment in a footnote is: "How the Japanese state copes with these [political and policy] dilemmas will be a true test of the liberal foundations of the regime." This implies that any government that moves to limit immigration or

to maintain the difference between the rights and responsibilities of its citizens and those of noncitizen residents is by definition statist and not democratic. If he responds to a more general failure of his predictions by charging that any democratic government that takes parliamentary action to amend its laws so as to control immigration and exercise the traditional rights of a sovereign nation has thus ceased to be democratic, he will be using a very narrow and highly debatable standard for defining democracy!

ROBERT A. BRAND

Pennsylvania State University
University Park

WILTENBURG, JOY. *Disorderly Women and Female Power in the Street Literature of Early Modern England and Germany.* Pp. x, 352. Charlottesville: University Press of Virginia, 1992. $39.50. Paperbound, $12.95.

A focus on gender relations has made us change the way we used to understand a whole range of phenomena. Feminist scholars have demonstrated that varying understandings of gender difference affect broad social realms—not only women's roles or family life but also political institutions, epistemology, and visions of the social order. In this tradition, Joy Wiltenburg's study of the representation of unruly women in early modern street literature goes well beyond the history of a literary genre. She employs insights derived from her reading of the tracts and broadsides so common in the early centuries of printing to make suggestions about the visions of social order that underlay them.

Her findings are fascinating and provocative, particularly those derived from her comparative reading of English and German sources. In one realm after another—from relations between husbands and wives to the depiction of notorious criminals—the English sources indicate a popular culture steeped in individualism and faith in the efficacy of individual action. German sources, on the other hand, suggest a world ruled by concern for the preservation of the collective order and fearful of the intervention of supernatural forces. With respect to women's power, the differences were significant, if not always in a consistent direction. For example, if English sources presumed that women shared their individualist orientation with men and thus were essentially like them, this meant that their motives for action could be seen as selfish fulfillment of their desires, especially through the wielding of sexual power. If German women were never granted equality of motivation with men and generally were represented as inferior and passive, at least they were occasionally honored for their special virtues as chaste virgins or devoted mothers.

Wiltenburg is very careful to avoid drawing unwarranted conclusions. As she herself writes, interpretation of sources like street literature "demands a full awareness of the uncertain congruences between literature and life." Nevertheless, her attention to the social visions of the rarely studied cultural milieus reflected in street literature does allow her to reach new insights. As mentioned earlier, some of these concern different notions of female power and powerlessness as these varied across cultures and over time. Other insights address specific historical issues like the origins of the companionate marriage and its connections to changing parent-child relations (Wiltenburg notes that the two did not necessarily change in tandem) or the relation between the visions of the educated religious reformers and more popular notions (she argues that English Protestant theorists echoed rather than caused

changing popular sentiments about relations between spouses). This is a rich and subtle study—as well as a very concrete contribution to our knowledge of the changing understandings of the difference that gender makes.

MARY JO MAYNES

University of Minnesota
Minneapolis

UNITED STATES

CONDIT, CELESTE MICHELLE and JOHN LOUIS LUCAITES. *Crafting Equality: America's Anglo-African Word*. Pp. xxi, 355. Chicago: University of Chicago Press, 1993. No price.

SMEDLEY, AUDREY. *Race in North America: Origin and Evolution of a Worldview*. Pp. xii, 340. Boulder, CO: Westview Press, 1993. No price.

"The American Negro problem is a problem in the heart of the American. It is there that the interracial tension has its focus. It is there that the decisive struggle goes on." So wrote the Swedish sociologist Gunnar Myrdal in the introduction to his magisterial study of American race relations, *An American Dilemma: The Negro Problem and Modern Democracy* (New York: Harper & Brothers, 1944). According to Myrdal, that "dilemma" was intrinsic to the national character, a product of the conflict between the egalitarian ideals of American civic culture and the harsh realities of racism.

If the last fifty years have erased the most grotesque features of the racial caste system that Myrdal took pains to depict, the competing claims of race and equality—prominent in the debate over such issues as political representation, employment, education, housing, welfare, and crime—have proved no more tractable. The volumes under review are to be welcomed for relating how these concepts have informed, and continue to inform, American public life.

Audrey Smedley's primary target is race, its etymology and scientific status. She makes the case that, in North America, race has been a cultural construct, manufactured to rationalize the dominance of those of northern European lineage. Further, she argues that until the present century, both the aim and the effect of much scientific investigation of race was to reinforce such notions; it is only lately that science has cast doubt on an idea that, despite significant changes in the structure of American race relations, retains popular currency.

Celeste Michelle Condit and John Louis Lucaites take equality in America as their principal object. In their view, equality's substance is continually reformulated through means of ordinary public discourse—a conversation entered into by white and black Americans alike. The authors' analysis suggests that (1) at any given point in America's past, African Americans have tended to argue for the most expansive understanding of equality mooted; (2) across American history, African Americans have tended to argue for progressively more expansive varieties of equality; (3) white Americans, while by no means unified in their understanding of equality, have addressed the American dilemma either by dehumanizing African Americans, regarding them as aliens and candidates for repatriation, or acknowledging their right to equality yet viewing them as culturally distinct and warranting special, and thus unequal, treatment—a reading of the evidence that Smedley's study endorses.

Each of the volumes deserves a wide audience, if not an uncritical one. Perhaps because of the breadth of Smedley's compass, her argument appears overly speculative in places. In particular, given that she leaves unexplained the mecha-

nism effecting the cross-fertilization of cultural and scientific ideas, the relationship at the heart of her essay remains more plausible than persuasive.

Condit and Lucaites are open to a similar charge. That African American leaders have spoken and written about equality does not necessarily mean that they have altered the way in which the nation has understood and implemented the concept. To establish the latter situation, one would have to know more about the institutional context through which African Americans have sought to exert their influence. Moreover, the authors' conviction that Americans share a common rhetorical culture, a culture that allegedly furnishes the unity of a heterogeneous society, is puzzling in light of the balance of their argument that at least one component of that culture—equality—has no essential meaning. If equality can cover both Jim Crow and affirmative action, one wonders just what the integrative properties of America's rhetorical culture are. Indeed, on that reading, one wonders whether the American dilemma is capable of resolution.

J. C. HARLES

Messiah College
Grantham
Pennsylvania

CORTNER, RICHARD C. *The Iron Horse and the Constitution: The Railroads and the Transformation of the Fourteenth Amendment.* Pp. xvi, 231. Westport, CT: Greenwood Press, 1993. $55.00.

HARRIS, WILLIAM F., II. *The Interpretable Constitution.* Pp. xv, 225. Baltimore, MD: Johns Hopkins University Press, 1993. $38.50.

While both books under review deal with constitutional interpretation, their approaches are quite different. Cortner uses historical narrative to recount the story of the railroad cases and their effects on the jurisprudence of the Fourteenth Amendment, while Harris relies on political theory, jurisprudence, and semiotics to advance a theory of an interpretable Constitution where words and policy are bonded in a coherent whole. Befitting a narrative, Cortner's style is brisk and straightforward. Consistent with his view that "the level of language must be adapted to the level of theory," Harris uses complicated terms and sprinkles his discourse with lots of parenthetical asides, numerous words emphasized by italics and capital letters, complex charts, and long explanatory—and often illuminating—footnotes.

Cortner's narrative actually encompasses two stories. The first recounts the response to the Supreme Court's rejection of substantive due process in *Munn v. Illinois* (1877), culminating in the doctrinal reversal in *Chicago, Milwaukee & St. Paul Railway Co. v. Minnesota* (1890) that subjected state regulatory legislation to judicial determinations of reasonableness. The second details how, under further pressure from the railroads, the Supreme Court in *Ex Parte Young* (1908) lowered the barriers to suits against state officials despite earlier conflicting interpretations of the Eleventh Amendment. Cortner shows that the rural Grangers were not alone in opposing what they perceived as unfair railroad practices, and he utilizes a host of original sources including briefs, newspapers, and railroad records. In emphasizing the railroad cases, Cortner slights the role of the *Dred Scott* decision in originating substantive due process. While he shows that railroads battled for their rights as consistently and tenaciously as modern interest groups, his final and somewhat anticlimactic chapter detailing the Court's decision to uphold state regulation in the

Minnesota Rate Cases of 1913 leaves me wondering how significant a barrier to state regulation of railroads the idea of substantive due process ultimately proved to be. Here, more theory and explanation would help.

By contrast, Harris's work is almost completely theoretical. Concerned with the links between the words of the large-*C* written Constitution and the small-*c* scripted policy, Harris follows this concern through chapters on writing, reading, explaining, and revising the Constitution, frequently resorting to metaphor and analogy and explications of philosophers like Hobbes and Locke. Harris's prescription for constitutional interpretation is ultimately vague. He suggests that the best interpretation would not be that of immanent positivism, immanent structuralism, transcendent positivism, or transcendent structuralism (his categories) but rather one that "would orchestrate all four partial styles and . . . clarify the tense juncture of liberalism and democracy."

Similarly, in describing constitutional amendments, Harris suggests that there may be substantive limits on amendments and that in initiating fundamental constitutional changes, "the theory of the Constitution's authority requires initiation and ratification by the convention track." However, Harris acknowledges that there is no institutional mechanism for enforcing the first constraint, and historical practice does not appear to validate the second requirement. Harris misses a good bit of contemporary literature, including a book by Peter Suber (*The Paradox of Self-Amendment* [New York: Peter Lang, 1990]) on the subject of self-referentiality, which so fascinates Harris. Similarly, while emphasizing the practice of adding amendments to the constitutional text rather than incorporating them within it, Harris never refers to debates in the first Congress that clarify the reason for this practice. While raising many fascinating questions, Harris ultimately leaves me with some large-C Confusion.

JOHN R. VILE

Middle Tennessee State University
Murfreesboro

GRIMSHAW, WILLIAM J. *Bitter Fruit: Black Politics and the Chicago Machine, 1931-1991.* Pp. xiv, 248. Chicago: University of Chicago Press, 1992. $24.95.

Twentieth-century Chicago politics, labyrinthine in nature and peopled with such larger-than-life figures as Mayor Richard J. Daley and Mayor Harold Washington, have proved a subject of enduring interest to scholars from various disciplines. In *Bitter Fruit*, William J. Grimshaw, a political scientist and activist in various insurgent campaigns against the machine in the last two decades, presents an account of the way the Democratic Party machine has exploited and neglected the city's black population over the last sixty years.

In the first two chapters, Grimshaw sets out to correct and update such classic works as Harold F. Gosnell's *Negro Politicians* (1935) and *Machine Politics* (1937) and James Q. Wilson's *Negro Politics* (1960). To me, admittedly a historian, these chapters seem flat, but once Grimshaw shucks off his concerns with turf battles in his discipline and examines what actually happened in Chicago, the book picks up considerably. The author's detailed analysis of the black switch from the Republican Party to the Democratic Party from 1936 through to 1944 is subtle and convincing, as is his debunking of the myth that "Boss" Dawson was a maverick bucking the machine. Similarly, Grimshaw gives an intriguing account of the

way Daley, initially associated with the reform wing of the Democratic Party and reliant on the black vote, not only ignored the needs of African American voters but also, as the civil rights movement began to challenge the status quo, presided over a machine that was as implacably racist as anything found in the South. In the final section of the book, Grimshaw gives us an insider's analysis of Harold Washington's campaigns and administration. The analysis, though somewhat mired in detail, shows clearly that because of Washington's refusal to institutionalize reform and his early death, black Chicagoans, in the end, gained little from the election of an African American mayor.

Unfortunately, the University of Chicago Press and its editors have not served their author well. The virtual repetition of a paragraph (pp. 43-44 and again on p. 100) is merely symptomatic of a structural looseness that leads to much of the material in the first two chapters being used again in later chapters. There are also too many typographical errors in the text, though I did like the idea that the judiciary could be broken down according to the "ethicity" of its members, surely a much more interesting measure than "ethnicity" (p. 105). *Bitter Fruit* is certainly worth reading, but I could not but conclude that the book fails to display fully the level of insight and knowledge that Grimshaw clearly has about blacks in Chicago politics.

SHANE WHITE

University of Sydney
New South Wales
Australia

KELLNER, DOUGLAS. *The Persian Gulf TV War.* Pp. xii, 460. Boulder, CO: Westview Press, 1992. $55.00. Paperbound, $19.95.

Douglas Kellner is a philosopher by trade, much influenced by the intellectual and moral perspective of the critical school, who has become a major voice in the study of mass media in contemporary society. The present book is a tribute both to Kellner's indefatigable talents and to the power of his chosen perspective to illuminate a specific event in terms of its larger implications. The event under scrutiny is the Gulf war, along with the process by which the American news media were co-opted and even transformed by it. Kellner recounts the press's role in the conduct of the first war seen in real time in great, and often astonishing, detail. But he does not lose sight of the big picture: his critical perspective impels him to think that there was more to the war than literally met the eye. He recounts in embarrassing detail the extent to which the "free press" yielded to the pressure to become a part of the official propaganda machine, and how much that contributed to the dearth of the criticism and the fragility of the opposition that might otherwise have emerged during the episode. Rich in detail and impassioned in analysis, Kellner's book is indispensable in understanding the war.

Two criticisms are in order. First, Kellner has a tendency to see things in much more conspiratorial terms than many of us are willing to accept. It may be that the origins, conduct, and consequences of this war were much more random and unintended than his book contends. Too, his language sometimes becomes a bit overheated, with his contempt for both military and media elites sometimes interfering with his analysis. What must be taken seriously, however, is his conclusion that this episode contributes further to "the militarization of U.S. culture and society," affecting everything from budgetary decisions to the marketing of toys. Even without reference to conspiratorial elites or culpable actors, this is a thesis

that bears close examination. For if, as he contends, the Gulf war was "the perfect war" (as Vietnam was not), then we might well see such televised wars again, conducted not only for foreign policy aims but also for domestic political purposes, including boosting budgets and popularity, as well as cathartic therapy for bored and restless populations. The Orwellian implications of that kind of activity are clear enough. Yet, as Kellner implies, the Gulf war turned out to be imperfect, since Saddam Hussein is still firmly in control in Iraq, Bush was defeated, and military budgets decline as bases close. It now remains to be seen what the role of the military-industrial complex will be in America in the twenty-first century, in which trading states with little military might but with great productive capacity may well dominate. In such a world, great war machines might become strangely obsolete, a relic of the previous century of war.

JAMES COMBS

Lebanon
Virginia

RICCI, DAVID M. *The Transformation of American Politics: The New Washington and the Rise of Think Tanks.* Pp. x, 310. New Haven, CT: Yale University Press, 1993. $30.00.

David Ricci has written an interesting book on a topic that deserves attention: the rise of the policy wonks. He underscores the importance of ideas, evidence, and argumentation rather than raw power in American politics, and he discusses the role of the policy analysts of various Washington think tanks in developing, advertising, and arguing for new interpretations of policy problems and solutions.

Among the strengths of the book is considerable emphasis on the topic of agenda setting, particularly the notion that the public agenda for major policy initiatives is a scarce good and that policymakers engage in competition for that space. In this competition, ideas, rather than brute political force, take on much greater importance than is often ascribed to them. (Ricci notes as well how the former can often be at the service of the latter.) In this sense, Ricci adds to a growing literature, though his focus on the think tanks in particular distinguishes his work from that of others.

Among the shortcomings of the book, which are considerably less substantial than this strength, is a tendency to explain the increased importance of the think tanks by reference to an almost encyclopedic array of social, political, and cultural trends of the past thirty years. We learn clearly that policy analysts play an important role in developing policy alternatives and intellectual justifications for government decisions. But we are led to infer as well that the assassination of Bobby Kennedy, the growth of congressional staff, the popularity of daytime television, the decline of party nomination powers, and a great variety of other factors may be equally responsible for this change. Finally, Ricci implies through his emphasis on the politics of ideas in the "new Washington" that somehow policies were justified in the past without reference to their intellectual underpinnings. This might come as a surprise to advocates of progress through science, atoms for peace, containment, and a variety of other intellectual theories that formed the bases for important government policies in years gone by.

Ricci has filled an important gap in our understanding of contemporary policymaking, and he has given us an important normative lens through which to evaluate what goes on in these Washington policy debates. Considering the importance of these issue networks in creating policy, we should indeed include them in our consideration of representative democracies. Ricci's book helps us along that path.

FRANK BAUMGARTNER

Texas A&M University
College Station

SKOCPOL, THEDA. *Protecting Soldiers and Mothers: The Political Origins of Social Policy in the United States.* Pp. xxi, 714. Cambridge, MA: Harvard University Press, 1992. $34.95.

A big, bold book, *Protecting Soldiers and Mothers* offers a fundamental rethinking of the origins and course of social provision in the United States. Skocpol notes the frequent lament on the part of scholars—particularly those of a social democratic bent—that the United States failed to create a "paternalist welfare state, in which male bureaucrats would administer regulations and social insurance 'for the good' of breadwinning industrial workers." Rather, the United States "came close" to creating a "maternalist welfare state, with female-dominated public agencies implementing regulations and benefits for the good of women and their children." This remarkable development, one that exploded from 1900 through the early 1920s, enjoyed an early and, at least at first glance, unlikely precedent: post-Civil War assistance to soldiers of the Army of the Republic. Writes Skocpol, "Through Civil War benefits, the federal government—long before the New Deal—became the source of generous and honorable social provision for a major portion of the American citizenry."

Because her thesis is revisionist. Skocpol builds her case carefully, noting that the data as they emerged challenged the assumptions with which she herself began this work. Provision for soldiers emerged because the young men had earned aid—for themselves and their dependents—by serving their country and, in many cases, suffering permanent harm. It was, of course, the Republican Party in this epoch that served as "the special vehicle" for delivering help. Coded into post-Civil War provision was the presumption that assistance went to those who were, in some abiding sense, civically deserving. Taking a cue from Civil War precedents, a nationwide network of women activists pushed for mothers' pensions during the Progressive Era, an epoch that saw most states in the country enacting such pensions. Aid, in these cases, went to mothers who, through no fault of their own, had been thrown into penury through the death or desertion of a spouse or, later, required protection in the workplace.

Skocpol is insistent on the importance and drama of these developments. For one thing, it meant the desertion of earlier models of charity as grassroots mothers' groups and prominent social reformers, including Jane Addams, gave support to mothers' pensions. The National Congress of Mothers was a particularly important player in a national effort as it "dramatized strong maternalist and social-justice arguments on [mothers'] behalf."

In addition to telling this fascinating story, in rich and rewarding detail, Skocpol challenges contemporary scholars, especially feminists, to rethink their own assumptions about maternalist social reform. She notes that from the perspective of feminist thinking at present, reform that, in some sense, idealized "separate spheres for the genders does not look progressive." Acknowledging the complexity of the historical moment she surveys so skillfully, Skocpol bids us to look again and to give due credit to those who so successfully forged a national move-

ment to gain social provision for mothers and children. *Protecting Soldiers and Mothers* makes a major contribution.

JEAN BETHKE ELSHTAIN

Vanderbilt University
Nashville
Tennessee

SONENSHEIN, RICHARD. *Politics in Black and White: Race and Power in Los Angeles.* Pp. xix, 301. Princeton, NJ: Princeton University Press, 1993. $29.95.

The purpose of this volume is to explore the ways in which biracial political coalitions work, "why they rise and why they fall." This is no small matter for an increasingly multiethnic, multicultural nation, such as our own, that actively and vocally resists the metaphoric bromides of a melting-pot society. Richard Sonenshein's effort to address this issue through a case study of biracial coalition politics in Los Angeles from 1960 to 1993 represents an important first step in coming to understand the transformative nuances that race and power have played and will continue to play in American politics.

The book is divided into four parts. Part 1 provides a theory of racial coalition politics that operates through the interaction between ideology, self-interest, and leadership. It then offers a historical perspective on the racial, political makeup of Los Angeles from its origins as an entrepreneurial city in the later years of the eighteenth century through the first victories of a tentative, biracial coalition for political representation and reform in the early 1960s. Parts 2 and 3 employ an analysis of demographic and voting patterns in four key council districts—the largely white, liberal, Jewish 5th, the black 8th, the white conservative

12th, and the Latino and moderate-white 14th—as a means of tracing the transformation of those early successes into a powerful biracial hegemony and its subsequent demise in the 1990s, capped by the events of the Rodney King case. Part 4 focuses attention on the example of biracial coalition politics in Los Angeles, contrasting it with the failure of biracial coalition politics in New York City, and on its implications for the future of a multiracial society writ large.

This is clearly a valuable volume that needs to be studied by anybody who is concerned with the pragmatic and moral problems of race and ethnicity in American politics. As I have suggested, however, it is only a first step, for there are shortcomings here that need to be engaged. As currently developed, the study operates with rather weak notions of ideology and hegemony, defined by their juxtaposition with self-interest, as if these three were discrete phenomena that could be identified and managed apart from one another or the sociopolitical contexts in which they exist. In a similar vein, the study ignores—or perhaps simply takes for granted—the symbolic environments or rhetorical cultures in which biracial political coalitions are crafted and the role that the ability to manage such environments and cultures plays in translating power into leadership. A comprehensive understanding of the ways in which biracial political coalitions are formed and function demands careful and sustained attention to the discursive practices through which such coalitions are produced and reproduced and the implications that such practices have for the course that the coalitions will follow. We do not get that here, but Sonenshein should be thanked for setting the stage for the next generation of study.

JOHN LOUIS LUCAITES

Indiana University
Bloomington

SOCIOLOGY

BARRINGER, HERBERT, ROBERT W. GARDNER, and MICHAEL J. LEVIN. *Asians and Pacific Islanders in the United States.* Pp. xx, 384. New York: Russell Sage Foundation, 1993. $42.50.

In *Asians and Pacific Islanders in the United States* the authors provide a comprehensive study of the size, diversity, and complexity of the Asian and Pacific Islander populations based on the 1980 census and subsequent mid-census assessments prior to the 1990 census. The volume could easily serve as a reference book for those involved in immigration history and ethnic studies or as valuable college library reference material. It is complete with comprehensive documentation of each Asian and Pacific Islander group enumerated in the 1980 census and contains invaluable comparative materials that explore the notable differences in demographic and economic structure between Asian groups. Although obviously a volume for those with a special interest in immigration history or demography in general, there are elements that will interest the sociologist as well.

The volume sheds a particularly interesting light on the shifting nature of recent Asian and Pacific Islander immigration and the related but often undocumented secondary movement of populations after arrival. Given the relatively recent arrival of the Asian and Pacific Islander populations with but a few exceptions, this portion of the study will be especially valuable to those interested in projections for the integration of the new immigrants into the mainstream of American life over time. Variables describing the dispersion of the Asian Indian community and the concentration of the Vietnamese community into enclaves illustrate the diversity factor. Likewise, the detailed documentation of earnings, family structure, and gender differentials confirms the diversity of the studied groups.

Special concern is voiced by the authors with regard to the tenuous nature of projections based on the 1980 census when the 1990 census is now able to carry the story forward. Also the facts that most Asian groups were not separate categories at all in the U.S. census until 1970 and that Pacific Islanders were separated out only in the census of 1980 give little opportunity for a historical overview. Nonetheless, there are numerous valuable, although often isolated, insights offered by this research. Particularly interesting is the continuing mobility and dispersion of Asian populations throughout the country, with notable increases in the South; few ethnic enclaves of any significance; and the potential growth of pan-Asian communities. The phenomenon of accelerating rates of inter-Asian marriage as well as Asian-Caucasian marriage bespeaks not only swifter assimilation than originally suggested but also a significant feature to explore in studies of the 1990 census. Equally interesting, Asian immigrants reach economic parity with native-born white populations within five to ten years, tend to bypass urban centers for the suburbs, and show clear signs of upward mobility over time. At the time of the 1980 census, even the Vietnamese refugee populations that settled into blue-collar categories, were already evincing mobility via the higher educational levels of their children. Moreover, all the studies show that Asians in general and the American-born members of virtually every Asian community have achieved higher educational levels than the average white American and dramatically higher levels than Hispanics and blacks. The authors note that all statistics show that Asian Americans, regardless of background, have avoided the castelike status of Hispanics and blacks.

The concluding portion of the book deals with the Pacific Islander population in a brief and necessarily limited fashion. Since this population has been isolated statistically only since 1980, documentation is limited. Nonetheless, this portion obviously serves as a beginning for future studies that will emerge from the 1990s. Even the few statistics included in this book emphasize, as with the Asians, a wide diversity between island groups.

ROBERT J. YOUNG

West Chester University
Pennsylvania

GITTELL, ROSS J. *Renewing Cities.* Pp. x, 232. Princeton, NJ: Princeton University Press, 1992. $39.50.

Ross Gittell has provided an excellent example of urban scholarship that should deepen our appreciation of the wisdom and efficacy of interdisciplinary research. Focusing on the experiences of four medium-sized manufacturing cities, Gittell uses their size and history to capture the interrelationships between economy, community, and public policy. Chapters 1 and 2 provide an overview of the problems facing industrial cities and theories of economic development and revitalization. In these chapters, Gittell sets up the remainder of his analysis, which depends on case studies of four declining manufacturing towns: Lowell and New Bedford, Massachusetts; Jamestown, New York; and McKeesport, Pennsylvania.

Each city was chosen based on its ability to provide a context for an in-depth analysis of local public policy, economic development, and the potential for revitalization. Lowell is used to capture the dynamics of a successfully revitalizing city; New Bedford is used to illustrate the effects of extended decline. While Jamestown has experienced some rejuvenation through locally based community groups, McKeesport is used as an example of continuing decline and the effects of public policies that exacerbate local economic problems.

The final two chapters provide a synthesis of the experience and lessons gleaned from the case studies. Gittell argues that several factors contribute to successful revitalization, but all are integrally related to the ability of a city to adapt, facilitate change, and construct new institutions that support economic growth. Thus regional approaches to economic development problems, combined with leadership and community organizing, can help construct new community-based institutions that encourage cooperation, public-private joint ventures, and mechanisms for retooling the local labor force and infrastructure.

Gittell's book is valuable to urban researchers and urban economists for several reasons. First, his approach demonstrates the value of interdisciplinary research, drawing heavily on theories and techniques in economics, political science, public administration, and sociology. Second, Gittell's analysis acknowledges the importance of both institutions and individuals in the development process. Thus local leaders are important in revitalization within the context of appropriate institutional frameworks that harness the entrepreneurial activities of local communities. Third, while lessons from case studies should be drawn cautiously, Gittell's method provides the analysis with a richness and complexity that are lost in studies that rely solely on large data sets where meaning is difficult to discern.

Gittell's analysis offers neither brilliance nor cutting-edge theory. On the contrary, the book's value lies in its journeyman's approach to disentangling the complexities and nuances of the development process. For this reason, serious researchers and students of economic development should find *Renewing Cities* a valuable addition to the literature.

SAMUEL R. STALEY

Wright State University
Dayton
Ohio

JHALLY, SUT and JUSTIN LEWIS. *Enlightened Racism: The Cosby Show, Audiences, and the Myth of the American Dream*. Pp. xvii, 152. Boulder, CO: Westview Press, 1992. $39.95. Paperbound, $14.95.

Enlightened Racism is a noteworthy contribution to the literature on popular culture. Two important aspects of contemporary culture are explored: how television influences thought processes and how Americans feel about race in the post-civil rights era. It is within this framework that a new type of racism is delineated that has permeated North American popular culture.

The mode of analysis used by Sut Jhally and Justin Lewis is qualitative; their conclusions are based on discussions with respondents from Springfield, Massachusetts. All interviewees had to be either frequent or occasional viewers of *The Cosby Show*. A comparison group of nonviewers is not used.

Jhally and Lewis's selection of *The Cosby Show* is judicious, as it represents a significant departure from most earlier programming, which depicted African American families in a working-class mode. The Huxtables enjoy an upper-middle-class lifestyle. This is where television distorts reality; most African American families are not like the fictitious characters. In addition, the Huxtables' race is perceived positively by the Caucasian audience, for the show absolves whites in general of the responsibility for the wide income differences between the races.

Interestingly enough, African Americans are also responsive to the Huxtables because of the myth of the American dream. The belief in equality of opportunity is universal, and programs like *The Cosby Show* help to perpetuate it. The reality, however, is that because of a rigid class structure, African Americans have become part of the permanent underclass.

Because of programs like *The Cosby Show*, Caucasians are not prepared to deal with class differences and, as a result, are not equipped to think clearly about race either. Such programming allows the majority population to be liberal and accepting of color differences and, at the same time, intolerant of cultural differences. Both Caucasian and African American respondents are opposed to the notion of a working-class Huxtable family. This is rather ironic in that it fuels the Caucasian stereotype of the culturally inferior African American and forces African Americans to accept a class system that is clearly disadvantageous to them.

To the authors' credit, they are not optimistic about pending reform in programming. Television producers will undoubtedly continue to depict the popular culture in a distorted fashion. After all, such programming is highly profitable in spite of its tragic effect on society. Jhally and Lewis demonstrate effectively that class is a better explanatory variable than race for differences between social groups.

BRIAN L. FIFE

Ball State University
Muncie
Indiana

KOPEL, DAVID B. *The Samurai, the Mountie, and the Cowboy: Should America Adopt the Gun Controls of Other Democracies?* Pp. 470. Buffalo, NY: Prometheus Books, 1992. $28.95.

Does the lack of strict gun control in the United States lead to unchecked violence? To answer this question, David Kopel surveys the firearm policies of Great Britain, Japan, Canada, New Zealand, Australia, Jamaica, and Switzerland. He argues that there is no causal link between stronger gun laws and a lower homicide rate. If there were, it would be difficult to explain Switzerland's low crime rate. While military firearms are prohibited in most European countries, the Swiss are not merely allowed to own assault rifles; they are required to do so. Norway and Israel also resemble Switzerland in having low crime rates and in encouraging civilian firearm ownership.

In this book, Kopel attempts to place the firearm laws of a variety of countries in their historical and political contexts. This is an audacious task, but Kopel succeeds rather well in pulling together a wide range of material. Kopel argues that the firearm bans may work better in Japan and Great Britain, but they would not work in the United States because of important cultural differences. The United States differs from other countries in that the general mistrust of government has been institutionalized, and, in Kopel's view, civilian ownership of firearms is seen by many Americans as being integral to individual freedom. This argument, however, is vulnerable to the critique that, since all countries change, why not the United States? The United States abolished slavery; why not firearms? Kopel retorts that firearm ownership is more intimately tied to fundamental American values than slavery and so is more resistant to change.

Kopel's analysis leads him to the controversial conclusion that the United States should promote responsible gun ownership instead of attempting to erase the gun culture. Citing relevant studies, he argues that firearm ownership, when linked with civic responsibility, offers a partial solution to the crime problem. Ulti-mately, though, gun control policy can do little to reduce America's high crime rate, which springs from America's greatest vices, such as racism and slavery, and its greatest virtues, such as individualism.

This book is meticulously researched. The chapter on Canada, the country I know the most about, is quite accurate. With over 1900 footnotes, Kopel provides sources for many juicy quotes and solid references. Fishing through so many foot-notes, however, can be extremely frus-trating! Nevertheless, I strongly recom-mend this book for anyone interested in the gun control debate. This is simply the most fact-filled international review available.

GARY A. MAUSER

Simon Fraser University
Burnaby
British Columbia
Canada

MANGIONE, JERRE and BEN MORRE-ALE. *La Storia: Five Centuries of the Italian American Experience.* Pp. 508. New York: HarperCollins, 1992. $30.00.

La Storia is the best book available on the Italian American experience, al-though insufficient attention to the third and subsequent generations render it just shy of being the definitive work. The saga is wonderfully told, unsurprisingly because Jerre Mangione is also the author of *Mount Allegro*, the most sensi-tively written memoir of growing up in an Italian immigrant family.

Although Columbus was one of the first Europeans to reach America, on the eve of the Civil War only 10,000 Italians lived in the United States. Within a dec-ade, Italian immigration began to esca-late, and it became a flood tide between 1900 and the start of World War I. But the

war and the strict immigration quotas instituted in the 1920s effectively halted the mass entrance of Italians as well as other Southern and Eastern Europeans viewed as undesirable. Thus the huge majority of Italian Americans today are descendants of the millions who immi-grated from primarily southern Italy dur-ing the brief quarter century period preceding World War I.

Mangione and Morreale's thorough discussion of the Italian and American economic and social factors that produced this mass immigration skillfully conveys both the larger forces involved and their human impact. Ironically, the productiv-ity gains responsible for American pros-perity also devastated the agricultural and mining industries that undergirded the southern Italian economy, which in turn resulted in mass departures. Two-fifths of Sicilians left the island, under-scoring the desperate conditions preva-lent there.

Most Italian emigrants left for the United States. Due to illiteracy, lack of salable work skills, and the absence of a group identity, they faced a formidable challenge in adjusting to American life. Prior to 1900, nearly half of Italian immi-grants were illiterate. Only a quarter of southern Italian immigrants spoke standard Italian: the rest spoke dialects often incomprehensible outside their na-tive region.

As a result of such obstacles, combined with severe prejudice, in 1910 only blacks had lower earnings than Italian Ameri-cans. Yet within three-quarters of a cen-tury, Italian Americans as a group were virtually indistinguishable from the av-erage American in terms of income and culture, including divorce rates and atti-tudes toward various social and political issues. *La Storia* sensitively depicts the adjustment difficulties of second-genera-tion Italian Americans, who had one foot in the Old World and the other in the New. But Mangione and Morreale fail to fully explore the explanations behind the upward mobility and rapid Americanization of Italian Americans. For example, American schools undoubtedly played a powerful role in socialization, but the book devotes only a few paragraphs to this subject.

La Storia has some minor flaws. It would have been improved if the authors had provided translations for all the Italian expressions used and if they had consistently noted whether the old Italian neighborhoods described exist today and, if they no longer exist, where they had been located. In addition, given the several pages of acknowledgments, there was no good reason for leaving the research assistants anonymous. But such deficiencies do not gainsay the splendid achievement of the book.

FRANK GALLO

Washington, D.C.

MASSEY, DOUGLAS S. and NANCY A. DENTON. *American Apartheid: Segregation and the Making of the Underclass.* Pp. x, 292. Cambridge, MA: Harvard University Press, 1993. No price.

This is a remarkable book that speaks not only to liberals but to all Americans about a serious civil rights problem, residential segregation.

It is to the credit of Douglas S. Massey and Nancy A. Denton that they can approach with freshness an area in which so much has already been said. The authors argue that segregation of black Americans is not comparable to the transient segregation experienced by other racial and ethnic groups. In fact, for blacks, their unique experience of segregation is at the core of their problems; it supports and binds together the other forms of discrimination. In chapter 1, Massey and Denton explore the four theoretical explanations for black segregation: the culture of poverty, institutional racism, economic restructuring, and welfare disincentives.

In chapter 2, the authors describe the evolution of all American black urban neighborhoods into what has been the residential configuration for the past eighty years. In chapter 3, they demonstrate how the residential configuration persists, by using data from the 30 largest black communities. One-third of all American blacks live in 16 metropolitan areas that are so racially segregated, with so little chance of interracial contact, as to warrant the descriptive term "hypersegregation."

In chapter 4, Massey and Denton explain why segregation persists for blacks at all levels of income. Prejudice, they argue, is supported by discriminatory practice used against home seekers. Personal attitudes and private behaviors are joined by institutional practices to create and sustain the black ghetto. This chapter carefully documents this situation and points to the larger implications, namely, how important the connection is between segregation and socioeconomic status. No contact, the authors show, means reduced social mobility, and "in U.S. metropolitan areas, the likelihood of white-black contact rarely exceeds 5%"!

In chapter 5, the authors explore the interaction between segregation and poverty to demonstrate how segregation creates an underclass. The authors create four hypothetical cities ranging from no racial segregation to complete racial segregation. These hypothetical cities allow them to demonstrate how the degree to which minority members experience concentrated poverty rises as segregation rises. Poverty has associated with it many social ills, among them family instability, welfare dependency, crime, and low educational achievement. Given the development of these associated social ills, Massey and Denton are able to show

how poverty affects neighborhoods, causing a spiraling downward. Racial segregation traps blacks in such environments. Trapped, they respond to their condition by creating a black street culture at odds with white society's culture, separating them further from white society. This cultural adaptation is the focus of chapter 6. It includes a description of black English, male joblessness, and the disappearance of marriage as a social institution.

Chapter 7 focuses on public policy that tolerated or supported segregation. Massey and Denton provide a detailed history of court decisions and legislation concerning fair housing, including the 1988 Fair Housing Amendments. In chapter 8, the authors outline policies that would promote residential integration, including more vigorous Fair Housing Act enforcement, integration-maintenance schemes, integration through Section 8 housing, and elimination of racist practices in the private urban housing market—no easy matter since it requires changes in the real estate and lending industries.

This well-written book accomplishes three things. First, it thoroughly examines one civil rights area, that of housing. Second, it demonstrates that, in spite of America's antisegregation commitment, both private and institutional practices perpetuate segregation. Third, and most important, the book proves how pivotal residential segregation is as an independent factor compounding a whole host of socioeconomic problems plaguing most black people in America today.

ROBERTA ANN JOHNSON
University of San Francisco
California

McKOWN, DELOS B. *The Mythmaker's Magic: Behind the Illusion of Creation Science.* Pp. 180. Buffalo, NY: Prometheus Books, 1993. $24.95.

It is practically a truism to observe that we live in an increasingly multicultural world. The United States welcomes nearly 7 million legal immigrants every decade, over 2 million of whom are Asian, from 19 Asian countries, including Iran, Iraq, Korea, and India. This fact alone demands that we learn more about diverse cultures and the religions to which each immigrant group adheres. But we cannot, it appears, teach religion with "dispassionate objectivity" in the public school systems of the United States without incurring the wrath of any number of fundamentalistic groups—what Delos McKown refers to collectively as "Fundagelicals," assorted fundamentalists and evangelicals who hold that the Bible is inerrant.

In our passion for fairness, we have, as one commentator put it, "Cloroxed" religion entirely out of the public school curriculum. In the absence of agreement about what to teach, we have decided to eliminate religion from the curriculum. It is not just that we do not have prayers, Bible readings, religious instruction, released time for religious meetings, and the like. We have a de facto policy of teaching nothing about religion. In addition, we allow the religious beliefs of parents to interfere with such things as teaching students about reproductive physiology, birth control, family planning, sexually transmitted disease, the historical and/or functional significance of sex roles, the role of mythology in cultural systems, values and value clarification, critical thinking, and so on.

Religious issues are so volatile among some groups that merely articulating public policy concerning the teaching of religion in the schools has become increasingly a matter for the federal judiciary rather than the states and the public school systems. But has the federal judiciary resolved the various dilemmas presented by those who would have us teach either nothing about religion in the schools or some specific brand of religion? This is one of the most brilliantly analyzed questions in Delos McKown's book. In answering this question, McKown looks carefully at the 1971 *Lemon v. Kurtzman* case, dealing with the question of how schools might know "when they are treating religion[s] properly under permissible state statutes."

" 'Scientific Creationists' would be up in arms," McKown writes, because introducing a course in comparative religion into the schools "would force a captive audience to encounter religions that, to the parents, are heathenish at best, satanic at worst." The author adds that it would have other undesirable results including "elevating other religions to the level of the favored religion (in our case Christianity) . . . [causing] students, potentially at least, to become critical of their own religion as a result of comparing and contrasting it with other religions . . . and . . . [causing] students to distance themselves from their own religion . . . [in order] to study it objectively."

Thus the dilemma we are confronted with is this: if we teach comparative religion in an academic way in the schools, we cannot avoid offending certain fundamentalists; whereas if we do not teach religion academically at all in the schools, we risk depriving students of the opportunity to enhance their general cultural literacy, their knowledge of the role of religion in history, or their ability to tolerate diverse religions. What are we to do? McKown carefully examines each judicial criterion given in the *Lemon* case and shows how, in following each, one is led to the same conclusion: one must either deprive students, surrender substantive components of the education curriculum, and not teach about these matters at all—geology or biology of human origins, for example—or one must risk offending the ever growing number of Fundagelicals in the United States.

The problems we create by trying to articulate public policy that will permit schools to pursue their secular purposes and to teach about religion in the schools are more profound than we realized. After following McKown's tightly reasoned analysis of *Lemon*, one must conclude that the religion of Fundagelicals and secular education are logically incompatible. Students who continue to hold Fundagelical beliefs are being wrongfully educated to the extent that they are taught beliefs that are incompatible with biological science, medicine, astronomy, geology, physics, and the like. Until courts wrestle with the problems presented by McKown's analysis, we will continue to slog through a policy wasteland that gives little guidance about either the limits of secular education or the benefits accruing from knowing more about the history and comparative importance of religion.

STEPHEN W. WHITE

Auburn University
Alabama

STROM, SHARON HARTMAN. *Beyond the Typewriter: Gender, Class and the Origins of Modern American Office Work, 1900-1930.* Pp. 415. Urbana: University of Illinois Press, 1992. $42.50.

Historian Sharon Hartman Strom provides a detailed view of the development of modern office work, placing it in the larger context of early-twentieth-century industrialization, mechanization, and rationalization and showing its ambiguities and contradictions. Strom's strength is her ability to present a richly textured analysis of the development of a less studied aspect of U.S. working-class history and thereby solidly challenge several major theories applied to this period.

Strom first provides an overview of the modern firm's economic and managerial structure, the emergence of scientific management, and the development of male business professions. New in this familiar story is Strom's focus on clerical work, which these developments relied upon and fostered. Frozen out of its upper reaches, women were confined to its lower levels, which became simultaneously feminized, mechanized, and subject to scientific management. Analogized to light manufacturing, clerical work adopted many of the attitudes and assumptions characterizing female factory work.

Strom then focuses on office workers and their work culture. She details class and gender relations in shaping the modern clerical worker, the workers' often contradictory expectations and ambitions, and the cross-cutting pressures that bosses, the work environment, and larger cultural values placed on female workers. Exploration of these factors suggests why collective action, unionism, and feminism made little headway among these workers. Class divided female clerical workers: native-born white workers from English-speaking homes were preferred; white immigrant women found themselves assembly-line stenographers rather than "professional" secretaries, who most often were college-educated native-born women. While the U.S. Postal Service hired African American clericals, jobs went primarily to black men. It was virtually impossible for well-trained African American women to find clerical work. Age, marital status, and individualistic competition further divided female clerical workers.

These constraints notwithstanding, Strom shows attempts to resist the most dehumanizing aspects of clerical work. She points to small acts of resistance and solidarity. In the long run, however, divisive factors blunted the new clericals' ability to shape their work conditions. Additional workplace ambiguities explain why this might have been the case: while much office work resembled light manufacturing, mechanization did not automatically mean deskilling, so some room was left for personal initiative and advancement; despite low wages, clerical work was better paid than most women's jobs; and immigrant and middle-class women alike saw clerical work as a route to upward mobility.

Strom's research demonstrates the limitations of two well-accepted theories. Labor market segmentation theory holds that there was little except gender to distinguish female workers. Strom clearly shows otherwise; segmentation of women workers along several lines of difference existed even within the office. Human capital theory maintains that failure to invest in higher education or training excluded women from advancement into managerial positions. Once hired, expectation of marriage and hence willing retirement made additional training unfeasible. Strom demonstrates women's desire to advance and to stay on the job after marriage, but discriminatory practices confined them to low-paying jobs while male counterparts advanced into management.

The contemporary office, with its gender and class hierarchy, was securely in place by 1930. Strom's analysis provides a clear understanding of the seemingly permanent and intractable aspects of that hierarchy.

JEANNE HAHN

Evergreen State College
Olympia
Washington

ECONOMICS

BRACE, PAUL. *State Government and Economic Performance.* Pp. xv, 152. Baltimore, MD: Johns Hopkins University Press, 1993. $28.95.

What are the limits of the effectiveness of local government policy in the context of a globalizing economy? This is the question that Paul Brace sets out to answer, with specific regard to the economic policies of state governments, in this brief monograph. The discussion is anchored in a comparison of the minimal-regulation, low-tax philosophy of southern and western states versus the more interventionist management strategies of northern states. Arizona, Texas, Michigan, and New York provide case studies, which receive the most in-depth attention, with background provided by statistical analyses of the economic performances of all fifty states.

Brace asserts that the idea that state policies make any difference in such areas as creating or retaining jobs, luring industry, and increasing per capita income is an unexamined article of faith. State-level policymakers must believe in it because their work otherwise is mere ritual, and their belief is reinforced by others who attempt to influence them in the hope that local policies will serve their particular interests. Brace's assertion that there is no proof that local policy has any effect is fascinating, and while it is probably overstated—can we assume that there are countless assessment studies gathering dust in state archives that would tell us something?—this book provides useful insights into the general efficacy of grossly differing state development strategies and the changing political and economic national and world arenas within which state policies continue to evolve.

Brace says that the idea, given currency by the rise of the Sunbelt, that the low-tax, minimal-regulation strategy works better in attracting and maintaining economic growth than interventionist state policies that require higher taxes is shortsighted. Minimal government may be attractive when the national economy is rapidly expanding, as it was in the 1960s, but the neglect of infrastructure and social expenditures in times of pitched international competition and slower economic growth creates mounting liabilities. The 1980s generated a new kind of partnership between local government and the private sector. In the period of slower growth that marked the decade, state governments turned from "buffalo hunting"—luring footloose industries and other businesses from other states— to a policy of market stimulation and research and development support for their resident industries. In the new competitive climate, states with professional government personnel, efficient government administrative structures, and a political culture that supported excellent educational institutions had the edge. As Republican administrations in Washington cut aid to the states and turned responsibility back to state and local government, those states that had remained committed to an activist role were able to cope best. At the same time, when federal expenditures were drying up, the Sunbelt myth of laissez faire exploded, and the dependency of states like Arizona and Texas on federal support, including defense spending, was fully exposed.

Brace's point in laying out this recent history is not that the more activist state government strategies work best in the long run. Rather, the point is that the efficacy of divergent local policies is in large part dependent on cycles within the national—and thereby international— political economy. There is an interplay between what is going on at the national level in terms of economic growth and attendant philosophies regarding the limits of federal responsibility for providing for services. Washington is not the ultimate context. States have even less power to manage the outcome of a worldwide restriction or glut of oil supplies. Brace's analysis reminds us that states, as open systems without the power to restrict the movement of capital or labor, have little impact on the creation or retention of jobs. On the other hand, his findings do indicate that the one area in which state economic policy may have an impact is per capita income.

Brace has provided a plausible interpretation of the limits of the effectiveness of state economic policy. There is some unevenness in the level of presentation, though: the introductory chapters and narrative history of the featured states are quite accessible to undergraduates, while the quantitative analysis appears to be intended for a professional (academic) audience. Both groups will wish that the author's interpretations and conclusions were more extensive. The choice of states for case study is bound to generate questions of representativeness, despite the fact that Brace broadens the empirical base in his analysis of employment and income indicators for all fifty states. Conceptually, Brace has contributed insights into the issue of the role of local actors and their capacity to affect local economic conditions, and he offers case study as well as cross-sectional evidence in support of his interpretations.

WILLIAM G. FLANAGAN

Coe College
Cedar Rapids
Iowa

GROSSBARD-SHECHTMAN, SHOSHANA. *On the Economics of Marriage: A Theory of Marriage, Labor, and Divorce.* Pp. xv, 349. Boulder, CO: Westview Press, 1993. $45.00.

This book collects the fruits of almost twenty years of developing and testing the theoretical implications of an original concept: spousal labor. The concept is defined as "any task people perform for the benefit of a spouse or partner and beyond

their own needs." Five of the 15 chapters have never been published in English. Most of the chapters that are based on previously published work have been expanded, rewritten, or translated from Hebrew.

The book is rich in hypotheses—70, numbered for convenience—and imaginative empirical tests. An economist, Grossbard-Shechtman enthusiastically invites scholars from sociology and anthropology to flesh out her general theory of marriage. Since "the exact composition of spousal labor varies . . . from culture to culture," the hypotheses cry out for tests by anthropologists.

Markets for spousal labor (marriage markets) are obtained when the demand for spousal labor, aggregated over individuals, is juxtaposed with the aggregate supply of spousal labor. In the marriage market for women (men), the demand is by men (women) and the supply by women (men). The equilibrium spousal wage rate for men is typically higher than that for women, because the supply of female spousal labor is typically larger for women. This means that in marriage, the husband typically compensates the wife for her services.

Grossbard-Shechtman describes the compensation as mainly nonmonetary. It has two components: a material component consisting of goods and services consumed by the wife, including food and shelter, and a nonmaterial component. Examples of the latter are a husband's help with child care and the relative power of the wife in the marriage. The more value attached to children, the more power women are likely to have in the household.

Given her acknowledged intellectual debt to Gary Becker's *Treatise on the Family* (1981), I find it surprising that Grossbard-Shechtman does not discuss the relationship between her concept of compensation and his concept of altruism. Altruists compensate their beneficiaries. How does one distinguish between altruistic transfers and spousal wages?

Nevertheless, the book is replete with evidence that men compensate women in marriage. For example, logit regressions in chapter 14, "A Study of Spousal Help among Israeli Managers" (written with Dafna Izraeli and Shoshana Neuman), show that compensation is negatively related to age; that is, husbands tend to help their employed wives when it is most productive to do so. An unpredicted result is that wives of Eastern origin receive more help than wives of Western origin.

This book is must reading for scholars interested in contributing to our understanding of marriage.

CHARLOTTE D. PHELPS

Temple University
Philadelphia
Pennsylvania

KING, RONALD F. *Money, Time and Politics.* Pp. viii, 536. New Haven, CT: Yale University Press, 1993. $45.00.

This massive work in political science should be noted and taken seriously by all the social sciences but especially sociology. The thesis of this book is that the American presidencies between Truman and Reagan developed an overall strategy for dealing with a capitalist economy and with major problems arising from an unequal and antagonistic system of classes. This strategy served to protect and advance the interests of capital, but in such a way that the disadvantaged sections of society would accede to the strategy. The strategy adopted was "growthmanship," a continual expansion of the economy so that all classes would share in its rewards, though capital would remain the major beneficiary. That

this policy was a success is manifest in the extent to which the laboring classes put aside their antagonism and adhered to what Ronald King calls a policy of "asymetrical, non-zero sum growthmanship." This adherence was not the result of the weakness of the labor movement or the cultural hegemony of the capitalist class or false consciousness. It was the result of a rational calculation on the part of the nonlaboring classes of where their true interests lay.

It is true that the various presidencies differed in the details of this strategy, particularly in the extent of the inequalities. In general, Democratic Presidents favored fewer and lesser inequalities, Republican Presidents greater advantages for business and others with large salaries or accumulations of wealth, with both parties reflecting the short-range interests of their constituencies. But so similar were the underlying strategy and assumptions of these administrations that it is justifiable to consider them as constituting a single regime.

This book ends with the installation of Reagan. The regime still had some way to go. But King recognizes that the strategy of growthmanship was the product of a particular period, marked by an unchallengeable industrial base and virtual hegemony over the non-Communist world. As these conditions recede, it is an open question of whether the policy of growthmanship can be continued. If that should happen, then the tensions latent in the class structure may very well reappear.

Money, Time and Politics is a valuable, thoroughly researched book, and this review cannot do justice to it. One hopes that its length and technical detail will not deny it the readership it deserves.

EUGENE V. SCHNEIDER

Bryn Mawr College
Pennsylvania

ORLOFF, ANN SHOLA. *The Politics of Pensions: A Comparative Analysis of Britain, Canada, and the United States, 1880-1940.* Pp. xii, 381. Madison: University of Wisconsin Press, 1993. $60.00. Paperbound, $24.95.

In *The Politics of Pensions*, Ann Orloff provides us with "an explanation of when, how, and why poor relief was replaced by modern social insurance and pensions for the elderly in Britain, Canada, and the United States." This is an issue that has been much debated of late by a host of historians and social scientists who have examined the coming of the "capitalist welfare state" not only in these three countries but in the rest of the industrialized world as well. (Among the more notable of these discussions can be found in two books by Orloff's fellow sociological historians. See Jill Quadagno, *The Transformation of Old Age Security* [Chicago: University of Chicago Press, 1983]; Theda Skocpol, *Protecting Soldiers and Mothers* [Cambridge, MA: Harvard University Press, Belknap Press, 1992].)

Orloff's contribution to the debate is a well-researched book that is organized into three sections: a careful review of the major approaches to the problems of the elderly in an industrial society; a very useful discussion of the historical roots of social assistance to the elderly; and a comparative historical analysis of the evolution of policies in each of the three countries. At the core of all this is a question that Orloff claims the prevailing literature has not successfully resolved: How can we account for the fact that the British were able to introduce old-age assistance and pensions in the first decade of the twentieth century, while the United States did not provide any significant federal assistance to the elderly until the Social Security Act of 1935?

To answer this question, Orloff presents a comparative approach that incorporates the importance of institutional features—most notably, the level of "state autonomy and capacity"—with a historical analysis that emphasizes "policy feedback" as a key element shaping the evolution of social policy. She describes all this as "a conversation between hypotheses and evidence."

The conversation is certainly plausible. Orloff skillfully shows how the combination of an outdated poor law that created pernicious conditions for the elderly and a well-developed bureaucracy in Britain allowed advocates of social insurance to succeed. A federal government with limited responsibilities, patronage politics, and a legacy of corruption from the Civil War pension system defeated proponents of social insurance in the United States who were pressing for reforms at about the same time. In Canada, patronage and federalism combined with the impact of World War I on Canadian politics to delay implementation of social insurance until the late 1920s.

While this may be a plausible story, some of us find it rather incomplete. Though rejecting what she and Theda Skocpol call the "logic of industrialization approach," Orloff concedes that "social insurance is an invention of an age marked by a capitalist and industrial economy; it was in this sense a 'response to [capitalist development].' " She fails to explain why this response can come from only the public sector. By ignoring private responses to the insecurities posed by the process of industrialization, Orloff misses one of the most significant differences between the British and American cases—differences that could shed considerable light on the question of timing for social insurance.

Evidence on private savings rates, ownership of homes, widespread purchase of insurance, and the fact that one of four men aged 60 and over in the United States had left the labor force all attest to the strength of a privately based system of economic security—bolstered by generous military pensions—that diluted both the economic and the political pressures for social insurance. A comparable safety net of private accumulation and soldiers' pensions did not exist in Britain.

Taking this into consideration, much of the puzzle about the timing of social insurance in the two economies vanishes. The presence of private accumulation not only explains the delay in social insurance in the United States compared to Britain; it also fits rather well with the sudden support for old-age assistance when the capital markets collapsed in the 1930s.

All of this is not to diminish the contribution that Ann Orloff has made with her excellent study of pensions in three countries. This is a book that cuts across disciplinary lines and should be of interest to a wide audience of scholars in both history and the social sciences.

ROGER L. RANSOM

University of California
Riverside

OTHER BOOKS

ABURISH, SAID K. *Cry Palestine: Inside the West Bank.* Pp. xvii, 205. Boulder, CO: Westview Press, 1993. $49.50. Paperbound, $15.95.

ADAMS, F. GERARD, ed. *The Macroeconomic Dimensions of Arms Reduction.* Pp. viii, 259. Boulder, CO: Westview Press, 1992. $49.95.

BALL, HOWARD. *Cancer Factories: America's Tragic Quest for Uranium Self-Sufficiency.* Pp. xiv, 188. Westport, CT: Greenwood Press, 1993. $49.95.

BARKER, ANTHONY and B. GUY PETERS, eds. *The Politics of Expert Advice: Creating, Using and Manipulating Scientific Knowledge for Public Policy.* Pp. x, 129. Pittsburgh, PA: University of Pittsburgh Press, 1993. $49.95. Paperbound, $19.95.

BARTRA, ROGER. *Agrarian Structure and Political Power in Mexico.* Pp. xvii, 221. Baltimore, MD: Johns Hopkins University Press, 1993. $45.00. Paperbound, $14.95.

BERGER, THOMAS R. *A Long and Terrible Shadow: White Values, Native Rights in the Americas, 1492-1992.* Pp. xiv, 183. Seattle: University of Washington Press, 1992. Paperbound, $12.95.

BODENHAMER, DAVID J. and JAMES W. ELY, JR., eds. *The Bill of Rights in Modern America: After 200 Years.* Pp. x, 246. Bloomington: Indiana University Press, 1993. $29.95. Paperbound, $12.95.

BRESNAN, JOHN. *Managing Indonesia: The Modern Political Economy.* Pp. xi, 375. New York: Columbia University Press, 1993. $55.00. Paperbound, $18.50.

BRODY, HOWARD. *The Healer's Power.* Pp. xiii, 311. New Haven, CT: Yale University Press, 1992. $30.00.

BROWN, MICHAEL BARRATT and PAULINE TIFFEN. *Short-Changed: Africa and World Trade.* Pp. xix, 220. Boulder, CO: Westview Press, 1993. $59.95. Paperbound, $18.95.

BULMAN, PHILIP MICHAEL. *Caught in the Mix: An Oral Portrait of Homelessness.* Pp. x, 211. Westport, CT: Greenwood Press, 1993. $49.95.

CHUBB, JOHN E. and TERRY M. MOE. *A Lesson in School Reform from Great Britain.* Pp. vii, 50. Washington, DC: Brookings Institution, 1992. Paperbound, $6.95.

COBBLE, DOROTHY SUE, ed. *Women and Unions: Forging a Partnership.* Pp. x, 452. Ithaca, NY: ILR Press, 1993. $52.00. Paperbound, $19.95.

COHEN, MORRIS RAPHAEL. *The Faith of a Liberal.* Pp. xv, 497. New Brunswick, NJ: Transaction, 1992. Paperbound, $22.95.

CONNAUGHTON, RICHARD. *Military Intervention in the 1990s: A New Logic of War.* Pp. xvi, 198. New York: Routledge, Chapman & Hall, 1993. $65.00. Paperbound, $17.95.

CONSTABLE, PAMELA and ARTURO VALENZUELA. *A Nation of Enemies: Chile under Pinochet.* Pp. 367. New York: Norton, 1993. Paperbound, $12.95.

COOK, BLANCHE WIESEN. *Eleanor Roosevelt.* Vol. 1, *1884-1933.* Pp. xviii, 587. New York: Penguin, 1993. Paperbound, $14.00.

ELIOT, THOMAS H. *Recollections of the New Deal: When the People Mattered.* Pp. xv, 169. Boston: Northeastern University Press, 1992. $24.95.

ERICSON, DAVID F. *The Shaping of American Liberalism: The Debates over Ratification, Nullification and Slavery.* Pp. ix, 238. Chicago: University of Chicago Press, 1993. $40.00. Paperbound, $14.95.

FOLEY, DOUGLAS E. *Learning Capitalist Culture: Deep in the Heart of Tejas.*

Pp. xix, 247. Philadelphia: University of Pennsylvania Press, 1990. $31.95. Paperbound, $14.95.

FRANKLIN, DANIEL P. *Extraordinary Measures: The Exercise of Prerogative Powers in the United States.* Pp. 172. Pittsburgh, PA: University of Pittsburgh Press, 1991. $24.95.

FRIEDMAN, EDWARD, PAUL G. PICK-OWICZ, and MARK SELDEN. *Chinese Village, Socialist State.* Pp. xxiv, 336. New Haven, CT: Yale University Press, 1993. $40.00. Paperbound, $17.00.

GEORGE, ALEXANDER L. *Bridging the Gap: Theory and Practice in Foreign Policy.* Pp. xxvi, 170. Washington, DC: United States Institute of Peace, 1993. $24.95. Paperbound, $14.95.

GERHARDT, UTA, ed. *Talcott Parsons on National Socialism.* Pp. vii, 357. Hawthorne, NY: Aldine de Gruyter, 1993. $52.95.

GIDDENS, ANTHONY. *Modernity and Self-Identity: Self and Society in the Late Modern Age.* Pp. 256. Stanford, CA: Stanford University Press, 1991. $35.00. Paperbound, $12.95.

GRAY, ANDREW, BILL JENKINS, and BOB SEGSWORTH, eds. *Budgeting, Auditing and Evaluation: Functions and Integration in Seven Governments.* Pp. xiii, 214. New Brunswick, NJ: Transaction, 1993. $39.95.

GRAZIANO, FRANK. *Divine Violence: Spectacle, Psychosexuality, and Radical Christianity in the Argentine "Dirty War."* Pp. xi, 328. Boulder, CO: Westview Press, 1992. $49.95. Paperbound, $18.95.

GREIDER, WILLIAM. *Who Will Tell the People: The Betrayal of American Democracy.* Pp. 464. New York: Simon & Schuster, 1993. Paperbound, $13.00.

HAYWARD, J.E.S. et al., eds. *De Gaulle to Mitterand: Presidential Power in France.* Pp. xi, 228. New York: New York University Press, 1993. $45.00. Paperbound, $15.00.

HINCK, EDWARD A. *Enacting the Presidency: Political Argument, Presidential Debates, and Presidential Character.* Pp. xiv, 255. Westport, CT: Greenwood Press, 1993. $49.95.

HONIG, JAN WILLEM. *Defense Policy in the North Atlantic Alliance: The Case of the Netherlands.* Pp. xii, 263. Westport, CT: Greenwood Press, 1993. $49.95.

HUCZYNSKI, ANDRZEJ A. *Management Gurus: What Makes Them and How to Become One.* Pp. 331. New York: Routledge, Chapman & Hall, 1993. $27.50.

HYCLAK, THOMAS and GERAINT JOHNES. *Wage Flexibility and Unemployment Dynamics in Regional Labor Markets.* Pp. viii, 116. Kalamazoo, MI: W. E. Upjohn Institute, 1992. Paperbound, $11.00.

IPPOLITO, DENNIS S. *Uncertain Legacies: Federal Budget Policy from Roosevelt through Reagan.* Pp. xiv, 297. Charlottesville: University Press of Virginia, 1990. $37.50.

ISSERMAN, MAURICE. *The American Communist Party during the Second World War: Which Side Were You On?* Pp. xvii, 305. Champaign: University of Illinois Press, 1993. Paperbound, $15.95.

ISSERMAN, MAURICE. *California Red: A Life in the American Communist Party.* Pp. viii, 263. Champaign: University of Illinois Press, 1993. Paperbound, $12.95.

ISSERMAN, MAURICE. *If I Had a Hammer: The Death of the Old Left and the Birth of the New Left.* Pp. xx, 259. Champaign: University of Illinois Press, 1993. Paperbound, $12.95.

JENNINGS, EDWARD T., JR. and NEAL S. ZANK, eds. *Welfare System Reform: Coordinating Federal, State, and Local Public Assistance Programs.* Pp. xii, 249. Westport, CT: Greenwood Press, 1993. $55.00.

JOLY, DANIELE. *Refugees: Asylum in Europe?* Pp. x, 166. Boulder, CO:

Westview Press, 1993. $58.00. Paperbound, $21.00.

KENNEDY, CHARLES H., ed. *Pakistan 1992*. Pp. viii, 201. Boulder, CO: Westview Press, 1993. $29.95.

KETCHAM, RALPH. *Framed for Posterity*. Pp. xii, 195. Lawrence: University Press of Kansas, 1993. $25.00.

KISHIMA, TAKAKO. *Political Life in Japan: Democracy in a Reversible World*. Pp. xvi, 142. Princeton, NJ: Princeton University Press, 1991. No price.

KRUGMAN, PAUL R. *Currencies and Crises*. Pp. xix, 219. Cambridge: MIT Press, 1992. $25.00.

LAVER, MICHAEL and NORMAN SCHOFIELD. *Multiparty Government: The Politics of Coalition in Europe*. Pp. xiii, 308. New York: Oxford University Press, 1990. $59.00.

LEGGE, JEROME S., JR. *Traffic Safety Reform in the United States and Great Britain*. Pp. xvi, 190. Pittsburgh, PA: University of Pittsburgh Press, 1991. $29.95.

LICKLIDER, ROY, ed. *Stopping the Killing: How Civil Wars End*. Pp. ix, 354. New York: New York University Press, 1993. $50.00.

LINCOLN, W. BRUCE. *The Great Reforms: Autocracy, Bureaucracy, and the Politics of Change in Imperial Russia*. Pp. xxi, 281. De Kalb: Northeastern Illinois University Press, 1990. $29.00.

LIVELY, DONALD E. *Foreshadows of the Law: Supreme Court Dissents and Constitutional Development*. Pp. xxvi, 168. New York: Praeger, 1992. Paperbound, $17.95.

MAHER, MICHAEL. *Lieutenants: The Evolution of Political Style*. Pp. xiv, 190. New York: Praeger, 1990. $42.95.

McCULLOUGH, DAVID. *Truman*. Pp. 1117. New York: Simon & Schuster, 1992. Paperbound, $15.00.

McFAUL, MICHAEL. *Post-Communist Politics: Democratic Prospects in Russia and Eastern Europe*. Pp. xix, 132. Washington, DC: Center for Strategic and International Studies, 1993. Paperbound, $14.95.

McGLEN, NANCY E. and MEREDITH REID SARKEES. *Women in Foreign Policy: The Insiders*. Pp. x, 351. New York: Routledge, Chapman & Hall, 1993. Paperbound, $15.95.

MEEHAN, EUGENE J. *Assessing Governmental Performance: An Analytical Framework*. Pp. 201. Westport, CT: Greenwood Press, 1992. $47.95.

MONMONIER, MARK. *Mapping It Out: Expository Cartography for the Humanities and Social Sciences*. Pp. xiii, 301. Chicago: University of Chicago Press, 1993. $37.00. Paperbound, $15.95.

MOORE, STANLEY. *Marx versus Markets*. Pp. x, 126. University Park: Pennsylvania State University Press, 1993. $22.50.

MORAN, THEODORE H. *American Economic Policy and National Security*. Pp. ix, 100. New York: Council on Foreign Relations Press, 1993. Paperbound, $10.95.

MUJAL-LEON, EUSEBIO M. *European Socialism and the Conflict in Central America*. Pp. xvi, 127. New York: Praeger, 1989. No price.

NAGENGAST, CAROLE. *Reluctant Socialists, Rural Entrepreneurs: Class, Culture, and the Polish State*. Pp. xiv, 239. Boulder, CO: Westview Press, 1991. $45.00.

NORRIS, CHRISTOPHER. *Uncritical Theory: Postmodernism, Intellectuals, and the Gulf War*. Pp. 218. Amherst: University of Massachusetts Press, 1992. $30.00. Paperbound, $9.95.

NOTHDURFT, WILLIAM E. *School Works: Reinventing Public Schools to Create the Workforce of the Future*. Pp. ix, 94. Washington, DC: Brookings Institution, 1989. Paperbound, $7.95.

NUGENT, NEILL. *The Government and Politics of the European Community*.

2d ed., revised. Pp. xiv, 434. Durham, NC: Duke University Press, 1992. $49.95. Paperbound, $19.95.

OLSEN, MARVIN E. and MARTIN N. MARGER, eds. *Power in Modern Societies*. Pp. xv, 327. Boulder, CO: Westview Press, 1993. $65.00. Paperbound, $18.95.

PALMER, VERNON V. *The Paths to Privity: The History of Third Party Beneficiary Contracts at English Law*. Pp. 250. San Francisco: Austin & Winfield, 1991. $64.95. Paperbound, $39.95.

PANGLE, THOMAS L. *The Ennobling of Democracy: The Challenge of the Postmodern Age*. Pp. vi, 227. Baltimore, MD: Johns Hopkins University Press, 1991. $25.95.

PARZYCH, KENNETH M. *Public Policy and the Regulatory Environment*. Pp. xvi, 268. Lanham, MD: University Press of America. $47.50. Paperbound, $25.50.

PETERS, B. GUY and ANTHONY BARKER, eds. *Advising West European Governments: Inquiries, Expertise and Public Policy*. Pp. xi, 228. Pittsburgh, PA: University of Pittsburgh Press, 1993. $49.95. Paperbound, $19.95.

PETERSON, MELVIN N. A., ed. *Diversity of Oceanic Life: An Evaluative Review*. Pp. xviii, 109. Washington, DC: CSIS, 1993. Paperbound, $14.95.

PIERCE, JAMES L. *The Future of Banking*. Pp. x, 163. New Haven, CT: Yale University Press, 1991. $25.00.

POND, ELIZABETH. *Beyond the Wall: Germany's Road to Unification*. Pp. xv, 367. Washington, DC: Brookings Institution, 1993. $28.95.

PYLE, KENNETH B. *The Japanese Question: Power and Purpose in a New Era*. Pp. x, 171. Washington, DC: American Enterprise Institute, 1992. $17.95.

REARDON, JOHN J. *America and the Multinational Corporation: The History of a Troubled Partnership*.

Pp. viii, 185. Westport, CT: Greenwood Press, 1992. $45.00.

ROGOWSKI, RONALD. *Commerce and Coalitions: How Trade Affects Domestic Political Alignments*. Pp. xvi, 208. Princeton, NJ: Princeton University Press, 1989. $24.50.

ROSE, RICHARD and IAN McALLISTER. *The Loyalties of Voters: A Lifetime Learning Model*. Pp. viii, 219. Newbury Park, CA: Sage, 1990. $45.00. Paperbound, $19.95.

ROSENBERG, WILLIAM G. and LEWIS H. SIEGELBAUM, eds. *Social Dimensions of Soviet Industrialization*. Pp. xix, 296. Bloomington: Indiana University Press, 1993. $39.95. Paperbound, $14.95.

RUSK, DAVID. *Cities without Suburbs*. Pp. xviii, 147. Baltimore, MD: Johns Hopkins University Press, 1993. $29.00. Paperbound, $13.95.

SALMI, JAMIL. *Violence and Democratic Society: New Approaches to Human Rights*. Pp. x, 134. Atlantic Highlands, NJ: Zed Books, 1993. $49.95. Paperbound, $19.95.

SALTMAN, MICHAEL. *The Demise of the "Reasonable Man."* Pp. vii, 168. New Brunswick, NJ: Transaction, 1991. No price.

SAWYER, RALPH D. *The Seven Military Classics of Ancient China*. Pp. xix, 568. Boulder, CO: Westview Press, 1993. $29.95.

SCHMIDTZ, DAVID. *The Limits of Government: An Essay on the Public Goods Argument*. Pp. xviii, 197. Boulder, CO: Westview Press, 1990. $38.50. Paperbound, $12.95.

SHIELS, FREDERICK L. *Preventable Disasters: Why Governments Fail*. Pp. xi, 204. Lanham, MD: Rowman & Littlefield, 1991. $42.50.

SMELSER, RONALD and RAINER ZITELMANN, eds. *The Nazi Elite*. Pp. xiv, 259. New York: New York University Press, 1993. $35.00.

SMITH, GORDON et al., eds. *Developments in German Politics.* Durham, NC: Duke University Press, 1992. $55.00. Paperbound, $19.95.

STANLEY, JAY and JOHN D. BLAIR, eds. *Challenges in Military Health Care: Perspectives on Health Status and the Provision of Care.* Pp. ix, 191. New Brunswick, NJ: Transaction, 1993. $29.95.

STARKS, MICHAEL. *Not for Profit, Not for Sale: The Challenge of Public Sector Management.* Pp. 168. New Brunswick, NJ: Transaction, 1991. No price.

STOWE, JUDITH A. *Siam Becomes Thailand: A Story of Intrigue.* Pp. xii, 394. Honolulu: University of Hawaii Press, 1991. $39.00. Paperbound, $16.95.

THOMPSON, WAYNE C. *The Political Odyssey of Herbert Wehner.* Pp. xxii, 487. Boulder, CO: Westview Press, 1993. $58.00.

UNGAR, SHELDON. *The Rise and Fall of Nuclearism: Fear and Faith as Determinants of the Arms Race.* Pp. 214. University Park: Pennsylvania State University Press, 1992. $32.50. Paperbound, $14.95.

VANDEN, HARRY E. and GARY PREVOST. *Democracy and Socialism in Sandinista Nicaragua.* Pp. xii, 172. Boulder, CO: Lynne Rienner, 1993. $32.00.

VENET, WENDY HAMAND. *Neither Ballots nor Bullets: Women Abolitionists and the Civil War.* Pp. xii, 210. Charlottesville: University Press of Virginia, 1991. $25.00.

WALTER, EDWARD. *The Rise and Fall of Leftist Radicalism in America.* Pp. viii, 194. Westport, CT: Greenwood Press, 1992. $45.00.

WATSON, DENNIS and CHRISTINE CRAIG, eds. *Guyana at the Crossroads.* Pp. 95. New Brunswick, NJ: Transaction, 1992. Paperbound, $14.95.

WEIL, KARI. *Androgyny and the Denial of Difference.* Pp. x, 212. Charlottesville: University Press of Virginia, 1993. $35.00. Paperbound, $12.95.

WHITE, ROBERT W. *Provisional Irish Republicans: An Oral and Interpretive History.* Pp. xiv, 206. Westport, CT: Greenwood Press, 1993. $55.00.

WILSON, THOMAS M. and M. ESTELLIE SMITH, eds. *Cultural Change and the New Europe: Perspectives on the European Community.* Pp. x, 244. Boulder, CO: Westview Press, 1993. $39.95.

WINSTON, KENNETH and MARY JO BANE, eds. *Gender and Public Policy: Cases and Comments.* Pp. xvii, 385. Boulder, CO: Westview Press, 1993. $55.00. Paperbound, $19.95.

WOLFENSTEIN, EUGENE VICTOR. *Psychoanalytic-Marxism: Groundwork.* Pp. x, 468. New York: Guilford Press, 1993. $40.00. Paperbound, $19.95.

WUNDERLICH, GENE, ed. *Land Ownership and Taxation in American Agriculture.* Pp. x, 277. Boulder, CO: Westview Press, 1992. Paperbound, $45.00.

WUTHNOW, ROBERT. *Acts of Compassion: Caring for Others and Helping Ourselves.* Pp. viii, 334. Princeton, NJ: Princeton University Press, 1991. $24.95.

YELVINGTON, KEVIN. *Trinidad Ethnicity.* Pp. vii, 296. Knoxville: University of Tennessee Press, 1993. $31.95.

ZARTMAN, I. WILLIAM, ed. *Europe and Africa: The New Phase.* Pp. x, 211. Boulder, CO: Lynne Rienner, 1992. $33.00.

INDEX

217

POLITICAL THEORY

An International Journal of Political Philosophy

Editor: Tracy B. Strong,
University of California, San Diego

Political Theory publishes articles on political philosophy from a variety of methodological, philosophical and ideological perspectives. It offers essays in historical political thought, modern political theory, normative and analytic philosophy, the history of ideas, as well as critical assessments of current work.

The journal serves as the leading forum for the development and exchange of political ideas. It's broad in scope and international in coverage. **Political Theory** has no single affiliation or orientation, and it's dedicated to serving the entire political theory community.

Political Theory brings you the latest thought and theory on political philosophy. The editorial board is truly representative and international, and it's dedicated to giving you thought-provoking and informative scholarship in a variety of forms, including:

- Feature Articles
- Critical Responses
- Books in Review
- Review Essays
- Special-Topic Symposia
- Annual Index

Policy Studies Journal and Policy Studies Review
Questions, Answers, and Experts

The *Policy Studies Journal* and the *Policy Studies Review* are designed to raise questions and offer answers. In doing so, both periodicals call upon experts on the general approaches and specific policy problems involved in policy studies. Some of the questions that have been addressed in recent issues of *PSJ* and/or *PSR* include:

1. How can one determine the effects of alternative public policies?
2. How can policy evaluation be used to maximize societal benefits minus societal costs in choosing among alternative policies?
3. How can we facilitate the utilization of policy evaluation research by policy-makers and policy-appliers?
4. How can governmental institutions be made more effective, efficient, and equitable in formulating and implementing policy decisions?
5. How can we facilitate more interaction across academic disciplines that are relevant to policy evaluation?
6. How can we facilitate more comparisons across nations, states, and cities concerning alternative public policies?
7. What policies are most appropriate for facilitating international peace and mutually beneficial trade relations?
8. How can we minimize inflation, unemployment, poverty, crime, discrimination, pollution, disease, and illiteracy through more effective public policy?
9. How can we maximize food, energy, technological innovation, freedom of communication, fair judicial procedure, and productivity through more effective public policy?
10. What goals should public policy be seeking to achieve and what obligations do policy analysts have for achieving those goals?

All these questions have been addressed in various PSO symposia and non-symposia articles which have been published in the *Policy Studies Journal* or the *Policy Studies Review*. Questions like these will be addressed in future symposia and non-symposia articles. For the names of the past and forthcoming PSO symposia editors, see the *PSJ-PSR* ad entitled "These Are the PSO Symposia Editors."

Send me the *PSO* journals, directories, and other benefits immediately. Here is my name address, and check for only $22.

Name _____

Affiliation _____

Address _____

City/State/Zip _____

Send to: *PSO*, University of Illinois, 702 S. Wright Street, Urbana, IL 61801

FROM CONFRONTATION TO COOPERATION

Resolving Ethnic and Regional Conflict

by JAY ROTHMAN, Haverford College, Bryn-Mawr College, & The Hebrew University of Jerusalem

What will the world look like in the next century? How will it get there: through great upheaval, chaos, and violence or through planned and peaceful adjustment? As the twentieth century nears its end, the global arena presents a paradox of simultaneous unity and fragmentation. On one hand, an international interdependence prevails. Modern communication links people in all corners of the globe. Yet, at the same time, a greater separatist nationalism is brewing, one that asserts ethnic identity and demands independence and statehood. **From Confrontation to Cooperation** is designed to explore these questions and provide hypotheses and constructive directions for conflict resolution.

Conceptually, this book suggests that politics be approached from the inside out: from the perspective of people and their communities. In the first chapter, an historical overview of the Israeli-Palestinian struggle is presented as a prototype of contemporary nationalism and nationalist conflicts. From this vantage point, Rothman then details a systematic approach for broadening conflict analysis and management as well as a specific method for facilitating constructive dialogue between disputants in deep conflict in the Middle East and beyond.

Practitioners, scholars, and students of Arab-Israeli studies, peace studies, conflict resolution, international relations, political science, and sociology will find **From Confrontation to Cooperation** to be a lucid and insightful contribution to the field of conflict resolution.

Violence, Cooperation, Peace: An International Series
1992 (Summer) / 250 pages / $44.00 (h) (46937) / $21.95 (p) (46945)

SAGE PUBLICATIONS, INC.
2455 Teller Road, Newbury Park, CA 91320
(805) 499-0721 / Fax (805) 499-0871

SAGE PUBLICATIONS LTD.
6 Bonhill Street, London EC2A 4PU, England

SAGE PUBLICATIONS INDIA PVT. LTD.
M-32 Greater Kailash Market—I, New Delhi 110 048, India